The Political Economy of
Education and Development

About the Author

Frank Youngman is Professor of Adult Education at the University of Botswana. He was educated at the universities of Nottingham and Hull, and the London School of Economics. He has worked at the University of Botswana since 1975 and has been Head of the Department of Adult Education and Dean of the Faculty of Education. In Botswana he has participated in a wide range of governmental committees responsible for areas such as rural extension, women in development, adult literacy, teacher education and distance learning. He was a member of the Presidential Commission which reviewed Botswana's education system in 1992–93 and is on the UNESCO National Commission. Elsewhere in Africa he has undertaken advisory and training work for various governments.

He has published widely on many aspects of adult education and is the author of a number of books, including *Adult Education and Socialist Pedagogy* (Croom Helm, 1986), *Education for All in Botswana* (coeditor) (Macmillan Botswana, 1993) and *Towards a Transformative Political Economy of Adult Education: Theoretical and Practical Challenges* (coeditor) (LEPS Press, Northern Illinois University, 1996).

The Political Economy of Adult Education and Development

FRANK YOUNGMAN

NIACE
Leicester

ZED BOOKS
London & New York

The Political Economy of Adult Education and Development was first published by
Zed Books Ltd, 7 Cynthia Street, London N1 9JF, UK,
and Room 400, 175 Fifth Avenue, New York, NY 10010, USA in 2000

Published in paperback in the United Kingdom by NIACE,
the National Organization for Adult Learning, 21 De Montfort Street,
Leicester LE1 7GE, UK

Distributed in the USA exclusively by St Martin's Press, Inc.,
175 Fifth Avenue, New York, NY 10010, USA

Typeset in Monotype Baskerville by Lucy Morton & Robin Gable, Grosmont
Cover designed by Lee Robinson, Ad Lib Design, London N19
Printed and bound in Malaysia

Library of Congress Cataloging-in-Publication Data
Youngman, Frank
 The political economy of adult education and development /
Frank Youngman.
  p. cm.
 Includes bibliographical references (p.) and index.
 ISBN 1-85649-675-9. — ISBN 1-85649-676-7 (pbk.)
  1. Adult education—Economic aspects—Developing countries.
 2. Adult education—Political aspects—Developing countries.
 3. Developing countries—Economic conditions. 4. Socialism and
education—Developing countries. I. Title.
 LC5261.Y68 1999
 374.9172'4—dc21   99-052390

ISBN 1 85649 675 9 (Hb)
ISBN 1 85649 676 7 (Pb)

NIACE ISBN 1 86201 080 3 limp

Global Perspectives on Adult Education and Training

Series Editors: Budd Hall with Carol Medel-Anonuevo
and Griff Foley

Series Advisors: Peggy Antrobus, Phyllis Cunningham,
Chris Duke, Patricia Ellis, Matthias Finger, Heribert Hinzen,
Agneta Lind, Peter Mayo, Derek Mulenga, Jorge Osorio, Lalita
Ramdas, Te Rippowe, Nelly P. Stromquist, Rajesh Tandon,
Carlos Alberto Torres, Alan Tuckett, Shirley Walters, Makoto
Yamaguchi, Karen Yarmol-Franko, Frank Youngman
and Abdelwahid Yousif

This new series is designed to provide for the first time a genuinely
global basis to the theory and practice of adult education and
learning worldwide. A key goal is to introduce readers to issues,
debates and understandings related to centrally important areas
in adult education and training, particularly but not exclusively in
the majority (or third) world, and to provide a forum where
practitioners from the South, women, and other social groups historically under-represented in AET, can find a voice. To this end,
the new series will contribute to redressing an imbalance in the
literature whereby our understanding and debates in adult education and training in the English-speaking world have been unduly
dominated by bodies of knowledge and theoretical perspectives
drawn from experience in the USA and Britain and relatively
unrepresentative of class, race and gender.

Among the issues of immediate and vital interest to adult educators throughout the world which new titles in this series will
address are: popular education, adult learning and civil society,
post-colonial perspectives, women's perspectives, informal learning in peoples' struggles, worker education, environmental adult
education, participatory research, the political economy of adult
education, indigenous knowledge and adult learning, and the
impact on them of globalization and other social trends.

Titles already available

Shirley Walters (ed.), *Globalisation, Adult Education and Training: Impacts and Issues*

Peter Mayo, *Gramsci, Freire and Adult Education: Possibilities for Transformative Action*

Griff Foley, *Learning in Social Action: A Contribution to Understanding Informal Education*

Frank Youngman, *The Political Economy of Adult Education and Development*

In preparation

Matthias Finger and José Asún, *Learning Our Way Out: Adult Education at the Crossroads*

For full details of this list and Zed's other subject and general catalogues, please write to: The Marketing Department, Zed Books, 7 Cynthia Street, London N1 9JF, UK or email Sales@zedbooks.demon.co.uk Visit our website at: http://www.zedbooks.demon.co.uk

Contents

Acknowledgements

The bulk of the work on this book was undertaken while I was on sabbatical leave at the University of Leeds, England. I would therefore like to thank the University of Botswana for granting me leave and express appreciation to my colleagues in the Department of Adult Education for undertaking extra duties in my absence.

The sabbatical period was spent attached to the Centre for Development Studies at the University of Leeds, which provided a congenial environment for my research. I would like to thank the Director, Dr Preston, and the Deputy Director, Dr Aydin, for their assistance. Appreciation is also due to Dr Ghazzali of the University of Hull for his help.

Friends at the University of Leeds provided a home from home in the period when I was away from my family in Botswana. I would like to thank them for their tender loving care – especially Ray Bush, Lionel Cliffe, Gordon Crawford, Delia Davin, Mahmood Messkoub and Mette Wiggen. When I was in England, my parents Frank and Kathleen Youngman provided their usual love and support. I am sad that they did not live to see this publication.

My students on the BEd (Adult Education) course EAS 480 at the University of Botswana have provided excellent feedback over the years on ideas presented here. For the final preparation of the book, I would like to thank Griff Foley, series editor, and Robert Molteno, editor at Zed Books, for their very helpful advice and encouragement.

Finally, I am pleased to acknowledge the unwavering solidarity of Phora Gaborone-Youngman. The book is dedicated to her and Tshepiso Rabasha, and to the ideal of substantive democracy and social justice in Botswana.

Le kamoso bagaetsho.

University of Botswana
Gaborone

CHAPTER I

Introduction

Adult educators in the countries of the South can be found in many organisational contexts, ranging from government departments to training units in business, and from universities to community-based organisations. Their activities are similarly diverse, including areas such as adult literacy, non-formal education, extension programmes, vocational training and continuing professional education. But whatever the organisational situation or area of activity, their work is dominated by the theories and practices of development. Policy-makers and practitioners set goals, establish systems, organise programmes and assess performance in terms of ideas about what adult education can contribute to national development.

The problems confronted by the countries of the South are considerable, as the South Commission, chaired by Julius Nyerere of Tanzania, made clear in its report *The Challenge to the South:* 'Hundreds of millions of people living in the South suffer from hunger, malnutrition, and preventable disease, and are illiterate or lack education and modern skills' (South Commission, 1990: 23). The Commission asserted that these conditions are unacceptable, and that the South must meet the challenge of transforming them. It maintained that transformation includes creating economic growth that will meet the needs of the people, strengthening democratic institutions, eradicating poverty, enabling people to realise their talents and creativity, applying science and technology, protecting the natural environment and restructuring global relations.

This list of the tasks facing the South is typical of discussions about what development should achieve.

In this context it is often argued that adult education has a key role to play. For example, the Fifth International Conference on Adult Education in Hamburg in 1997 concluded:

> Adult education ... is a powerful concept for fostering ecologically sustainable development, for promoting democracy, justice, gender equity, and scientific, social and economic development, and for building a world in which violent conflict is replaced by dialogue and a culture based on justice. (UNESCO, 1997a: 1)

This kind of general statement on adult education's role is based on the expectation that adult education programmes can address specific development tasks. For example, it is assumed that agricultural extension programmes can improve agricultural production and food security, thereby reducing malnutrition; that skills training can strengthen income-generating projects and help to eradicate poverty; that literacy classes can increase women's involvement in public affairs and extend democratic participation. It is expected that in such ways adult education programmes can contribute to the economic, political and social dimensions of development.

It is important to consider to what extent adult education in the South is actually capable of meeting these expectations. To do this, it is necessary to analyse critically the nature of adult education, and to understand its limitations and its potentials. The role of adult education has to be questioned. Does adult education in fact help to create more secure livelihoods? Does it really empower marginalised groups in society? Does it genuinely contribute to democratisation? It is essential that adult educators ask such questions, and go beyond rhetorical statements. In particular, they must ask what development really means, and who really benefits from the provision of adult education programmes. This entails taking a critical stance towards their work and its impact on people and society. An important task is therefore to acquire a better understanding of the relationship between adult education and development.

However, the writing in this field consists mainly of descriptive accounts of adult education activities, reports of programme evaluations, and the results of small-scale empirical research projects. There have been few attempts to address the question of adult education and development at a theoretical level, and to elaborate general propositions about the relationship between adult education and society in the countries of the South. This book addresses this problem, and is therefore primarily a work of theory. It is based on a deductive approach which is concerned mainly with the construction of a theoretical framework and the delineation of research agendas derived from that framework. It applies these research agendas in country case studies in order to examine empirically the adequacy of the theory's concepts and general propositions. These applications seek to demonstrate the explanatory power of the theoretical framework, and thus provide an alternative approach to the atheoretical empiricism which often prevails in research on adult education and development (Paulston and Altenbaugh, 1988: 115). In so doing, the book aims to provide adult education policy-makers and practitioners with an approach to social analysis that they can use to investigate the role of adult education in development. Its usefulness will be measured by the extent to which it helps them to clarify their own circumstances and adopt appropriate goals, systems, programmes and curricula.

The analytical approach taken is one which seeks to uncover the contextual factors that shape adult education. The dominant approaches in adult education scholarship are based on individualised conceptions of the adult learner and the adult educator. These approaches are derived from the standpoints of psychology and philosophy rather than social theory, and they embody liberalism's concept of the free and autonomous individual. For example, the humanist theory of adult learning advocated by Malcolm Knowles (1978) pays no attention to the significance of different class or gender backgrounds among learners. The mainstream approaches tend to abstract adult education from society, and ignore the wider social forces that shape its organisation and processes. The political economy approach adopted here deliberately moves the focus of analysis from individual choice and behaviour to a consideration of the historical and structural context within which individual action takes place. In particular, it looks at how the historical evolution and contemporary nature of the capitalist mode of production conditions the relationship between adult education and society. The book seeks to clarify the historical-structural constraints on the choices about adult education policies and programmes in the South. A range of choices can be made in any given situation, but that range is not unlimited. It is circumscribed by economic, political and social factors.

The boundaries on individual agency are made evident in the everyday experience of adult education in the South. In many countries, for example, structural adjustment policies have been implemented by governments under the direction of the World Bank and the International Monetary Fund. These have reduced public expenditure, necessitating cutbacks in the state's adult education programmes. In this situation, the individual adult educator heading a government department has to decide which activities to continue and which to terminate, and which programmes must charge fees to users. The choices are made within a context in which the state's social policies have been determined by the material and ideological realities of the global political economy. They are genuine choices, but their scope has been set by social forces beyond the individual who has to take them. Thus it is necessary for adult educators to achieve a high degree of self-awareness about the contextual limits on their activities in order to be able to recognise both the constraints on action and the possibilities for change. Hence an important task for adult educators is to analyse the determining factors in their situations so that the influences on their choices are well understood. To do this, adult educators in whatever organisational setting must undertake systematic inquiry into specific socioeconomic contexts.[1] The theoretical discussions in the chapters that follow are intended to provide appropriate tools of analysis for adult education in peripheral capitalist countries. The research agendas at the end of Chapters 4, 5 and 6 give specific conceptual frameworks that can guide inquiry by adult educators into central aspects of these contexts.

The book is based on a broad concept of adult education that embraces all forms of organised learning which adults undertake. Thus adult education denotes the organisational arrangements in society to provide people at any stage in their adult lives with opportunities for learning. The term does not in itself specify anything about levels or methods or settings, but derives its definition from the nature of its participants, who are those regarded as adults by the society in which they live. However, it is a fact that many of those who teach adults (say, family planning or business management) do not identify themselves as being involved in adult education. In many ways, therefore, the term 'adult education' is an analytical construct that gives intellectual coherence to a range of activities which appear on the surface to be unconnected, and which are usually perceived by their practitioners as unrelated. For example, it is doubtful whether literacy workers, industrial training officers and lecturers on part-time university courses often consider the commonalities in their work of helping adults to develop particular skills, knowledge, values and attitudes. The assumption here, however, is that these commonalities do exist, and that adult education has validity as a term to denote a field of study and of practice. The scope of the book therefore encompasses all forms of organised learning for adults. Hence a wide variety of adult education activities are considered, ranging from adult literacy, agricultural extension and trade-union education to home economics courses, radio learning groups and political consciousness-raising.

The term 'development' refers to the idea that deliberate action can be taken to change society in chosen directions which are considered desirable. It is an idea that has had currency since 1945 in the context of policies and programmes intended to promote the economic, political and social progress of those areas of the world which were formerly colonised. From the early 1950s these areas were referred to as the Third World, to indicate countries outside the First World of advanced industrial capitalism and the Second World of industrialised state socialism. However, the Second World collapsed in 1989–91; therefore the terminology South and North is now commonly used to refer to the contemporary division between rich and poor in the global political economy (South Commission, 1990). This book focuses on the capitalist countries in the South, as these constitute the vast majority. Very few countries in the South have attempted to follow a socialist model of development since 1945, and by the 1990s little remained of these experiments. Moreover, the adult education and development relationship within socialist models is distinctive, and would require separate analysis. Thus this study concentrates only on capitalist countries in the South. These countries are on the periphery of the main centres of the world's capitalist economy: the USA, Japan and Europe. Peripheral capitalism provides a common denominator that gives them a certain identity despite their heterogeneity in levels of economic development, political institutions and national cultures. It is this identity which enables a degree of generalisation about the relationship between adult education and development. However, it is the existence of differences which means that these generalisations have to be examined within specific national contexts. Hence three country case studies from Botswana in Southern Africa have been included to illustrate the theoretical discussion. The case studies apply the book's theoretical framework to aspects of adult education during the first twenty-five years of the country's post-colonial experience.[2]

This book seeks to fill the gap created by the lack of recent in-depth studies on adult education and development in the English language. A number of books on adult education and development appeared between the late 1960s and the early 1980s, notably those by Prosser (1967), Townsend-Coles (1969), Lowe (1970), Coombs and Ahmed (1974), Hall and Kidd (1978) and Bock and Papagiannis (1983). Since then, however, consideration of the topic has been confined to conference papers, research reports, programme evaluations, and articles in journals such as *Convergence* and *Adult Education and Development*. A major exception is Rogers's recent book *Adult Learning for Development* (1992). This, however, is an idiosyncratic and eclectic work. It does not provide a systematic review of the concept of development in relation to development theory; nor does it take a critical position on the role of adult education in development. In particular, it does not give a critical appraisal of the major shifts in development thinking during the 1980s embodied in neoliberal theory and populism. There remains a gap in the literature in terms of a comprehensive, up-to-date study of adult education and development from a consistent theoretical perspective.

Reviews of research in adult education, such as that by Deshler and Hagan (1990: 161), suggest that theory-building is important at this stage in the evolution of adult education as a field of study, and that 'research related to economic and social development' is one of the 'promising directions' for the future. It is hoped that the theoretical approach to adult education and development presented here will advance adult education research related to the specific circumstances of the South and, in turn, lead to more informed and clear-sighted practice.

Plan of the Book

In Chapter 2 I initiate discussion of the theoretical framework used here. I discuss the key elements of political economy and appraise recent critiques. On this basis, I make a summary of the political economy approach to social analysis. In Chapter 3 I use this summary to assess the theoretical foundations of previous works on the political economy of adult education. After this review, I present the theoretical framework of the book.

In Chapter 4 I consider the main theories of development that have evolved since 1945, focusing on: (a) modernisation theory; (b) dependency theory; (c) neoliberal theory; (d) populism; and (e) political economy. I discuss the way in which changing ideas about the nature of development have had an impact on conceptualisations of the relationship between adult education and development. I conclude that the theoretical framework established in Chapter 3 provides a valid and relevant basis for the analysis of adult education in the context of development.

In Chapter 5 I consider the place of peripheral capitalist countries within the global political economy in terms of the theory of imperialism. In particular, I theorise the role of aid in developing the necessary conditions for capitalist accumulation on a world scale. Foreign aid is identified as having a significant impact on the nature of domestic development policies. The chapter then analyses the relationship between aid and adult education, identifying a research agenda for analysing the economic, political, social and ideological consequences of foreign aid to adult education in the countries of peripheral capitalism. A country case study is used to illustrate the agenda.

In Chapter 6 I analyse the nature of social inequality in peripheral capitalist societies, focusing on the inequalities of class, gender, ethnicity and race, and their interactions. I show that social inequality is an important factor in shaping the development process and its outcomes. I then consider the relationship between social inequality and adult education, including the ideological role of the curriculum. On the basis of the discussion, I present a research agenda for the study of social inequality and adult education within peripheral capitalism. This is exemplified in a country case study.

In Chapter 7 I consider the political dimension of the development process, elaborating the concepts of the state and civil society in peripheral capitalism. This discussion provides the theoretical basis for clarifying the political consequences of the role of adult education in development. The chapter concludes with a research agenda for studying the state, civil society and adult education in the countries of peripheral capitalism. The agenda is applied in a country case study.

Chapter 8, the final chapter, provides a summary. It concludes with a consideration of the implications of the book for future theory-building and research on the topic of adult education and development.

Notes

1. S.B. Merriam and E.L. Simpson, *A Guide to Research for Educators and Trainers of Adults* (1989) introduces adult educators to the systematic enquiry of research and encourages their involvement as practitioners.

2. Botswana is a landlocked country in the centre of the Southern Africa region with a large landmass and a small population of 1.5 million. Formerly the colony of Bechuanaland, it became independent from Britain in 1966. For information on its economy, politics and society, see W.A. Edge and M.H. Lekorwe (eds), *Botswana: Politics and Society* (1998); and S.J. Stedman (ed.), *Botswana. The Political Economy of Democratic Development* (1993).

CHAPTER 2

The Political Economy Approach

The aim of this book is to provide adult educators with conceptual tools for analysing the contextual factors which influence the nature of adult education policies and programmes in the countries of the South. The conceptual framework which has been adopted is that of political economy, an approach which analyses social reality in terms of the economic organisation of society and the relationships between classes. This approach attempts to situate and understand individual behaviour and experience within adult education in relation to its wider sociohistorical context. It is derived from Marxist social theory, which provides a coherent foundation for comprehending adult education and development at both the macro and micro levels of analysis. One of the strengths of Marxist social theory is its comprehensive scope and transdisciplinary nature. It transcends the conventional boundaries of philosophy, history, economics, political science, sociology and psychology, and this makes it a powerful tool for comprehending the complexities of adult education.

These complexities can be illustrated by considering an adult education class on computing in a private commercial college in Harare. The class is not simply a place of psychological activity where individual learners acquire new knowledge and skills. It is also part of an economic process of producing the skilled labour required by new technology and competition in the global capitalist economy. The provision of the course is an outcome of public policies adopted by the state under pressure from the World Bank/ IMF to promote private adult education institutions and a

9

competitive training market. The class is an instance of cultural interaction as Zimbabweans engage with software produced by an American transnational corporation. Participation in the class has been determined by, among other things, the economic situation of the learners and their ability to pay the fees. The social relations of the classroom – among learners, and between learners and educators – are structured by the patterns of social class, gender, ethnicity and race in Zimbabwean society, patterns which are themselves a product of historical events such as colonialism and the development of capitalism in Africa. Thus the everyday activity and experience of the adult educator and adult learners in this class are shaped by the wider economic and political realities of Zimbabwe and its place in the world economy. The tradition of Marxist social theory offers a fertile source of concepts for a comprehensive approach to analysing the complexities illustrated by this typical adult education situation.

The use of the expression 'political economy' denotes an analytical approach based on Marxist theory. But it also indicates a particular approach *within* the Marxist tradition, as will be elaborated in subsequent sections. This is an important point, as Marxism is not a monolithic body of social theory but contains a variety of internal perspectives, which arise from the varying interpretations that can be placed upon the extensive body of work that Marx and Engels produced between 1840 and 1895. In the original writings there were diversities of emphasis, differing depths of analysis, gaps in coverage and ambiguities of formulation, which have provided the basis for a wide variety of subsequent interpretations and applications. Marx and Engels's work was the product of a specific historical period, and its subsequent uses are also historically bounded. The value of their writings is that they provide a source of research problems, concepts and methods for the analysis of society, not a set of fixed truths.

The conception of Marxism on which this book is based is therefore an undogmatic one, antithetical to the tradition of 'official' Marxism associated with communist parties, and the institutionalised role it played in the Soviet bloc. It is a conception shaped by the economic, political and intellectual history of the last thirty years. The current stage of capitalist development is characterised by the dominance of transnational corporations, the microelectronics technological revolution, expanded consumerism, ecological crisis and the intensified (though uneven) incorporation of post-colonial societies into the global capitalist economy. Clearly such changes have produced new problems for analysis that were unforeseeable in earlier eras. In the political domain, developments such as the state's defeat of the general strike in France in 1968, the rise of the women's movement and other social movements, the transition of national liberation movements into governing parties, and the collapse of the Soviet bloc regimes have generated challenges for Marxist political theory and new ideas on appropriate modes of political practice. Responding to and influencing these changes have been intellectual developments involving not only debates within Marxism itself but sustained critiques from outside the tradition, particularly by feminism, post-structuralism and postmodernism. The current situation is that

> Marxism has been challenged and rewritten, both by its dialogue with other bodies of theory and by its effort to acknowledge the diverse political realities of the postwar world ... it has become a much more varied discourse. (Nelson and Grossberg, 1988: 11)

The need to address new realities and the range of theoretical challenges has led some writers on the Left in Western Europe and North America to identify a 'crisis' in Marxism, and question its adequacy as a theory. Indeed, some former Marxist writers have adopted other theoretical positions either against or 'beyond' Marxism. On the other hand, the collapse of 'actually existing socialism' in Eastern Europe has encouraged political theorists of the Right, such as Fukuyama (1992), to pronounce liberal democracy and free-market economics as a political-economic system which cannot be improved upon, and hence the final stage of social evolution. Against this background, some writers consider political economy outdated and eclipsed by more recent social theory, especially postmodernism. However, a tenable position remains of continuing to develop the Marxist tradition so that it responds to the evolutions that have taken place within capitalism and reflects critically upon the experience of state socialism. Marxism is still a viable and creative social theory which can provide powerful tools of analysis for research into contemporary capitalist society, and in particular for the study of adult education within its societal context. This book demonstrates how Marxist political economy can provide insights into the form and content of adult education in the peripheral capitalist countries of the South.

The following sections provide an outline of Marxist political economy and discuss the implications of some of the recent critiques of Marxist theory and practice.

Marxist Political Economy

Here I present a summary of the main elements of Marxist political cal economy as found in the writings of Marx and Engels and elaborated by subsequent writers. The starting point of Marxist political economy is the theory of society and social development which, in 1846, Marx and Engels (1970) called 'the materialist conception of history'. This theory posits that the system of economic organisation in society is the key to understanding the various dimensions of social reality. This theoretical proposition is explicitly presented by Marx in a well-known passage in the 'Preface to *A Contribution to the Critique of Political Economy*' (1859):

> In the social production of their life, men enter into definite relations that are indispensable and independent of their will, relations of production which correspond to a definite stage of development of their material productive forces. The sum total of these relations of production constitutes the economic structure of society, the real foundation on which rises a legal and political superstructure and to which correspond definite forms of social consciousness. The mode of production of material life conditions the social, political and intellectual life process in general. It is not the consciousness of men that determines their being, but, on the contrary, their social being that determines their consciousness. At a certain stage of their development, the material productive forces of society come into conflict with the existing relations of production, or – what is but a legal expression for the same thing – with the property relations within which they have been at work hitherto. From forms of development of the productive forces these relations turn into their fetters. Then begins an epoch of social revolution. With the change of the economic foundation the entire immense superstructure is more or less rapidly transformed. (Marx, 1969: 503)

The essence of the theory expressed here is that there are different stages of economic development, each of which is characterised by particular kinds of labour process, technology and property relations. Thus societies in Europe in the Middle Ages typified as feudal were based on agricultural production using hand-tools and animal draught power, with serfs producing for themselves and for the nobles who owned the land. Each stage of economic development has distinctive productive forces (including raw materials, technology, human skills, division of labour) and a particular set of production relations (based on who owns and controls productive resources). The importance of analysing the way in which the economy is organised is that the mode of production has an effect on ('conditions') all the other aspects of social life, including the social psychology of how people view the world ('consciousness'). Hence the essential emphasis of Marxist theory on the mode of production.

A number of modes of production can be identified as different epochs in history, such as slavery, feudalism and capitalism. In all except the earliest stage ('primitive communalism'), there has been an economic surplus produced by society, namely the difference between the total output of the direct producers and what they consume. It is this surplus which releases some people from direct production, and in different modes of production this economic surplus is appropriated in different ways. It provides the basis for class relations, which are defined by who owns the productive resources and thus appropriates the surplus product. As we have seen, in the feudal mode of production, for example, the class of landowners appropriated the surplus from the class of serfs.

The concept of the mode of production is therefore not narrowly economic, because it embraces the social relations of class. The idea of class is pivotal to Marxist political economy. The procedure of class analysis to identify the nature of the class formation at any given time is central to its mode of empirical inquiry. Class relations are determined by the relationship of different groups to productive resources – within capitalism, for example, the capitalists own means of production such as factories, while the working class owns no productive property and has to work for wages. However, the relations of class encompass not only the economic dimension of exploitation but also the dimension of power, since they are characterised by domination and subordination, and they shape many areas of social experience. Indeed, it is the different situation of groups within the economic system that is a major source of social conflict and struggle for power as members of the different groups pursue their class interests – for example, in struggles over the ownership of land or over wages and conditions of work. The political economy approach argues that the existence of class divisions conditions social and political phenomena, and that class conflict is the major engine of social change.

The mode of production given most attention by Marx and Engels and subsequent Marxist writers is capitalism. The central aim has been to explain the dynamics of capitalist accumulation and reproduction, and show their impact on society. The capitalist mode of production is defined by capital being the main means of production and by characteristic relations of production, in which one class (the capitalist class or bourgeoisie) has private ownership of capital, while another class (the working class or proletariat) owns no means of production and sells its capacity to work. Marxist political economy has revealed evolution and changes (in technology, economic characteristics, political institutions) as capitalism has passed through a number of phases from its origins in the fifteenth century. Its present phase is characterised by its global nature and the dominance of large transnational corporations. Marx identified the tendency of capitalism to spread around the world and develop a world market. The intensification of this process in the twentieth century has made it an important area of study for later writers, from Lenin's work on imperialism early in the century to contemporary studies of the global political economy and socioeconomic development in the peripheral capitalist countries of the South.

An important purpose of social investigation for Marx – and for many others drawing on his legacy – has been to develop a theoretical analysis of capitalism that would help to identify the internal contradictions which would provide the conditions for its transformation and the establishment of a new stage of social development. These contradictions include the developments in technology that cause strains in the existing relations of production. For example, the growth of manufacturing technology and the development of the bourgeoisie as a class in France led to the

Revolution of 1789 and the overthrow of the feudal aristocracy by the new class, which instituted political and legal arrangements to serve its own interests. A key element of Marx's theory is that the proletariat – which was created by the development of industrial production, and exists in an antagonistic relationship with the bourgeoisie – can develop self-awareness as a class, and the necessary political organisation, to overthrow the ruling bourgeoisie and establish a new form of society. The essential contradiction in the capitalist mode of production between the social nature of production in large enterprises and the private appropriation of the economic surplus could then be overcome. In the new mode of production – initially socialism and ultimately communism – there would be no private ownership of the means of production. It would be based on a system of economic organisation that would enable the direct producers to have collective control over production, and thus end the subordination of one class to another. The end of class exploitation and domination would end alienation and make human emancipation possible for all oppressed groups in society. Thus, within the tradition of Marxist political economy, the working class is identified as the historical agent with the strategic location in the economy and the material interest to carry out the revolution that will end capitalist society and create a new stage of social development.

The concern with class conflict, class consciousness, struggles over power, agencies for social change, and so forth are part of the political theory embedded in the paradigm of Marxist political economy. The passage from the 'Preface' quoted above refers to the 'legal and political superstructure' in society, which in essence means the institutions of the state: laws, courts, armies, legislatures and government bureaucracies. The 'Preface' argues that the state arises from the foundation constituted by the relations of production. The state received some attention in the writings of Marx and Engels, who regarded it as a class institution, a means through which the economically dominant class advances its interests. In a famous phrase, they spoke of the state as 'a committee for managing the common affairs of the whole bourgeoisie' (Marx and Engels, 1969: 110–11), thus rejecting Hegel's position – that the state represents the general interests of society as a whole. The precise ways in which the state relates to class-divided society within the capitalist mode of production have been a subject of extensive investigation within Marxism since the 1960s. Although there is controversy over the extent to which the dominant class directly controls the state, and the extent to which the state has autonomy as an institution, there is general agreement that the state serves the interests of capitalist accumulation and reproduction. Indeed, its capacity to do this (and to stabilise the disruptions inherent in the mode of production) is an important feature of contemporary capitalism; this is why it has been so closely analysed.

The power of the state within capitalist society is a significant political fact for conceptions of the process of social change. An important concern of Marxist political theory, therefore, is how the proletariat can develop politically to undertake socialist revolution – that is, to take control of state power and bring capitalism to an end. Marxist politics focuses on the development of the subjective conditions of human agency and the organisation of working-class struggles in the context of the structural contradictions which are endemic to capitalism. The development of modern political parties of the working class at the end of the nineteenth century raised a range of questions concerning the nature of socialist political practice. One central issue has been the appropriate relationship between class and party. A dominant tradition, symbolised by Lenin and the Bolshevik Party in Russia, is that of the elite 'vanguard' party of professional revolutionaries which seeks to bring socialist consciousness to the workers from outside and guide their activity. An alternative view – expressed, for example, by Rosa Luxemburg – has laid greater stress on mass participation by workers, whose involvement in various forms of political and economic activity (trade unions, co-operatives, workers' councils, political campaigns) would develop their class consciousness in a process of working-class emancipation through its own efforts. In this concept the party expresses and organises the self-activity of the working class. Despite their differences, both these traditions see the party as the key political form of working-class politics.

The issues of political theory and practice in Marxist political economy raise questions of social psychology – why do people hold a particular world-view, and in what circumstances do they change their outlook? In the 'Preface', Marx (1969: 503) argued that 'the mode of production of material life conditions the social, political and intellectual life process in general', and that it is people's 'social being that determines their consciousness'. His social psychology is therefore based on a materialist theory of knowledge that sees ideas, attitudes, values and beliefs as being shaped by the class divisions of capitalist society. People's world-view arises from their position within the social relations of pro-duction and their everyday experience, particularly in the labour process. But ideas and beliefs are also used to advance class inter-ests in the conflicts between the classes. As Marx and Engels put it in *The German Ideology*:

> The ideas of the ruling class are in every epoch the ruling ideas i.e. the class which is the ruling material force of society is at the same time the ruling intellectual force. The class which has the means of material production at its disposal, has control at the same time over the means of mental production. (Marx and Engels, 1970: 64)

They argued that bourgeois ideology is propagated through a number of social institutions and is the dominant way of thinking in capitalist society. For example, values of individualism, consumer-ism and private profit are taken for granted. The power of this world-view in society is such that it becomes difficult for the working class to recognise its own interests. The task of Marxist politics is thus to oppose the ideas of the ruling class and provide alternative ideas and experiences which will help the working class to become aware of its own interest and its capacity for action – that is, to acquire class consciousness.

These issues of consciousness and ideology have received a lot of attention in Marxist theory, particularly in the current known as Western Marxism, which has focused on the demonstrated capacity of the capitalist class to exert its control over society and block the emergence of working-class consciousness. The most important explanatory concept here is that of hegemony, developed by Gramsci, who sought to understand how the ruling class en-gineers consent to its rule among the mass of the population (in parallel to the coercion it can mobilise through the state when necessary). He used the concept of hegemony to signify political leadership by consent, and showed how it was achieved by the diffusion of the dominant ideology through social institutions such as religion, the media, education and popular culture, so that it permeates social life and becomes 'common sense' which is reproduced through daily experience. It was his contention that hegemony is not a given, and that it is a terrain of struggle, as it is contradicted by some of the ideas and everyday experiences of the majority of the population. Gramsci argued that the struggle for hegemony takes places in all spheres of cultural and intellectual life, and of social practice. He believed that there was a need for the working class to develop a new world-view which would undermine the legitimacy of ruling ideas and create an oppositional culture, a counter-hegemony. He concluded that socialist political activity should create intellectual leadership within the working class to develop a counter-hegemony through which that class could achieve its own emancipation.

In this brief review of Marxist political economy I have presented it as a comprehensive theory of society which goes beyond customary disciplinary boundaries such as sociology or economics. This theory provides a coherent conceptual framework. Its main concepts are historical materialism, the mode of production, class, capitalism, imperialism, social revolution, socialism, the state, the party, consciousness, ideology and hegemony. These concepts provide the basis for a distinctive mode of analysis which aims to uncover the relationships between the mode of economic organisation on the one hand, and social and political phenomena on the other. It is a general social theory which provides the concepts and methodology for the study of particular activities in society, such as adult education.[1]

At this point it is appropriate to consider some of the recent critiques of Marxist theory and practice in order to examine their implications for the political economy approach.

Recent Critiques of Marxism

Ever since the early formulations of Marxist social theory there have been arguments within and outside Marxism over its interpretation and application in social analysis, and its implications for political practice. Some recent critiques have been made by those who are sympathetic to Marxism and wish to reconstruct the tradition so that it provides a more adequate theory and is more able to address present-day social realities – see, for example, Wright, Levine and Sober, *Reconstructing Marxism* (1992). But alongside such internal debates, there have been external critiques from feminism, post-structuralism, post-Marxism and postmodernism. There is therefore a range of contemporary critiques (some sympathetic, some hostile) of Marxist theory and practice. Six areas of critique are examined below, because they have particular significance for the political economy approach discussed above.

Marxism as a theory

The first area of critique relates to Marxism's status as a theory which claims to provide a general account of society and its development. One dimension of this critique is the extent to which Marxism can or should be regarded as a 'science'. Working within nineteenth-century paradigms, Marx and Engels clearly regarded their work as scientific, and concerned with uncovering the laws governing social phenomena in a manner comparable to methods used in natural science. This positivist view permeated classical Marxism, and the current of thinking known as Western Marxism is based on a reaction to this scientism. It constitutes a critique not only at the philosophical level but also at the practical level, as the appeal to scientific authority legitimated communist parties, so that official Marxism ('scientific socialism') became uncritical and a body of doctrine. The issue led to controversy within Marxism, exemplified by Althusser's attack on humanist Marxism in the 1960s (Smart, 1983). It can be usefully considered in terms of broader thinking about the nature of social science.

The position adopted in this book concurs with Anthony Giddens's view that social sciences do not need to imitate the natural sciences in terms of procedures or the nature of their findings, because human/social phenomena are different from natural phenomena. However, they can still be considered sciences in terms of their 'use of systematic methods of investigation, theoretical thinking, and the logical assessment of arguments to develop a body of knowledge about a particular subject-matter' (Giddens, 1989: 21). This position is similar to that of Wright, Levine and Sober (1992), who regard Marxism as a social science, the validity of whose findings are open to the normal criteria of evaluation in terms of assessment of the evidence produced, the logic of the arguments and the adequacy of the theory in explaining the data. Hence the conception in this book of Marxism as a social theory open to development as it responds to new evidence and arguments. This conception agrees with Carver (1982) that a statement like Marx's 'Preface to *A Contribution to the Critique of Political Economy*' should be regarded as a set of propositions (a 'research hypothesis') to guide empirical inquiry rather than a fixed set of laws about society. Thus this study is aligned with those within the Marxist tradition who wish to develop it so that its explanatory strengths are retained and its weaknesses (in terms of internal consistency, flaws or ability to address new realities) are resolved.

This, however, implies that I regard as indispensable for holistic social inquiry a theory which enables a systemic analysis of society and a search for causal explanations. In this view, capitalism is regarded as a social system, so that analysis of specific aspects of social existence benefits from a theoretical starting point that sees society in its totality. Without a general theory it is not possible to analyse society as a whole and search for the underlying causes of social inequality, domination, and so forth. An overall theory of social structures enables the macro-level analysis of the contexts of people's actions and beliefs, and of how they 'create, consent to and struggle against these social arrangements' (Gordon, 1996: viii). This support for a general theory of society conflicts with the second dimension of critique of Marxism as a theory. This critique is articulated by post-structuralism and postmodernism, which is critical of all grand theory ('master narratives', 'meta-discourses') as typified by Marxism. Writers such as Foucault and Lyotard have criticised Marxism in terms of its claim to be a science, its concept of historical progress, its concern with causality and its global theorising (Sarup, 1993). From the postmodern perspective, Marxism's 'totalising discourse' is seen as coercive and as the basis for the authoritarianism characteristic of Soviet-style state socialism. The logic of this position is questionable, however, as there is no necessary connection between the nature of a social theory and a particular form of political regime. The analytical value of Marxism remains, and it is tenable to utilise the political economy approach based on Marxist theory as a means of explaining the dynamics of capitalist society.

Economic determinism

Another area of critique surrounds the question of economic determinism. In the 'Preface' Marx argues that the economic base of society shapes the political and cultural superstructure, an idea summed up in the formulation 'The mode of production of material life conditions the social, political and intellectual life process in general' (Marx, 1969: 503). This concept of determination is central to Marxism, but it raises theoretical difficulties. First, how direct or indirect is the relationship between the economic foundation and various aspects of social life? Second, how general and inclusive is the formulation, and to what extent is it applicable to *all* social phenomena? Classical Marxism inclined towards a position which sought to interpret all historical events, political activities and social practices in terms of economic factors. The critical and humanist current in Marxism reacted against this and placed its emphasis on issues of consciousness, experience and agency. A major debate on the issue took place between structuralist and culturalist Marxists during the 1970s over the question of the relationship between structure and agency in social life. In this study I accept Smart's conclusion after reviewing this debate about the base/superstructure metaphor and the question of economic determinism:

> In the works of Marx and Engels it is clear that the economy is determinant in the final instance and therefore the superstructures are in some sense determined. However, the latter are accorded some degree of effectivity which is not simply reducible to the economy. (Smart, 1983: 30)

Despite the criticism of so-called economic determinism or reductionism from inside and outside Marxism, a distinctive and defensible feature of Marxist analysis is that the mode of production does provide the structural context of social existence. However, any particular institution, event or practice may be relatively autonomous of economic factors, and other influences have to be taken into account. Furthermore, there is reciprocal interaction between the economic foundation and the political and cultural levels of society, so that these levels have an influence on the base. The nature of determination in any particular case is thus a question of empirical analysis. The relationship between structure and agency is quite clearly described by Engels:

> Men make their history themselves, only they do so in a given environment, which conditions it, and on the basis of actual relations already existing, among which the economic relations, however much they may be influenced by the other – the political and ideological relations – are still ultimately the decisive ones, forming the keynote which runs through them and alone leads to understanding. (Marx and Engels, 1962: 467)

In this book I use the concept of 'political economy' to make clear its assumption that the contexts within which people act are best analysed within the conceptual framework of historical materialism derived from the 'Preface'.

The primacy of class

Related to the discussion on the role of the economic structure in determining social phenomena is a third area of critique focused on the primacy given to class relations in orthodox Marxist accounts of social inequality and domination. This critique raises the issue of how Marxist analysis should account for systems of inequality which are not specific to the capitalist mode of production and do not arise out of social relations of production such as those of gender, ethnicity and race.

This question has been a theme within feminist scholarship. At issue has been the relationship between the system of patriarchy based on the power of men over women, and that of capitalism based on the exploitation of one class by another. One trend within feminism has engaged with Marxist theory in an effort to provide a historical-materialist understanding of patriarchy and its specific nature within the epoch of capitalism, including the intersections of class relations and gender relations (Lengermann and Niebrugge-Brantley, 1992). For example, the majority of women in the workforce have poorly paid and insecure jobs, so that patriarchal oppression intersects with the dynamics of capitalist accumulation to lower the costs of labour. The social situation of women – including in relation to other women – is inescapably bound up with class relations.

Alongside efforts to understand the interaction of class and gender there has been the recognition that configurations of ethnic and racial inequality also have their own specificity and distinctive patterns of intersection with the class structure (and gender relations). Anti-racist writers who have applied a Marxist perspective, such as Miles (1989), have dealt with similar problems to feminists in terms of addressing not only the specific aspects of racism but also how it articulates with class (and gender) relations. Miles's conclusion is that racial inequality has to be seen in the context of the capitalist mode of production: 'The influence of racism and exclusionary practices is always a component of a wider structure of class disadvantage and exclusion' (Miles, 1989: 9).

In parallel to these kinds of considerations has been the analysis of the nature of power by post-structuralism and postmodernism. Particularly important has been the work of Michel Foucault, who has argued that power is not located in relations between classes or in a central point, such as the state, but is 'decentred', diffused throughout society in many different forms. From the post-structuralist and postmodernist viewpoints, there are multiple patterns of domination within social life (and concomitant resistances), none of which should be privileged in relation to any other.

The effect of this feminist, anti-racist, post-structuralist and postmodernist theorising has been to present a more complex configuration of inequality in society than that suggested by those Marxist accounts which identify the cause of all oppression as class exploitation. The challenge for contemporary Marxism is how to situate its concept of class causation within what Wright, Levine and Sober (1992) call a context of 'multiple causality'. They argue that Marxism, which has traditionally accorded causal primacy to class, must acknowledge that other causal processes of domination which are not reducible to class, such as gender relations, are also important. Significance must be given to cultural factors as well as to economic ones. This is a vital area for the development of Marxist political economy, and this study incorporates the idea of multiple causality into its model of inequality. However, this does not diminish the importance given to the concept of class and the methodology of class analysis. Gender, ethnic and racial inequalities may have sources and consequences independent of the relations of production, but they are not totally autonomous of economic factors. These forms of social inequality are shaped by the capitalist mode of production and by the existing class structure. They have a class character. The analytical task of political economy is to clarify the linkages between the class basis of society and these other forms of social domination.

The politics of social change

The debate over the sources and modes of operation of power in society connects with a fourth area of critique which concerns the politics of social change in capitalist society. Marxism as a social theory has always sought both to analyse social change and to contribute to the process of social change. The rise of radical politics in the West in the 1960s – and especially the events of May 1968 in France – raised significant questions about orthodox Marxist thinking on the politics of social change. The protests in France were based on mass movements, and arose outside the conventional structures of left-wing parties and trade unions. Similarly, the protests in the USA around civil rights and the war in Vietnam took the form of social movements. Such struggles not only had an organisational form different from that of the working-class party; they also had a content that could not be conceived simply in terms of class conflict. The development of what are known as the 'new social movements' (that is, political activity by groups organised around specific issues such as peace, the environment, black nationalism, women's liberation and gay rights) has posed important problems for Marxist political theory and practice.

At the level of theory, this development has provoked new thinking about the nature of the 'revolutionary subject' and the extent to which the working class is necessarily the strategic centre of opposition to capitalist society. The new social movements and other organisations in civil society may question aspects of the capitalist social order, but they do not do so from experience located in economic relations. Moreover, they do not seek to take control of the state. They therefore raise questions on the nature of power in society and the significance of the state. The idea of diverse social groups pursuing different issues resonates with post-modernist thinking about multiple subject positions and decentred power, and with the feminist view that the antagonisms in capitalist society cannot be seen only in economic terms. The political strategy emanating from this theoretical position was clearly articulated in the post-Marxist views of Laclau and Mouffe in *Hegemony and Socialist Strategy: Towards a Radical Democratic Politics* (1985). They identify multiple sites of power and domination in society, and argue for an articulation of political forces which cuts across classes: namely, an alliance of various autonomous social movements. The goal of such a coalition is to struggle for radical democracy against all forms of social domination, and for the extension or defence of rights in civil society as much as the state. Radical democracy thus represents the transformation of the social relations of everyday life towards greater equality. These democratic struggles are separate from workers' struggles, and are carried out by a plurality of subjects, so that the working class cannot be seen as a 'privileged revolutionary subject'.

At the level of practice, the new social movements represent alternative modes of organisation to working-class political parties (particularly in the hierarchical Leninist tradition of the vanguard party) and seek alternative modes of engaging their membership in political activity. The idea of plural sites of power and resistance negates 'the Leninist organisational practice of subsuming heterogeneous social, sexual, economic and political struggles under one political struggle controlled by a single party' (Ryan, 1982: 195). The preferred practices of these movements are egalitarian and participatory, rather than hierarchical and elitist, in order to prefigure radical democracy. Of enormous significance in this respect has been the women's movement, which has developed distinctive ways of organising along these lines, including the use of personal experience in group discussion as the starting point for raising awareness of the need for personal, social and political change.

Single-issue identity politics have been controversial for Marxists because there is no clear basis on which coalitions and political leadership can be built, and because it is unclear how such politics can defeat the logic of capitalism embodied in the social relations of production and defended by the state. None the less, the expansion of social movements and other organisations of civil society, their challenges to aspects of the capitalist socioeconomic order, and their prefigurative modes of operation mean that they must be seriously considered in a Marxist rethinking of the politics of social change. This requires a clarification of the role of the working class in relation to groups resisting other forms of domination, and must therefore be informed by the kind of multicausal analysis suggested above. The political economy approach used in this book therefore includes a broad concept of politics in terms of the agents and processes involved in struggling for the goal of a post-capitalist society.

Alternatives to capitalism

Another area of critique relates to Marxism's conception of the alternative to capitalist society. An essential element in the historical materialism of Marx and Engels is that capitalism would eventually break down through its internal contradictions and the political activity of the working class, and would be superseded by a new stage of social development, socialism. Their work was motivated largely by the desire to show that what was morally and ethically desirable (an alternative society) was historically inevitable because of the very nature of capitalism. They envisaged socialism as an egalitarian and democratic society which would expand human freedom. However, they wrote very little about it in detail because they thought it would be developed as the product of working-class struggles, not as a result of blueprints for the future.

Between 1917 and 1991 there were a number of countries in Eastern Europe whose political-economic structures were influenced by conceptions of Marxism. These countries called themselves socialist or communist, and were widely regarded as a form of socialist society. The reality of 'actually existing socialism' confronted Marxists with severe problems, because the model of Soviet socialism was clearly flawed from a very early stage. Indeed, the critical currents in the Marxist tradition developed largely in reaction to the failings of this model, regularly exposed over the years by dramatic events such as the denunciation of Stalin in

1956, the crushing of the Czechoslovakian experiment in 1968 and the invasion of Afghanistan in 1979. The final collapse of the model – between 1989 and 1991 – created a new situation for thinking about post-capitalist society. The key question is whether Marxist theory is so responsible for the conception and legitimation of 'actually existing socialism' that the collapse of Eastern Europe terminally discredits the entire Marxist project – or does the end of these regimes enable Marxism, through critical analysis of what happened and theoretical reconstruction, to restate the arguments for socialism?

The postmodernist view is that Soviet-style socialism is a direct result of Marxist theory and the nature of that theory, totalitarianism being the product of a 'totalising' theory. But this is too simplistic an analysis of the complex economic and political processes which led to the emergence of state socialism. Although conceptions of Marxism played a role within these processes, the nature of these societies was not the inevitable result of Marxism. The case of the Soviet Union is well discussed by Gottleib (1992: 77–105), who shows how the Russian Revolution took place within an economically underdeveloped country with no democratic tradition. It was undertaken in the name of a tiny working class by an elite vanguard party that lacked widespread support. Immediately there was a civil war waged by internal groups backed by the surrounding capitalist countries. The new state sought a way out of economic chaos through industrialisation based on state control of economic life. However, it lacked popular support, especially from the peasant majority, and came to rely on coercion. In this situation, a regime of repression was instituted in which Marxism was used to justify the central power of the state and the Communist Party. The outcome of totalitarianism was thus a product of specific economic and political conditions rather than ideas inherent in Marxist theory.

Additionally, while postmodernism provides a negative critique of the Enlightenment and its values (including those values embodied in Marxism's vision of social progress, equality, justice and human emancipation), its own vision of an alternative society is not always clear, especially with respect to the capitalist mode of production (Sarup, 1993). The continuing failures of capitalism – its exploitation, inequalities and injustices, which are particularly salient when they are viewed in a global perspective – make the articulation of an alternative as relevant as ever. It is therefore concluded that the critical stance towards capitalism and the ideas of socialism remain relevant characteristics of Marxist political economy.

Eurocentrism

Finally, in this review of recent critiques it is necessary to consider the issue of whether a theory whose origins are in nineteenth-century Europe can have relevance for countries outside Europe at the start of the twenty-first century. Is Marxism Eurocentric? Can it comprehend the nature of contemporary global capitalism and the social reality of countries which have been historically on the fringe of capitalist development? The first question arises from the postmodernist antagonism to universal theories. Indeed, Jean Baudrillard has attacked Marxism for its 'theoretical racism' (Callinicos, 1989: 126) in applying its categories of analysis outside the context of industrial capitalism. It is true that Marx and Engels had limited information about other parts of the world, and may have been wrong in some conclusions about areas outside northern Europe and the nature of their pre-capitalist societies (for example, in the concept of the Asiatic mode of production). But this does not invalidate the use of the political economy approach as a mode of inquiry in varying circumstances. All societies, at whatever stage of development and in whatever geographical location, undertake economic activities for survival and reproduction, and the way these activities shape their political and social life is a justifiable focus of analysis. There seems to be no logical argument for characterising Marxism *a priori* as 'Eurocentric' in terms of its potential as a mode of social inquiry.

As for the second question, on Marxism's relevance to the analysis of global capitalism, Marx and Engels were well aware of the development of a world market and the worldwide spread of capitalism. This process was at a relatively early stage, and was not a major focus of their attention (although Marx planned to write books on international trade and the world market). However, the continued geographical expansion of capitalism has stimulated a lot of Marxist analysis of both the global dynamics of this process and its impact on the peripheral capitalist countries of the South. Many writers in the South, such as those referred to in this book (including Amin, Alavi, Cardoso, Faletto, Mamdani, Onimode and Thomas), have found Marxism a fruitful theory for analysing their situation. In fact, this is one area where the refinement of Marxist theory has clearly responded to changes in contemporary society. It is therefore quite valid to apply the political economy approach to the analysis of socioeconomic development in the South.

Summary

In this chapter I have presented an outline of the major concepts of the political economy approach, and an appraisal of some recent critiques of Marxist theory and practice. It is now possible to summarise the analytical position which has emerged from the discussion. My perspective embodies the view that Marxism continues to develop, and is able to provide a theoretical framework which is valid and relevant to the analysis of contemporary capitalist societies, including those of the South. It assumes that, despite criticisms by exponents of recent theoretical trends, especially post-structuralism and postmodernism, there is validity in applying the political economy approach.[2] I also believe that Marxist social theory generates findings which are open to the standard criteria of evaluation within the social sciences, and I therefore expect the book's analysis to be assessed accordingly. Thus it is argued that the conceptual tools of Marxist political economy are not outdated but remain of practical use for analysing the relationship between adult education and development.

The political economy approach that has been adopted posits that:

1. Social phenomena exist within a historical and structural context shaped by the mode of production and its class relations. The dynamics of the mode of production and the nature of the class formation change over time and can be analysed and delineated.
2. The manner and extent of the influence of the economic foundation on particular aspects of society is a matter for specific investigation in each case.

3. The dominance of the ·capitalist mode of production at the world level means that country-level studies must situate their analysis within the context of the global political economy. The dynamics of socioeconomic development in the peripheral capitalist countries of the South have to be located within the international context of imperialism.

4. The different classes which exist pursue their own interests in society, and these interests are fundamentally conflictual. These conflicts permeate all aspects of social life.

5. While class relations are the main determinant of social phenomena, they are not the sole determinant, and other social inequalities, such as those of gender, ethnicity and race, have significant effects. A comprehensive analysis of social phenomena must consider these multiple effects and how they interact.

6. The conflicts in society arising from class differences and other social inequalities are reflected in the state, which institutionally serves the interests of capitalist accumulation and reproduction. Public policy must therefore be analysed in terms of how it relates to the inequalities in society.

7. Intellectual and cultural life is shaped by the capitalist mode of production and by the contestation between different classes and groups in society as the legitimacy of the socioeconomic order is simultaneously defended and challenged. The struggle for ideological hegemony takes place both in the institutions of the state and in the organisations of civil society.

8. Opposition to the existing capitalist socioeconomic order is expressed not only by political parties but also by social movements and other organisations in civil society which articulate alternative conceptions of society and how it should develop. These organisations seek to transform people's understanding of society and thereby engage their support in struggles to change society.

The position summarised here provides the basis for developing a political economy approach specifically for the study of adult education. In Chapter 3 I assess the theoretical foundations of some previous works on the political economy of adult education prior to putting forward the theoretical framework of the book.

Notes

1. This conceptual framework will be elaborated as it is applied to adult education and development in subsequent chapters. However, the reader who wishes to explore it in greater depth is referred to the following books as a starting point: T. Bottomore et al. (eds), *A Dictionary of Marxist Thought* (1983); R.S. Gottleib, *Marxism 1844–1990* (1992); D. McLellan (ed.), *Marx. The First 100 Years* (1983).

2. For a recent Marxist critique of postmodernism, see E.M. Wood and J.M. Foster (eds), *In Defense of History. Marxism and the Postmodern Agenda* (1997).

CHAPTER 3

The Political Economy of
Adult Education

The Radical Tradition in Adult Education

A distinctive tradition within adult education practice and scholarship is the radical tradition (Elias and Merriam, 1995). This tradition encompasses adult education concerned with social justice and struggles for social change (Lovett, 1988). It is characterised by its emphasis on the link between adult education activities and social action, particularly through collective participation (in contrast, for example, to the liberal tradition's individualism and emphasis on education for its own sake). It has been an aspect of adult education since the nineteenth century, and has been influenced by various political and philosophical positions, including Marxism.

Since the early days of Marxism there has been a close connection between Marxist theory and the practice of adult education. In 1847, in Brussels, Marx himself delivered a course of lectures on wage labour and capital to the German Workers' Education Association, which he had helped to establish (McLellan, 1973: 177). Eminent Marxist theorists such as Lenin in Saint Petersburg in the early 1890s and Gramsci in Turin in the early 1920s engaged in workers' education. Such activity was consistent with their political conception of the role of the proletariat in social revolution and the need to develop working-class consciousness. Mao Zedong was involved in the adult education of communist political cadres in Yenan in the late 1930s and 1940s, and a number of his well-known works were delivered as lectures.

There is therefore a long-standing heritage within radical adult education in capitalist societies that has been based explicitly on Marxist theory. In the USA, for instance, Marxist socialists developed the Working People's College in 1907, linked to the trade-union movement. The goals of the College were stated in 1923:

> This [college] recognizes the existence of class struggle in society, and its courses of study have been prepared so that industrially organized workers, both men and women, dissatisfied with conditions under our capitalist system, can more efficiently carry on an organized class struggle for the attainment of industrial demands, and realistically of a new social order. (Cited in Paulston and Altenbaugh, 1988: 123)

The College sought to educate workers to provide leadership in industrial unionism and socialist activism from a definite Marxist viewpoint. More recently, in Kenya between 1976 and 1982, the Kamirithu Community Education and Cultural Centre developed an adult education programme based on literacy teaching and community drama which challenged the cultural imperialism characteristic of post-colonial Kenya from a position influenced by Marxist perspectives (Youngman, 1986: 226–32).

However, although some elements of the radical tradition have been Marxist, on the whole the linkage between adult education and social action has been inspired by reformist thinking, often derived from social democratic politics. Indeed, the two perspectives have on occasion been in direct conflict, as in the dispute in England (1909–29) between the Marxist Central Labour College (which emphasised independent working-class education) and the Workers' Educational Association over the latter's acceptance of funding from the capitalist state (Armstrong, 1988). It is also important to recognise that the radical tradition has embraced a close relationship between adult education and non-class-based social movements. This has been the case both historically – for example, in the anti-colonial movements of the 1940s and 1950s in Africa and Asia – and during the contemporary period in the women's, peace and environment movements.

Marxist theory has therefore been one of a number of influences on the radical tradition in adult education practice since the mid-nineteenth century. However, the use of Marxism as a theoretical framework for adult education scholarship is relatively recent, and developed only in the 1970s. The more widespread usage of Marxist theory in the English-language literature on adult education is a result of two factors: first, the renaissance of Marxism in the 1960s in Europe and the USA, and second, the writings of Paulo Freire.

Political Economies of Adult Education

The revival of political economy within the Marxist tradition that took place in Anglo-American scholarship in the late 1960s spread to the study of education, initially in the work of radical American economists. The idea of a political economy of education emerged in the early 1970s. For example, Martin Carnoy published a collection entitled *Schooling in a Corporate Society: The Political Economy of Education in America* (Carnoy, 1972). He then extended this mode of analysis to the countries of the South in *Education as Cultural Imperialism* (Carnoy, 1974), which focused on the international nature of capitalism, and argued 'that the spread of schooling was carried out in the context of imperialism and colonialism – in the spread of mercantilism and capitalism – and it cannot in its present form and purpose be separated from that context.... The structure of schooling, since it came from the metropole, was based in large part on the needs of metropole investors, traders and culture' (Carnoy, 1974: 15). The insight of the political economy approach that schooling serves the needs of the dominant capitalist classes was thus applied within the circumstances of the unequal international relationship between nations.

The most influential of the early political economy studies was *Schooling in Capitalist America*, by Bowles and Gintis (1976), who put the capitalist mode of production and its constituent social relations of production at the centre of educational analysis. They elaborated the 'correspondence principle' (based on Marx's 'Preface'): the education system serves to reproduce the social relations of production and corresponding forms of consciousness through the social relations of education replicating the hierarchical division of labour. The school system itself has different levels to produce workers for different levels within the occupational structure. Changes in schooling that have taken place 'have been dictated in

the interests of a more harmonious reproduction of the class structure' (Bowles and Gintis, 1976: 132–3) at periods when the restructuring of production and its relations have created changed educational requirements for their reproduction. Bowles and Gintis
presented detailed evidence to support their argument that it is
the underlying economic structure of capitalist society which shapes
the nature of schooling. This structural emphasis was influential
within the sociology of school education, and the book soon made
an impact within adult education – for example, in the collection
Adult Education for a Change (J.L. Thompson, 1980).

Subsequent writings on schooling from within Marxist theory
substantially developed this initial political economy approach.
There was a major critique of the base/superstructure model used
by Bowles and Gintis (1976) because it was seen as overly determin-
ist. Their correspondence principle was criticised for providing
too simple an account of the relationship between economic factors
and the nature of the education system. Other writers developed
a more complex conceptualisation which accorded greater
autonomy to education, and in which the role of the state received
more attention in terms of how the interests of capital are mediated and embodied in educational policies. For example, the role
of the state was extensively discussed by Carnoy and Levin (1985)
in *Schooling and Work in the Democratic State*, where they argued that
the state is a site of struggle between the different classes and
groups in society. Thus while the capitalist class seeks to ensure
that schools reproduce workers for the unequal division of labour,
this is resisted by subordinated classes and groups who seek greater
equality of opportunity through education. This analysis developed the view of a number of writers that there are processes of
contradiction as well as reproduction in education.

The idea of struggle over the nature of education was linked
with conceptions of education's role not only in economic reproduction but also in cultural reproduction. Michael Apple (1979,
1982) stressed issues of ideology, and the role of schools in the
constitution and contestation of hegemony. Studies with a focus
on the cultural practices of education looked at what actually goes
on within schools in terms of curriculum, textbooks, social relations, the work of the teacher, and so forth, to uncover the mechanisms whereby social inequality is reproduced and legitimated on

the one hand, and resisted and contested on the other. Apple also explored the dynamics of gender and race in education – areas neglected in Bowles and Gintis's analysis – from a multicausal position that regarded them as related to but not reducible to the dynamics of class relations. The significance of Apple's work in the 1980s for the political economy of education is that while he focused on processes of culture and social domination, he retained the importance of the mode of production and the class structure. Indeed, he subtitled his book *Teachers and Texts* (Apple, 1986) 'A Political Economy of Class and Gender Relations in Education'. In his endeavour to combine 'a structuralist focus on the objective conditions within a social formation and the culturalist insistence on seeing these conditions as ongoingly built, and contested, in our daily lives' (Apple, 1988: 119) he produced a theoretically sophisticated approach to the political economy of school educa-tion. Many of his ideas synchronise with the position summarised at the end of Chapter 2, with the exception that he concentrated solely on the USA and did not address the context of imperialism and the global political economy.

Marxist writers on school education have been a major source of influence on the development of the political economy of adult education. It seems to be generally the case that developments in the study of adult education lag behind those in school education. In Paulo Freire, however, adult education found a theorist who influenced radical school educators as well as providing a source of Marxist thinking in adult education scholarship.

Freire's impact on English-speaking adult educators was signifi-cant after the publication in the early 1970s of his books *Cultural Action for Freedom* (Freire, 1972a) and *Pedagogy of the Oppressed* (Freire, 1972b). In general terms, his position as a voice of the Third World and his philosophical-political stance resonated with the anti-imperialist and New Left ideas which characterised the radicalism that had emerged in Europe and North America in the 1960s. In the field of adult education, the writings which appeared in the early 1970s gave new impetus to the key idea of the radical tradition that adult education should contribute to social change in favour of the poor and oppressed. Freire's work espoused the view that adult education was inherently political, and that it was a force either for reproducing social domination ('domestication') or for emancipation ('liberation'). It was distinctive because Freire was from Latin America, and his ideas were related to his experiences of adult literacy and agricultural extension in peripheral capitalist countries of the South. It was especially significant because the practices of adult education that Freire advocated (centred on the process of demystifying patterns of domination, which he called 'conscientisation') were based on an elaborated theoretical foundation. The philosophical basis of Freire's early work included humanist Marxism, which found expression in his concern with alienation, consciousness, dialectics and praxis, and in his suspicion of Leninist political practice, as well as in his clear opposition to existing capitalist society. Thus Freire generated a new and wider awareness of the relevance of applying Marxist theory to the study of adult education and the effort to understand its nature, effects and potential.

Freire's importance for the development of the political economy of adult education is that in the 1970s he gave currency to the use of Marxist theory. However, his own position in his early writings was aligned with the culturalist tradition within Marxism, and did not focus on the structural context of consciousness and cultural practices. Indeed those early writings were overtly hostile to orthodox Marxism and its emphasis on the economic structure of society; therefore Freire himself did not initially use the conceptual framework of Marxist political economy. In 1978, however, in his book on his work in Guinea-Bissau, *Pedagogy in Process* (Freire, 1978), he did show a new concern with the structural determinants of adult education, and utilised concepts such as the mode of production, material conditions, social relations of production, and so forth, for the first time.

It can be concluded that Freire's work was a critical influence on the ideas of a political economy of adult education that emerged in the late 1970s. He did not himself elaborate a political economy perspective in his subsequent publications in English. His main concerns remained essentially around adult literacy and critical pedagogy conceived in terms of cultural politics, identity, subjectivity, knowledge, language, and experience. This position resonated with the concerns of postmodernism, as *Paulo Freire. A Critical Encounter* (McLaren and Leonard, 1993) illustrates. Nevertheless, his own position can be clearly differentiated from that of post-

modernism by its persistent emphasis on political action for freedom and social justice. Furthermore, it retained a clear political
economy perspective, explicitly informed by the work of Marx,
which located adult education within capitalism as a system, and
stressed the need for class analysis. Therefore, while Freire repudi-
ated economic reductionism, he did not reject a materialist stance:

> Liberating education can change our understanding of reality. But this
> is not the same as changing reality itself. No. Only political action in
> society can make social transformation, not critical study in the class-
> room. The structures of society, like the capitalist mode of production,
> have to be changed for society to be transformed.... The issue of social
> conflict is absolutely important here. In the last analysis, conflict is the
> midwife of consciousness. (Freire and Shor, 1987: 175–6)

Freire's body of work addresses many elements of the political
economy approach summarised in Chapter 2, though not in a
systematic way. Its strength is in its analysis of the processes of
social domination, ideology and hegemony within adult education, and in its linkage of liberating education with oppositional
social movements. Above all, its basis in the context of peripheral
capitalism in the South addresses the problem of Eurocentric bias,
and locates adult education within the international context of
imperialism. Its major weakness in terms of the summarised approach is its neglect of the state.

One of the earliest published uses of the concept of a political
economy of adult education was made by Hall (1978) in his important article 'Continuity in Adult Education and Political Struggle', where he provided a historical review of the radical tradition
of adult education, particularly in Europe and North America. In
assessing the role of adult education in social change, he wrote:

> A political economic view of adult education would not allow for the
> conclusion that adult education, or in fact any education alone, is an
> instrumental factor in changing society. The relationship of adult edu-
> cation to struggle, to social change, to the improvement of the distri-
> bution of wealth and resources amongst all classes is one of integral
> support ... not instrumentality. Economic history gives us the basis for
> an analysis of social and political trends. (Hall, 1978: 13)

The article indicated his awareness not only of the history of adult
education's links to the labour movement and other social move-

ments but also of Marxist political economy's concerns with the economic basis of social phenomena and with class struggle and social change. Its significance is that Hall subsequently became Secretary-General of the International Council for Adult Education (ICAE), and promoted a research project under its aegis entitled 'The Political Economy of Adult Education'. The first phase of the project involved a planning meeting in 1980 at which ten working papers were discussed (Healey, 1983). Two of those papers focused particularly on conceptual and methodological issues in the political economy of adult education.

Filson and Green's paper *Toward a Political Economy of Adult Education in the Third World* (1980) was obviously a 'working paper', being poorly structured and not very coherent. However, an approach to the political economy of adult education clearly surfaced, based on the works of Marx and Engels and recent Marxist writers. Its starting point was within the tradition of historical materialism:

> we are assuming that these societies' forces and relations of production fundamentally limit and condition their political and educational forms even though the political-educational realm has a relatively autonomous existence in relation to those productive forces and relations. (Filson and Green, 1980: 1)

The theoretical framework that emerged emphasised the mode of production and the significance of class relations. The writers argued strongly for a recognition of the specificity of the countries of the South, paying particular attention to the colonial period and the relationship of the new capitalist mode of production to the pre-capitalist modes of production. The paper discussed issues of consciousness, knowledge and ideology in relation to class-divided society, referring briefly to the role of the colonial and post-colonial state. Most of the examples of educational development were drawn from school and university education, and there was little analysis of adult education *per se*, apart from some references to literacy and agricultural extension. For example, agricultural extension in the countries of the South was seen as incorporating the peasant class into the international market in a programme of 'modernisation' that usually benefited other classes. Filson and Green's framework is not applied in any sustained manner to adult education. However, a political economy approach was clearly outlined, and it has similarities with the position summarised in Chapter 2. Its theoretical weaknesses are threefold: (a) it focuses solely on class, and neglects other social inequalities such as gender; (b) it does not accord enough significance to the role of the state; and (c) it pays little attention to resistance and opposition to the dominant ideology.

The second paper, *Towards a Methodology in Political Economy of Adult Education in Tanzania*, by Mbilinyi (1980), is also unpolished and rather incomplete. Nevertheless, it provides an important discussion of some of the issues surrounding a historical materialist approach to the study of adult education. Although Mbilinyi did not use the term 'mode of production', she did use the Marxist concept 'social formation', and emphasised the significance of class relationships. She identified class struggles at various levels, including the level of the state (defining Tanzania as 'state capitalist' in nature) and the level of ideology, where the ruling class's 'dominance is constantly under attack ... and must be continually reconstituted' (Mbilinyi, 1980: 4). Of great consequence is her identification of social contradictions which are not synonymous with class, and her discussion of gender relations and patriarchy is extensive. Some reference was made to Tanzania's colonial history and the impact of international capital but no general case for the specificity of countries of the South was argued, though this is implied in her clear methodological emphasis on concrete investigation. The strong theoretical sections of the paper were followed by a largely descriptive account of the development of education in Tanzania, which failed to apply her approach and said very little about the political economy of adult education. The theoretical framework of Mbilinyi's paper is congruent with the political economy approach established in Chapter 2, though it gives less attention to imperialism and the state, and does not address the question of organised opposition to the socioeconomic order.

Healey's article, 'Who Gains and Who Loses? The Political Economy of Adult Education' (1983), provided a review of the ICAE project, giving information on it and making an accessible statement of a political economy approach to adult education which is admirably clear and well-presented. Healey summarised the theoretical framework of the project and offset some of the deficiencies in the individual papers – for example, by stressing the importance of the global nature of the capitalist mode of production and the significance of social divisions other than class, including not only gender but also ethnicity and race. He went beyond the two papers by emphasising the capacity for action by subordinate classes to alter social and economic structures, and by making a linkage to adult education, which 'can have a major role in equipping subordinate classes for their struggles on their own behalf' (Healey, 1983: 53). The major theoretical weakness of this article is Healey's total omission of the role of the state.

From the two papers and the article it can be concluded that the theoretical framework which had begun to emerge during the first phase of the project was close to the one articulated at the end of Chapter 2. Unfortunately, the project did not proceed to the second phase, so that the framework was not elaborated and no applied studies were undertaken. An important opportunity to develop the political economy of adult education was therefore missed.

The next major discussion of a political economy of adult education was my own *Adult Education and Socialist Pedagogy* (Youngman, 1986). The book was the first in English to attempt an extended application of Marxist theory to the study of adult education. Its main focus was teaching and learning, but it situated the micro-level of pedagogy within the wider social context. The first chapter therefore contained a section on the political economy of adult education which drew attention to the structural context of the content and processes of adult education practice: 'This is not to say that all aspects of adult education are in some way directly determined by economic factors but simply to assert that adult education is not an autonomous institution which generates all of its own characteristics' (Youngman, 1986: 11). As the basis for its analysis of the context of adult education, the book presented certain central concepts of Marxist social theory – the mode of production, base and superstructure, class, the state and imperialism. It illustrated how adult education is used by the ruling capitalist class to advance its own economic interests and consolidate its political position – for example, courses in Britain for the unemployed in the late 1970s which, in effect, legitimated structural unemployment. But it also stressed that adult education is an area of class struggle and that the dominated classes have also sought to use it to serve their own interests – for example, in the 150 hours' paid educational leave achieved by the Metal-workers' Union in Italy in 1973. Later sections of the chapter expanded the idea that adult education could play an important role in the struggle to transform capitalist society by being linked to organised socialist politics. The next chapter, which considered issues of consciousness, knowledge and learning, included an extended discussion of the concepts of ideology and hegemony as a means of theorising the relationship between the cultural and the structural.

The theoretical framework presented in that book is similar to the one summarised above in Chapter 2. It was, however, unevenly developed, partly because the book's focus was on pedagogical practices rather than structural analysis. In terms of the approach summarised above, this meant that questions of ideology and hegemony were given greater prominence. The book did not elaborate on imperialism and the international context of adult education, nor did it consider the specific nature of peripheral capitalism. While it did discuss, at some length, the importance of class divisions for adult education, it paid little attention to the divisions of ethnicity, race and gender, and it did not identify the need for a theoretical understanding which could encompass patterns of multiple causation. Its treatment of the state was superficial, although its significance for the study of adult education was recognised. The book gave extensive consideration to the role of adult education in opposition to the capitalist social order, but it focused almost exclusively on the centrality of the working class, and did not accord importance to the role of new social movements in challenging social domination.

All in all, *Adult Education and Socialist Pedagogy* presented a comprehensive sketch of an approach to the political economy of adult education, but this outline was not systematically developed and contained a number of deficiencies. Some of these weaknesses were subsequently addressed in 'The Political Economy of Literacy in the Third World' (Youngman, 1990), which focused on the particularities of the South, highlighted non-class social divisions such as gender, ethnicity and race, and gave prominence to the state.

But within the confines of a short article it was not possible to elaborate these developments of the political economy approach.

One national study in the South was influenced by the framework established in *Adult Education and Socialist Pedagogy*. In *A Political Economy of Adult Education in Nigeria* (Filson, 1991), a team of researchers reported on an empirical study of access to government-sponsored non-formal education in three contrasting states within the Nigerian federation. The book was 'an attempt to situate Nigeria's existing adult education programmes in relation to its political economic structure' (Filson, 1991: 13). There was no systematic discussion of the theoretical framework of the study but reference was made (Filson,1991: 4, 14, 24) to *Adult Education and Socialist Pedagogy*, and discussion was couched in terms of the different modes of production within the Nigerian social formation and its class structures. The structural context of adult education was explained through historical accounts of Nigeria's economic development and its incorporation into the world capitalist economy, with the resultant penetration of the capitalist mode of production and displacement of pre-capitalist modes. However, the underlying theoretical position was not always satisfactorily integrated into the overall analysis – for example, the concept of adult education as a site of class struggle was rather tacked on to the discussion of Nigeria's economy in the second chapter and was not explored elsewhere in the analysis of particular programmes. The theoretical perspective is not sustained, and much of the book consists of descriptive accounts and presentations of questionnaire data on differential access to programmes which are not related to a political economy analysis.

One important chapter, however, did go beyond the outline in *Adult Education and Socialist Pedagogy*, and considered the impact of gender relations on access to adult education. This chapter considered the interplay of class and patriarchy and the significance of cultural and religious factors – including, for example, the resistance in Muslim areas to the perceived hidden curriculum of Western cultural norms of gender relations in state-sponsored non-formal education. But, on the whole, the book does not capitalise on the opportunities for theoretical development. The state's role in adult education, for instance, is described, but there is no clear theory of the state, and hence no substantial analysis. Above all, there is no systematic treatment of the international context and the nature of imperialism. Thus external aid to adult education, for example, is referred to but not problematised and investigated.

Overall, the book is disappointing in terms of the development of the political economy approach to adult education in the specific circumstances of the South. Its focus is narrower than its title suggests (in geographical coverage, forms of adult education and focus of research), and there is a lack of theoretical discussion and reflection. The intention of linking the theory of political economy to an empirical investigation was excellent, but – perhaps because of its multiple authorship – the book does not have a satisfactory degree of theoretical coherence.

Specially pertinent to the present study is a Ph.D. thesis by Gaborone, 'The Political Economy of Adult Education in Botswana with Special Reference to the Agricultural Sector' (Gaborone, 1986a), which was based on Marxist theory and used the concepts of the mode of production, imperialism and class to analyse the nature of the state's adult education programmes. It concentrated on the rural economy and the relationship of agricultural extension to the rural class structure created by Botswana's role in the regional economy. The thesis used many elements of the framework summarised in Chapter 2 but its conceptualisation and application are uneven. For example, the mode of production and imperialism are more fully elaborated than the state and hegemony. The study is strong in its analysis of patriarchy and gender relations, but it does not consider ethnicity and the organisations of civil society. The thesis used Marxist theory and fieldwork data to present an in-depth analysis of one facet of Botswana's political economy and one branch of adult education. It provides an important signpost for a more inclusive empirical study of a peripheral capitalist country that elaborates all the elements of a Marxist political economy and gives a comprehensive analysis of all forms of adult education.

An important study which explored the significance of the state was Torres's *The Politics of Nonformal Education in Latin America* (1990). Its major concern was to study adult education and the state in peripheral capitalist countries. Torres argued:

> to clarify the social settings where adult education takes place, it is essential to develop a political sociology of adult education on theo-

retical grounds. To understand the peculiarities of adult education in peripheral or semi-peripheral societies, we must understand the development of public education and the rules of policy formation in the dependent state.... In these dependent states adult education tends to have a clear-cut class orientation, in its target clientele and its policy formulation, as well as in its links and relationships to economic, social and political development. (Torres, 1990: 115)

Building on the work of Gramsci and more recent Marxist writers, Torres developed a theory of the capitalist state and public policy formation based on the premiss that the state serves to maintain capitalist accumulation and reproduction, and to legitimate the political domination of the capitalist class, while adjusting in various ways to pressures exerted by the subordinate classes and other groups in civil society. Thus adult education policy is a product of economic and political factors and especially of class conflict. The author explored and illustrated these dynamics in studies of adult education in Latin America and the Caribbean. Torres's work provided a significant advance in this area of the political economy of adult education.

Another important contribution is Foley's 'Adult Education and Capitalist Reorganisation' (1994), which applied historical materialism to an analysis of the current processes of capitalist reorganisation within the global political economy, and their reflection in state policies on economic 'restructuring' and vocational training. Foley revealed that the language of post-Fordism, flexible specialisation, the skilled workforce and human resource development was part of an ideological process that masked the basic dynamic of capital seeking new ways to increase productivity and reduce labour costs. His key point was the fundamental conflict between capital and labour – capitalism is not only 'a system of economic, political and cultural domination', it is also 'continually contested by those it exploits' (Foley, 1994: 122). By so doing he sought to emphasise the importance of what he called the 'contestation problematic' for radical adult education theory and practice. He illustrated his argument with a concrete example from Australia of adult learning by workers involved in conflicts over restructuring in the workplace. The importance of Foley's article was that it re-emphasised the significance of class struggle for the political economy of adult education, and stressed the potential for adult education either to accommodate or to resist the reproduction of capitalism.

The final example is Wangoola and Youngman's edited collection *Towards a Transformative Political Economy of Adult Education* (1996), which included contributions by fourteen different authors. The chapters covered many of the important concepts of political economy (such as imperialism, the state and civil society, and relations of class, gender, race and ethnicity), and often considered them in the context of adult education in the South. However, the contributors utilised the concepts in varied ways, reflecting a diversity of theoretical positions that ranged from orthodox Marxism to Third World feminism. Hence, while particular chapters provide valuable contributions to the political economy approach, the volume as a whole lacks theoretical coherence in terms of historical materialist analysis.

In this chapter I have provided a critical review of some of the writing on the political economy of adult education by assessing it in relation to the position summarised at the end of Chapter 2. On the basis of this review, it is now possible to present the book's theoretical framework for analysing adult education in the peripheral capitalist countries of the South.

The Theoretical Framework of the Book

The review of political economies of adult education above suggests that there has been an uneven coverage of the implications for adult education of the main elements of the political economy approach identified in Chapter 2. Certain writers – such as Torres on the state – have produced significant elaborations of particular dimensions, but no one has achieved an integrated approach of all the elements that would enable a comprehensive analysis of adult education in the South. In the light of the review, the earlier summary has been adapted to provide a framework for the political economy of adult education in peripheral capitalism. The theoretical framework of the book is as follows:

1. Adult education activities take place within a structural context shaped by the mode of production and its class relations. The study of adult education in a specific context must therefore

provide an analysis of the development of the capitalist mode of production and its relation to the pre-capitalist mode of production. It must also provide an analysis of the changing class structure and the processes of class formation. It is assumed that this analysis will give the structural background for explaining developments within the field of adult education.

2. The manner and extent to which the mode of production and the class relationships have influenced particular aspects of adult education constitute an area of investigation. It is assumed that these factors have a significant impact on adult education activities, but also that these activities have a relative autonomy from the economic basis of society, and can influence its development.

3. The dominance of the capitalist mode of production at the world level means that socioeconomic development in peripheral capitalist countries of the South must be located within the context of the global political economy. It is assumed that the dynamics of imperialism have an impact on the policies and practices of adult education.

4. Different classes have different interests, and conflicts arise as they pursue these interests. It is assumed that these conflicts have effects on the nature and consequences of adult education at every level, including policies, organisation and curricula.

5. Besides the relations of class, there are other important social inequalities, especially those based on gender, ethnicity and race. It is assumed that these inequalities have profound influences on adult education and its outcomes, including in ways which interact with those derived from class relations.

6. The conflicts within society that arise from class differences and other social inequalities are reflected in the state, which is a significant provider of adult education. It is assumed that the formation, implementation and outcomes of public policies on adult education can be meaningfully analysed in terms of how they relate to the inequalities in society.

7. Intellectual and cultural life is shaped by the capitalist mode of production and the contestation between different classes and groups in society over the legitimacy of the existing socioeconomic order. It is assumed that adult education provided by the state and the organisations of civil society constitutes an

area in which struggles for ideological hegemony are carried out.

8. There are different views on the nature of society and how it should develop, some of which question aspects of the capitalist socioeconomic order. It is assumed that the activities of political parties and of organisations in civil society which question the status quo have an adult education dimension, because they seek to change people's ideas about society.

CHAPTER 4

Adult Education and Development Theory

The study and practice of adult education in the countries of the South are framed by the context of 'development', the idea of the necessity and possibility of progress towards a 'more desirable kind of society' (Bernstein, 1983: 48). This idea has a particular history, one that is inextricably bound up with world economics and politics. The concept itself is value-laden, as the notion of 'more desirable' indicates. Who defines 'progress'? Who benefits from it? Who loses? It also embodies assumptions about deliberate action to change society in chosen directions. Theories of development have therefore been generated largely as a form of applied social science, intended not only to provide explanatory models of change but also to give guidance for policy-making. The location of adult education as an activity regarded as contributing to development makes it important to clarify these theories and their policy implications. In this chapter I review the evolution of different conceptions of development and their implications for adult education. I conclude that the theoretical framework of political economy established in Chapters 2 and 3 provides a valid and relevant basis for the analysis of adult education in the context of development.

The focus of development is societal change, and the social theory of Marx, Durkheim and Weber is an important intellectual legacy because of their work on the transition to modern (industrial, capitalist) society. The main basis of contemporary development studies, however, is economics, because the definition of the field of study in the period after 1945 was rooted in a concern with 'economically backward' areas of the world and the identification of appropriate strategies for their economic development, seen essentially in terms of industrialisation. This concern with the question of economic development in Africa, Asia and Latin America had a number of origins in the 1930s and 1940s. One source was the reaction of Latin American policy-makers to the disruptions to their economies caused by the Depression of the 1930s and the 1939–45 World War. The collapse of international trade had exposed the economic vulnerability of their reliance on the export of primary products; they therefore sought paths to more self-sustained economic growth. Another source was the reconstruction of Europe after the devastation caused by the war. The large-scale programme of economic aid to Europe by the USA (the Marshall Plan) showed the possibilities of planned intervention in national economies.

The most important source, however, was related to the shifts in global politics after 1945. This period was marked by the decline of the European colonial powers and the momentum to decolonisation, the emergence of the USA as the world's strongest economy, and the development of the Cold War, in which the USA sought to contain the spread of communism. One dimension of the perceived threat of the USSR was that it was the only country to have industrialised outside capitalism; it therefore provided an alternative model of development. In the early 1950s the concept of the 'Third World' emerged to indicate an area outside the First World of advanced industrial capitalism and the Second World of industrialised state socialism in which the two models of socio-economic development contended. The dominance of capitalism within the world economy has meant that the major theme within conceptualisations of development has been one of capitalist development. However, there has been a minor theme of critique, derived theoretically from the legacy of Marx and practically from the experience of the USSR, China, and countries such as Cuba.

Since 1945, the idea of development has been a powerful one in international affairs and in the internal affairs of those countries which have been on the periphery of the historic centres of capitalism. It has influenced a wide range of policies by international organisations and national governments, and many activities by non-governmental organisations and grassroots bodies. Its meaning has been contested, and thinking about development has changed over the years. Although approaches derived from economics have been predominant, the ideas and processes of development clearly involve polities and cultures too; therefore it is preferable to take a transdisciplinary perspective. Indeed, as I argued in Chapter 2, one of the advantages of Marxist social theory is its trans-disciplinary character, which makes it particularly useful for the analysis of development.

Adult education is a form of social policy, the product of de-liberate action by organisations to influence society (Griffin, 1987; Torres, 1990). It involves a variety of bodies, including the state and organisations of civil society, which seek to meet the needs, interests and values of different groups in society. The policy-making processes involving these organisations are shaped by competing definitions of what kinds of intervention in society are appropriate, hence what forms of adult education should be under-taken. In the countries of the South, the rationales for different kinds of social intervention are articulated in terms of ideas and values underpinned by theories of development. The nature of adult education in the South has therefore been influenced by the evolution of the different schools of development theory.

The literature on adult education and development reflects changing ideas about development. In some cases, writers on adult education consciously align themselves with a defined theory of development; in others, their adoption of particular assumptions about development indicates that they have accepted (perhaps unwittingly) a certain theoretical perspective. Thus a pattern can be traced in the literature, although it must be acknowledged that theoretical positions and forms of adult education in practice are often eclectic and defy neat categorisation. In this chapter, how-ever, I refer to selected writings to illustrate the impact of the major schools of thought on ideas about the relationship between adult education and development. I therefore focus on the main theories of development that have arisen since the mid-1940s. This provides a broad overview, although – as Hunt (1989) has empha-sised – the categorisation of approaches to development neces-sarily oversimplifies and obscures the variety of differences within a given category. She also notes that those who have provided reviews of the field differ in their categories and in whom they group together. Nevertheless, it is useful to show in broad terms the different trends that have arisen over time, and the relationship between theoretical efforts at explanation and unfolding economic and political realities, while noting that new paradigms do not necessarily completely displace the influence of others. The identification of the main schools of thought will clarify the linkage between adult education and development. In this chapter I consider five paradigms of development: modernisation theory, dependency theory, neoliberal theory, populism and political economy.

Where it is appropriate historically, the term 'Third World' is used. With the collapse of the Second World in 1989–91, however, the expression lost its referents, so the terms 'South' and 'North' have been adopted for the major division in today's global political economy.

Modernisation Theory

The variety of approaches that can be grouped in the category of 'modernisation theory' provided the consensus view of development until the mid-1960s and continued to dominate mainstream thinking until the 1980s. The extent to which the work of Maynard Keynes had a direct influence on these approaches is a cause for dispute. It is undoubtedly the case, however, that the adoption of his rationale of the role of the state in macro-economic policy in Europe and North America after the Depression of the 1930s provided a legitimation for state intervention in the processes of economic development in underdeveloped countries. Indeed, the idea of government planning was integral to the modernisation approach, which was generally sceptical of neoclassical assumptions about the effectiveness of market mechanisms to stimulate appropriate investment for growth.

Modernisation approaches had their basis not only in economics but also in sociological and psychological theories. In terms of economics, they saw 'backward' economies as dominated by subsistence agriculture, with low rates of capital accumulation and investment, a small foreign trade sector and a low rate of economic growth. These economies were seen as poor because of low productivity, but as having potentially abundant labour. The proposed economic strategy was therefore to develop a 'modern' sector based on industrialisation and commercial agriculture by mobilising the underemployed labour in the 'traditional' rural sector. Development was seen essentially in terms of economic growth based on the expansion of the modern sector and the export of primary products. This process required support by appropriate governmental measures, accompanied by external investment and foreign aid.

The concerns of economic theory with the internal constraints on economic growth and how to overcome them merged with ideas about how societies as a whole change. The dominant school of sociology in the USA in the 1950s was the structural functionalism of Talcott Parsons, working in the tradition of Émile Durkheim. This school viewed social change as a process of evolution from simple, pre-industrial traditional society to complex, industrial modern society as exemplified by the USA. It identified the characteristics of each type of society and considered how traditional societies might make the transition to modern life, with its market economy, democratic polity, urbanisation, high levels of literacy, and so forth. A psychological dimension to this dichotomy between the two kinds of society was also theorised, and the idea of a modern personality was postulated, with characteristics such as rationality and achievement motivation. Inkeles and Smith (1974), for example, argued that changes in attitudes and values were necessary to reproduce modern behaviour, and the effective functioning of modern economic and political institutions. Their central assumption was that development required a shift from traditionalism to individual modernity. These sociological and psychological concerns supplemented economic theory and suggested areas of social intervention, for example in education, which would help to promote economic changes.

The fundamental premiss of modernisation theory was that there is a single process of social evolution, the highest stage having been reached by the USA in the 1950s. This view received its most celebrated articulation in Rostow's *The Stages of Economic Growth* (1960), which sought to chart a series of historical stages in economic growth from traditional society to the 'high mass consumption' societies of the USA, Western Europe and Japan. The modernisation approach expressed an optimism about Western society that derived from the post-1945 period of sustained economic growth and full employment, and reflected the international economic and political hegemony of the USA. Although modernisation theory tended to use the concept of 'modern industrial society', its focus was in fact *capitalist* society, and Rostow's book had the revealing subtitle 'A Non-Communist Manifesto', reflecting the location of ideas about development within the ideological conflicts of the Cold War.

A major assumption of modernisation theory was that overall economic growth (measured in terms of gross national product and increases in average *per capita* income) would benefit everyone in society – it would 'trickle down' so that everyone's incomes and standard of living would improve. One of the divergent trends within the modernisation school of thought took a more egalitarian approach. This approach was associated with European (as opposed to American) writers, such as Gunnar Myrdal from Sweden, whose ideas on planning and welfare-orientated policies reflected the wide degree of consensus about the welfare state in Europe in the 1950s and 1960s. It emerged prominently following the recognition that even after the efforts of the United Nations' First Development Decade (1960–69), inequality and widespread poverty remained a characteristic of Third World societies. Writers such as Seers sought to redefine the meaning of development to include not simply economic growth but also trends in poverty, income distribution and employment:

> The questions to ask about a country's development are therefore: What has been happening to poverty? What has been happening to unemployment? What has been happening to inequality? If all of these have declined from high levels, then beyond doubt this has been a period of development for the country concerned. If one or two of these central problems have been growing, more especially if all three have, then it would be strange to call the result 'development' even if per capita income doubled. (Seers, 1969: 3)

This current in modernisation theory may be regarded as social democratic in its concern with redistribution within the framework of capitalist development. It gained a brief period of importance in the mid-1970s following the intervention of the International Labour Organisation in 1976 to increase attention to poverty alleviation in the Third World through its proposals for a 'basic needs' strategy. This strategy advocated priority for meeting the basic needs of all, focusing especially on the poor. It proposed setting targets for meeting survival needs (such as food, clean water and shelter), for providing social services (such as education and health) and for creating opportunities for work. It also included the social dimension of broadening popular participation in the development process. The strategy was based on continuing concern with growth in the modern sector while also redistributing investment in order to raise the incomes of the poor, through increased opportunities for productive work, and to extend public services. The underlying economic rationale was that an expansion in the employment opportunities and incomes of the poor would broaden the base of domestic demand in the economy, and thus provide a stronger foundation for sustained economic growth than overreliance on exports. Its policy implications included the promotion of small-scale, labour-intensive production in manufacturing and farming, and the expansion of government social services. Because the majority of the poor live in the rural areas, the strategy had a rural development emphasis. Foreign aid was seen as having a supportive role in assisting governmental efforts to meet targets.

This reformist approach to development was equity-based, and assessed progress in terms of gains in public welfare and the reduction of poverty. Although international institutions such as the World Bank showed some concern with poverty and basic needs in the mid-1970s, the reformist approach did not have a significant impact on the policies of Third World governments. A major weakness of the approach was that it avoided the issues raised by the fact that those who would gain from greater equity would have to confront the political domination of those who benefit from inequality. However, it retained some appeal for non-governmental organisations, and had a continuing influence on UNICEF (Oman and Wignaraja, 1991). It reappeared in the United Nations Development Programme's series of *Human Development Reports*, which started in 1990.

In relation to education, from the early 1960s modernisation theory advocated a large expansion of schooling. This idea was based on the 'human capital theory' which had been advanced by Theodore Schultz. In an influential speech in 1960 he had argued that education was not a form of individual consumption but a productive investment indispensable to rapid economic growth. His speech focused on industrialised countries but he also argued for aid to underdeveloped countries to support education: 'It is simply not possible to have the fruits of modern agriculture and the abundance of modern industry without making large investments in human beings' (Schultz, 1961: 322). This idea had a major influence on governments such as that of the USA, and on international bodies like the World Bank, which promoted the theory in relation to the Third World. It coincided with the argument of modernisation theory that countries were undeveloped because of their internal characteristics, such as the lack of educated and skilled people. In line with the evolutionary thinking of this theory, educational development was seen in terms of developing systems similar to those in the industrialised countries.

In the 1960s the countries of the Third World therefore rapidly developed school systems because they would create the people (the 'human capital') with the skills and attitudes to develop and manage a modern economy. A strong, centralised education system was also seen as politically important in the process of nation-building, creating national unity and the authority of the state, often in territories whose boundaries had been defined by colonialism. Significant investments of public resources and foreign aid were made in expanding school systems, with universal primary education as a key goal.

Modernisation theory and adult education

The rapid expansion of schooling, however, led to problems in many countries. These problems included levels of social demand which exceeded the resources available, escalating costs and internal inefficiencies, and the growth of the educated unemployed. The crisis was evident by the late 1960s and was widely publicised by Philip Coombs in his influential book *The World Educational Crisis* (1968). Coombs proposed a variety of solutions to the crisis, including non-formal education. He argued for investment in non-formal adult education: (a) to provide those who had never been to school with the knowledge and skills for national development; (b) to upgrade partially qualified people to be more effective in their jobs; and (c) to give training to the educated jobless. He gave priority to modernising the agricultural and rural sectors through farmer training, extension services and the training of rural leaders. His book helped to focus attention on the potential of adult education programmes to contribute to development within the modernisation paradigm. Subsequently, many government and aid agencies gave increased support to the development of adult education, often under the rubric of non-formal education.

Much of the writing on adult education and development in the late 1960s was couched in terms of modernisation theory. This is typified by three books published at this time. In the first section of *Adult Education for Developing Countries*, Prosser (1967) discussed the relationship between adult education and national development 'with the intention of highlighting its prime role'. His main emphasis was on the role of adult education in helping people to absorb the rapid social change associated with the transition from 'simpler societies' to 'a modern democratic state with its fundamental cash economy and maximum social mobility' (Prosser, 1967: 3). His perspective reflected uncritically the structural-functionalist sociology of modernisation theory. In a similar vein, Townsend-Coles argued in *Adult Education in Developing Countries* (1969: 19) for investment in adult education, because 'The first priority in developing countries is to improve human resources, on which national development plans depend.' His starting point was that developing countries were poor because their human resources were poorly developed, and he explicitly endorsed the human capital theory integral to the modernisation approach to development.

Finally, Lowe brought together a number of national and regional case-studies in *Adult Education and Nation Building* (1970). The book's basic assumption was the benign relationship between adult education and development:

> The reason why governments in developing countries have to treat adult education seriously is plain enough. Resolved to achieve rapid economic and social growth and to promote national unity they must somehow produce a skilled and informed adult population. Capital investment alone will avail them nothing if human skills are wanting. (Lowe, 1970: 1)

Adult education was seen as indispensable to national development, and the case studies presented descriptive accounts of adult
education, focusing largely on technical issues such as planning,
co-ordination, administration, finance, methods and the training
of adult educators. While the writers acknowledged failures – for
example, in mass literacy campaigns – and problems such as
inadequate resources, they seldom questioned the prevailing
conception of development. Occasional discussion of the objectives
of adult education – for example, as the 'modern means to
material progress' (Lowe, 1970: 19) – showed little critical analysis
of the nature of national development. There was a general
optimism about the nature of development and the positive
contribution of adult education, supported by international aid.
Only the final commentary chapter raised questions about the
conventional assumptions of development and considered
alternative ideas. In doing so, it prefigured the debates of the
mid-1970s.

As I mentioned above, the critique of the UN's First Development Decade led to the emergence in the mid-1970s of a reformist trend within modernisation theory that focused on the problems
of inequality and poverty, and the importance of meeting basic
needs. This trend was reflected in adult education. Again a key
figure was Coombs, whose *Attacking Rural Poverty: How Nonformal
Education Can Help* (Coombs and Ahmed, 1974) was an early advocate of using adult education to address the problem of rural
poverty. This book, commissioned by the World Bank, was based
on twenty-five case studies of rural adult education programmes,
including agricultural extension, farmer training, skill training for
rural artisans and small entrepreneurs, and community development. Its focus was on increasing rural incomes and participation
in the cash economy as a means of modernising rural society: 'For
a subsistence farmer to become a better commercial farmer he
must first visualize his farm as an economic unit – a business –
and not simply as a way of life' (Coombs and Ahmed, 1974: 119).
The book did not fundamentally question the modernisation paradigm. Rather, it located the problem of development in the fact
that the rural poor had been left outside the modern life which
the development process had hitherto brought only to the urban
areas. The role of adult education was therefore articulated within

a perspective of reforming the modernisation strategy to reduce the urban/rural gap and create greater equity.

The reformist trend of the mid-1970s was crystallised in the International Labour Organisation's 'basic needs approach' to development in 1976. This approach struck a chord with the social democratic tradition within adult education, symbolised by a large international conference on the theme of 'Adult Education and Development' held by the International Council for Adult Education (ICAE) in Tanzania in 1976. (At that time Tanzania was seen as a model of a country following a development strategy with emphasis on meeting basic needs, especially through popular participation in rural development.) The conference was dominated by the new 'basic needs' conception of development. A book sponsored by the ICAE (Hall and Kidd, 1978) contained major documents and reports from the conference which disseminated ideas about the role of adult education within this conception.

The original modernisation approach remains the theoretical basis of much mainstream adult education, such as government agricultural extension programmes. Its reformist variant has also continued to be influential, although from the 1980s it was increasingly absorbed into the populist approach to development.

Dependency Theory

From the mid-1960s, the modernisation theory of development came under attack by various writers who can be categorised as working within a dependency paradigm that regarded development in the Third World as conditioned by the domination of the advanced capitalist countries. The most influential writers worked within a neo-Marxist approach whose origins lay in the work of Paul Baran (1957). During the 1950s Baran analysed the problems of development from a neo-Marxist perspective, using concepts such as class and imperialism to study the relationship within the world economy between the advanced industrialised capitalist countries and the countries of the periphery. He focused on the idea of the economic surplus, and on the processes of imperialism by which this surplus is extracted from the periphery to the centre. He argued that Western capitalism, from its earliest contacts with regions outside Europe, had exported the surplus and thus blocked capital accumulation in the periphery. In consequence, industrial development in the periphery, undertaken by a domestic capitalist class, was unlikely to happen. Foreign capitalists dominate these economies, investing mainly in the production of primary commodities from mining and agriculture and partly in low-wage light industry, and they repatriate their profits to the centre. Therefore there is no national dynamic of capital accumulation controlled by an indigenous capitalist class. In fact the dominant domestic classes (particularly the landowners and commercial capitalists) use their control over the state to facilitate foreign investment and maintain the status quo, which serves their interests. Baran concluded that a socialist revolution and disengagement from the world capitalist economy would be needed to enable full socio-economic development to take place in the Third World.

Baran's conclusion that capitalist development was blocked in the peripheral economies departed from Marx's opinion that the process begun by the spread of mercantile capitalism to countries outside Europe would destroy pre-capitalist modes of production and lead to capitalist development in those countries. It was such departures from Marx's views that led to the classification 'neo-Marxist' (Foster-Carter, 1974) to indicate the modifications to Marx's formulations undertaken by Baran and later writers who followed his lead in elaborating dependency theory.

The idea of blocked development also contradicted the fundamental premiss of modernisation theory. Baran's views thus went against the dominant thinking of development theorists in the 1950s and they had little influence at the time. However, they were picked up and developed in the mid-1960s by Andre Gunder Frank, whose work began to be published at a time when the confidence of Western society was being undermined by factors such as slowing economic growth, the disillusion of young people with the 'affluent' society, opposition to the Vietnam War and other political and social conflicts. At the same time, the initial optimism of the 1950s around prospects for development was ebbing, as poverty and inequality persisted, and internal conflicts and authoritarian regimes emerged in the aftermath of decolonisation. Frank's publications therefore coincided with a time when both the model of society proposed by modernisation theory and the effectiveness of development policies undertaken within its prescriptions were coming into question. In this milieu, the neo-Marxist challenge to the orthodoxy of mainstream development theory received a degree of prominence.

Frank focused on the relationship between the centre and the periphery of the world capitalist system from the perspective of his historical analysis of the experience of Latin America. He argued that capitalism had penetrated Latin America in the sixteenth century from Western Europe, and that colonial rule established a trading system which ensured that minerals and other primary products flowed to Europe. Merchant capital therefore integrated the peripheral economies into the international capitalist system in a subordinate role which extracted their surplus and dissolved their feudal structures. The fundamental feature of world capitalism is its polarisation into metropolitan centres and peripheral satellites, a commercial relation in which the periphery exports cheap primary products and imports manufactured goods. The development of advanced capitalist countries in Europe was based on this relationship, and the export of surplus has led to the *under*development of the Third World.

Frank argued that the present situation of poverty and low productivity in the countries of the Third World had been produced historically by their subordination into the world market, and was not an original condition resulting from their internal characteristics. In a famous essay entitled 'The Development of Underdevelopment', he wrote:

> even a modest acquaintance with history shows that underdevelopment is not original or traditional and that neither the past nor the present of the underdeveloped countries resembles in any important respect the past of the now developed countries. The now developed countries were never *under*developed though they may have been *un*developed. (Frank, 1969: 4)

Frank identified the dominant capitalist class in the periphery as 'comprador' – that is, collaborationist. Its alliance with foreign capital meant that the dependent relation of Third World countries would be perpetuated. The domestic capitalist class is unable to generate an autonomous and self-sustaining form of capitalist development. His analysis was thus similar to Baran's, with some differences of emphasis – for example, on the extent of capitalist penetration of pre-capitalist modes of production. Like Baran, Frank reached the political conclusion that a socialist revolution was required. He advocated class struggle against 'the immediate enemy' of the domestic ruling classes rather than support of the national bourgeoisie to build capitalism and oppose foreign domination – that is, 'the principal enemy' of imperialism (Frank, 1969: 371–2). In this he contradicted the current political strategies of the orthodox communist parties in the region. The revolution in Cuba in 1959 and its subsequent development path provided a political model.

Frank became the most well-known in English of a group of writers who analysed development from the perspective of neo-Marxist ideas about underdevelopment and dependency. The Caribbean writer Walter Rodney, for example, published a celebrated book entitled *How Europe Underdeveloped Africa* (Rodney, 1972), which provided a historical account of the causes of underdevelopment in Africa. Other writers, such as the the prominent Egyptian dependency theorist Samir Amin, explored further the idea of the single world capitalist system in which the peripheral countries are structurally dependent because of the domination of foreign capital over their economies. From this viewpoint, the dynamic of the world system is generated by capitalist development in the centre. This process involves the appropriation of the surplus from the periphery through unequal exchange (because terms of trade favour the manufactured products of the centre and devalue the primary products of the periphery) and the repatriation of profits (based mainly on the low-wage character of production in the periphery). For the peripheral countries, the impetus for economic development comes from the outside. Thus even if there are shifts in the international structure of production, for example, with some industrial activity being moved to the periphery, control remains in the hands of foreign capital, and economic development is not self-controlled and self-sustaining.

The analysis put forward by dependency theorists, many of whom came from the Third World, challenged various assumptions of modernisation theory. Against the idea that there were stages of economic development through which all countries pass in evolution to advanced industrialisation, dependency theory argued that the advanced capitalist economies were developed on the basis of surplus drawn from the periphery, and that this route cannot be replicated by present-day underdeveloped economies. Indeed, the world system is structured in a way that makes Third World countries remain dependent on the centres of capitalism. Thus the possibilities of independent industrialisation in the periphery are blocked by external factors rather than internal ones such as lack of capital and entrepreneurial skills, as argued by modernisation theory, with its focus on development as an endogenous process.

Dependency theory challenged the notion that present-day underdevelopment is an original condition, and argued that it was created by the unequal international relationship that has developed since the sixteenth century. This historical process had undermined the potential for internal development, as exemplified by British colonial action against cotton weaving in India in favour of raw material export to mills in Britain. It also attacked modernisation theory's dichotomy of 'traditional' and 'modern' as superficial and Eurocentric, neglecting the history of colonialism and the nature of capitalist penetration of pre-capitalist societies (some of which were more developed than Europe at the time). Furthermore, international trade is essentially exploitative, and modernisation theory's encouragement of trade as mutually beneficial masks this inequality.

Dependency approaches had an impact at the level of theory in the late 1960s and during the 1970s, but they had little impact on policy. The main conclusion of dependency analysis was that development must be based on a socialist revolution and disengagement from the world capitalist market. Certain development policies stemmed logically from this position: controls on foreign capital, reduction of imports, encouragement to self-reliance and the development of technological capacity. But ideas on policy were usually left at the level of generalities, though in *Dependence and Transformation* the Caribbean academic Thomas Thomas (1974) did address in detail how a worker–peasant alliance holding state power might carry out a planned socialist transformation. Given the context of the Cold War and the global economic and political dominance of capitalism, however, it was predictable that dependency theory had little influence on national policies. It had some influence on certain Third World leaders, such as Salvador Allende in Chile, Julius Nyerere in Tanzania and Michael Manley in Jamaica, and it was reflected in the arguments of the Third World in the mid-1970s for a 'New International Economic Order' (Hettne, 1990: 97). But it seems reasonable to conclude that while dependency theory stimulated a lot of academic debate over development theory, it had little impact on development policy. In the end, this is because its analysis was linked to radical political conclusions rather than the provision of technical guidance for development planners.

It has been shown that the emphasis of modernisation theory was on the internal characteristics of a nation which constitute an obstacle to development. Within this paradigm, education (supported by foreign aid) has the role of addressing obstacles such as the lack of human capital and the absence of modern attitudes. The focus of dependency theory is on the external factors which block development. The implications for education were outlined by Amin, who criticised the failure of imported educational models which were copied from the developed world in the same way as production techniques and consumption models. He advocated

> a self-oriented development strategy and ... an education radically different from the borrowed model. The strategy must start with a direct definition of the needs of the masses, without reference to the European model; it must necessarily be egalitarian; it must be essentially self-reliant; it must awaken a capacity for autonomous technological innovation. (Amin, 1975: 52)

Amin did not give examples of such a strategy but his writings at the time suggested that China under Mao Zedong provided an appropriate development model.

Dependency theory and adult education

The presumption that a socialist government was necessary for ending underdevelopment meant that dependency theory had little practical impact on educational policies in the Third World. However, it did provide an analytical perspective on education and development, which was reflected in research studies on the external influences on school systems (Altbach and Kelly, 1986). A similar situation obtained in adult education. For example, Amin, in another version of his argument, addressed the question of adult education in a paper to the 1975 International Symposium for Literacy in Persepolis. His proposals embodied the belief that successful literacy and adult education campaigns can take place only when they are 'accompanied by profound changes in the economic and social system' (Amin, 1976: 90), and are therefore premissed on the existence of a socialist revolution. As in school education research, some writers used the dependency perspective to analyse aspects of adult education in the Third World. Harrington (1987), for instance, considered non-formal education in Papua New Guinea from a dependency viewpoint. She concluded that non-formal education could meet national needs and provide equal opportunities, and thereby contribute to a different, participatory model of development.

The most important reference point for dependency approaches within adult education was the early work of Paulo Freire. The intellectual milieu from which Freire emerged, the Latin America of the 1960s, was the source of the original thinking about the concept of dependency. Freire's practical activity in adult literacy and rural extension in Brazil and Chile in the 1960s was conceived in terms of challenging the underdevelopment produced by dependency. Through the publication in English of *Cultural Action for Freedom* (Freire, 1972a), *Pedagogy of the Oppressed* (Freire, 1972b) and *Education for Critical Consciousness* (Freire, 1974) and through his travels under the aegis of the World Council of Churches, Freire disseminated his ideas to the English-speaking world in the early 1970s. He stressed that his pedagogy had its roots in the Third World, specifically in the experience of South America, where colonialism had resulted in economic dependency. He contended that in these societies, 'The principal contradiction ... is the relationship of dependency between them and the metropolitan society' (Freire, 1972b: 130).

For Freire, an important dimension of this dependency is cultural, as the process of Europeanisation in the colonial era had been a 'cultural invasion', leading to alienation and a culture of silence. He therefore argued that the struggle for national independence must be accompanied by cultural action for freedom:

The dependent society is by definition a silent society. Its voice is not an authentic voice, but merely an echo of the voice of the metropolis – in every way, the metropolis speaks, the dependent society listens.

The silence of the object society in relation to the director society is repeated in the relationships within the object society itself. Its power elites, silent in the face of the metropolis, silence their own people in turn. Only when the people of a dependent society break out of the culture of silence and win their right to speak – only, that is, when radical structural changes transform the dependent society – can such a society as a whole cease to be silent towards the director society. (Freire, 1972a: 59–60)

Thus there is a need to oppose both the comprador bourgeoisie (the 'power elites') and the metropolis. The political thrust of Freire's approach to adult literacy, based on 'conscientisation', was to develop in marginalised rural and urban classes a critical consciousness that would question the dominant socioeconomic structures. Hence the topics ('generative words') in the adult literacy groups ('cultural circles') were chosen not only for their linguistic usefulness but because they were aspects of people's lives which would stimulate discussion of the prevailing development situation. In the example from his work in Brazil in 1963–64 that is recorded in *Education for Critical Consciousness*, the seventeenth and last generative word was 'wealth', which had the following explanatory note:

> Aspects for discussion: Brazil and the universal dimension. The confrontation between wealth and poverty. Rich man vs. poor man. Rich nations vs. poor nations. Dominant nations and dominated nations. Developed and underdeveloped nations. National emancipation. (Freire, 1974: 84)

It is clear that dependency theory was an important feature of Freire's early work; it was therefore an element in the influence he exerted on thinking about adult education and development in the 1970s. This influence reached its height at the UNESCO International Symposium for Literacy in Persepolis in 1975, and it permeated the final declaration (Bataille, 1976). Hence dependency theory, through Freire and other sources, was one of the intellectual influences on thinking about adult education and development in the 1970s.

Neoliberal Theory

In the section above I discussed a critique from the Left of main-stream thinking about development within the modernisation paradigm. There has also been a critique from the Right, and this has been highly influential since the early 1980s. This neoliberal critique is derived from neoclassical economics and the theory of *laissez-faire* capitalism, in which the unimpeded operation of the market is seen as leading to an optimal economic situation ('equilibrium'). For international organisations and national governments, neoliberalism has become the new orthodoxy on development (Jenkins, 1992). Although neoliberal theorists fall within the overall framework of the proponents of capitalist development, their views diverge significantly from modernisation theory in their emphasis on the market. This has led to profound changes in development policies.

Neoclassical economics centres on the idea that market mechanisms are the means to ensure an efficient and productive economy, and maximise economic welfare. This school of economics regards interventions by governments as disruptive distortions of free competition in the marketplace. For example, theorists such as Milton Friedman argue that it is governments which print money and thereby create inflation, so that the solution is to reduce the money supply and cut government spending. Thus they envisage that monetarist policies derived from this argument would restore the role of markets so that after a short-term drop in output and rise in unemployment, there would be economic growth without inflation. A central concern of neoclassical economists is therefore the need for reduced government intervention in the economy. They explicitly oppose Keynesian ideas about government spending and taxation policies, and seek to dismantle the welfare state. The accompanying political philosophy is that free-market capitalism is essential for democracy and individual freedom.

The slowdown of the economies of the advanced capitalist countries in the 1970s and the growth of inflation provided an economic climate in which these monetarist challenges to the prevalent Keynesian approaches to economic policy fell on fertile ground in right-wing political parties. During the 1970s these ideas were also articulated in relation to development economics. This can be seen in attacks on the perceived Keynesianism embodied in development policies, and in arguments for the privatisation of public enterprises and deregulation of government controls. Such proposals mirrored those for domestic policies; indeed, in Britain an influential protagonist in the debate over development economics, Peter Bauer (1972), was an adviser to the British Conservative Party, and helped to shape its monetarist polices. With regard to the international sphere, the neoliberal theorists advocated the expansion of free trade and opposed protectionist measures. They argued that countries should compete according to their 'comparative advantage' in providing particular goods and services.

Between 1979 and 1982 right-wing governments were elected in Britain (Margaret Thatcher), the USA (Ronald Reagan) and Germany (Helmut Kohl), and they proceeded to implement monetarist domestic policies, which became influential throughout the advanced capitalist countries during the 1980s. Inevitably these ideas came also to dominate the bilateral aid policies of these governments and the multilateral bodies under their control, such as the World Bank and the International Monetary Fund. An early statement of this perspective appeared in 1981 in a major World Bank report on development in Africa entitled *Accelerated Development in Sub Saharan Africa: An Agenda for the Action* (World Bank, 1981). The report reflected the neoliberal view that poor development performance was a result of erroneous policies by Third World governments which had allowed too large a public sector, had overemphasised physical capital formation to the neglect of human skills, and introduced too many economic controls and regulations. The practical conclusion of the neoliberal perspective was that Third World governments must introduce new policies.

This argument has provided the basis for a massive intervention by the World Bank and the International Monetary Fund in the internal policy-making of governments in the Third World. Since the early 1980s lending has been made 'conditional' on prescribed changes in economic policies. The possibilities for this prescriptiveness lay in the debt crisis in the Third World which emerged at this time, making countries more reliant on aid and vulnerable to external 'conditions'. In this context they turned increasingly to the World Bank and the International Monetary

Fund for assistance to meet their foreign debts. These bodies have given loans on condition that governments undertake 'structural adjustment programmes' that would alter their economic policies. In this way a policy of 'global monetarism' (Cypher, 1988) has been enforced whose neoliberal prescriptions for the Third World involve the removal of restrictions on foreign investment and trade, the promotion of exports, the privatisation of public enterprises, the reduction of government spending, the removal of price controls, the imposition of wage restraints, and currency devaluation. The majority of countries in the Third World have accepted structural adjustment loans. The overall aim of the World Bank and IMF policy is to liberalise capital flows and trade worldwide, and to strengthen reliance on market mechanisms. This is intended further to integrate the world economy, in which Third World countries have the role of exporters in their areas of 'comparative advantage'. The establishment of the World Trade Organisation in 1995 created a strong international institution to promote the neoliberal goal of free trade in a globalised economy.

The neoliberal theory of free-market capitalism currently dominates international policy on development. The advanced capitalist countries use conditional aid to pressurise governments in the South to reduce their public sectors, open up their economies to foreign trade and investment, and adopt democratic reforms. This has significantly reduced the sovereignty of many countries of the South, limiting their autonomy over economic and social policy and political affairs.

The implications of the neoliberal perspective for education in the South have been twofold (Colclough, 1991). First, it is argued that the education services provided by governments should be orientated to the needs of business. Education and training are seen in terms of developing the human resources necessary for economic growth and successful competition in the world market. In the context of globalisation, technological change and more flexible work organisation, schools are required to produce a workforce with the necessary skills and an educational base for future learning. Thus the criteria for the development of education are enhancing individual productivity and entrepreneurship, and improving national economic performance. Second, such a perspective encourages reduced public expenditure on education, the introduction of user charges and increased private-sector involvement. Neoliberalism sees inequality as a source of individual incentive, so its educational prescriptions reject the concern of welfare capitalism with the issue of equity secured through state intervention. Instead it stresses the extension of individual choice, especially through the private provision of education and training. The main impact of its prescriptions in the South has been a reduction in government spending on all levels of education, leading to a relative decline in school enrolments and educational quality, as shown by UNESCO's *Report on the State of Education in Africa – 1997* (UNESCO, 1997b).

Neoliberal theory and adult education

The impact of neoliberal policies on adult education in the countries of the South has been significant (Mulenga, n.d.). The major overall effect of structural adjustment policies has been a reduction in adult education services as part of general cutbacks in government expenditure, and a trend towards cost-recovery fees in programmes that are retained. Both measures have had an impact on access to adult education. But neoliberalism also involves two key prescriptions for a new approach to adult education. First, it gives priority to adult education meeting the needs of the economy. Thus there has been a new emphasis on 'continuing education', 'skills training' and 'human resource development' which is displacing earlier paradigms of compensatory adult education as a redistributive mechanism and radical adult education as a movement for social change (Millar, 1991). Second, it seeks a reduced role for the state, and gives the private sector a more important role in adult education provision.

A clear statement of this approach is to be found in the 1991 policy of the World Bank on vocational and technical education and training, which signalled a change in the previous policy of support to public institutions and pre-employment training. The following quotation captures exactly the neoliberal conception of adult education and training:

> The development of a skilled labor force makes an important contribution to development. The challenges are to use employer, private and public training capacities effectively to train workers for jobs that

use their skills and to do so efficiently in developing economies increasingly influenced by technological change and open to international competition.

Training in the private sector – by private employers and in private training institutions – can be the most effective and efficient way to develop the skills of the work force. In the best cases employers train workers as quickly as possible for existing jobs. Costs are low compared with training before employment, and trained workers are placed automatically in jobs that use their skills. Larger employers often have the technology, and their supervisors have the expertise, to train in both traditional and newly emerging skills. Even the very small unregulated enterprises of the rural and urban informal sectors can provide the training needs for existing technologies and production practices. Private training institutions must function in the marketplace and be adept at changing enrolments and curricula to fit with the employment opportunities for graduates. The costs and benefits of employer and private training are equitably shared by workers and employers. (World Bank, 1991a: 8–9)

The new policy stresses the need for all training to be market-orientated, and promotes training by the private sector.

The prescriptions of the neoliberal approach have affected the orientation of many adult education policies and programmes in the South. The emphasis of the first prescription on work-related training for adults is perhaps most visible in expanded concerns with urban adult education, especially adult training linked to the development of manufacturing and commerce. This is especially apparent in those countries of the South in which a significant degree of industrialisation has taken place, as in Southeast Asia. In Singapore, for example, rapid industrial expansion has been accompanied by rising levels of technology in production and a concerted strategy to upgrade the skills of the adult workforce through programmes of continuing education and training (Pillay, 1992). This strategy seeks to raise skill levels, increase productivity, develop a quality workforce and thereby enhance Singapore's competitiveness in the world market. Recent initiatives include the modularisation of part-time skills training programmes to make access more flexible, and schemes to provide school-level education to prepare workers for skills training, including a special scheme for workers over forty who lack primary education. Initially the strategy was based on public training institutions but increasingly it is undertaken either by employers in the workplace or by private training agencies.

The evolution of the training system in Singapore converges with the second prescription of neoliberalism that encourages the privatisation of adult education, which historically has been dominated by state provision. The focus here is on employers themselves providing training for their employees, and on the expansion of private colleges, institutes and training centres. An increasing number of private organisations provide adult education programmes to the public, and contract their services to employers and governments. Zimbabwe, for instance, has a large private training market, with private colleges, training consultancy firms and correspondence colleges. The idea of a market approach to other forms of adult education is increasingly influential. In Botswana, for example, a recent government policy document on rural development suggests that communities should be given budgets to spend on extension services; this would 'allow NGOs, community organisations and private companies to compete with the government extension services for this type of work' (Ministry of Finance and Development Planning, 1997: 30). Given the predominance of the neoliberal paradigm of development, it is inevitable that its prescriptions significantly affect the nature of adult education policies and programmes in the South.

Populism

I have argued above that the dominant influences on development policies since 1945 have been modernisation theory, which envisages capitalist development through significant intervention by the state, and neoliberal theory, which sees capitalism developing though reliance on private enterprise and the market. During the 1980s it became increasingly clear that these policies in practice had not benefited large sectors of the population in the countries of the South. Indeed, development policies had often had a negative impact on their quality of life. This fact led to a variety of critiques of development thinking derived from an analysis of ordinary people's actual experience of the development process.

These critiques originate from different perspectives but their proposals for alternative approaches to development converge in a model of 'people-centred development' which can be labelled populist because of its focus on the empowerment of ordinary people. Its emphasis on the values and interests of agrarian societies in the face of industrialisation and urbanisation, and its antagonism to the state and monopoly capital in favour of decentralised self-managed modes of organisation, echo the philosophy of the populist rural movements in Europe and the USA in the late nineteenth century (Pomata, 1986; Kitching, 1989).[1]

The populist model emerged in the 1980s in response to two circumstances. First, the continuing penetration of the capitalist mode of production incorporated into the global market even remote areas of the world, such as the tropical forest zones. With the expansion of urbanisation and capitalist relations of production, the mode of existence, ecology and culture of agrarian societies was increasingly under pressure. Second, the economic crisis in the South reduced formal employment, diminished markets and created a decline in the services provided by the state. The failure of the market and of the state after a long period of expansion stimulated self-reliance strategies, which included the formation of many non-governmental organisations and grassroots groups, often based on indigenous values and practices.

Against this background, the theoretical articulation of the populist model as an alternative approach to development was influenced by feminism, environmentalism and ethnoculturalism.

Feminism

The resurgence of feminism in Europe and North America from the late 1960s meant that feminist thinking on the oppression and subordination experienced by women permeated many fields of social action, including development. Women's struggles over economic and social policy in the North were reflected in international thinking about development – for example, when the United Nations declared 1975 the International Year of Women and 1976–85 the Decade for the Advancement of Women. These events focused international attention on the fact that development policies, especially those promoted by international agencies, were not meeting the interests of women, particularly poor women. There was evidence that development programmes either excluded women or worsened their situation, as in cash crop schemes which increased women's workload and lowered their nutritional intake. After 1975 many aid agencies and Third World governments promoted 'women in development' programmes which were influenced by liberal feminism and were designed to improve the social and economic situation of women. These programmes sought to increase women's participation in the existing development process – for example, through income-generating projects to provide a cash income. However, it became clear in the 1980s that despite these programmes the socioeconomic status of women was not improving, and pervasive structures of gender inequality remained. The sense of failure in relation to women was exacerbated by the debt crisis in Latin America and the food crisis in Africa, which created a general perception of the inadequacy of development policies.

By the mid-1980s a more radical critique by feminists in the South had emerged. This was well articulated in *Development, Crises and Alternative Visions: Third World Women's Perspectives* (Sen and Grown, 1988). Sen and Grown argued that the assumptions behind the 'women in development' approach were incorrect: 'that women's main problem in the Third World was insufficient participation in an otherwise benevolent process of growth and development', when in fact the real problem was 'the nature of the development process into which women were to be integrated' (Sen and Grown, 1988: 15–16). They contended that the 'trickle-down' postulate of modernisation theory and the 'structural adjustment' of neoliberal theory had not addressed either the unequal location of Third World countries in the international economy, which makes them vulnerable to fluctuations in commodity prices, or the acute internal inequalities that leave many people unable to meet their basic needs. Above all, development programmes had been 'top-down' and had ignored the voices of the poor. Sen and Grown argued for an alternative approach to development rooted in a feminist vision of women as full and equal participants in all areas of society, and in a struggle against the multiple oppression based on nation, gender, class and ethnicity. The alternative approach advocated was a 'genuine people-oriented development' (Sen and

Grown, 1988: 49) focusing on the goal of eliminating poverty and inequality, and on processes of participatory democracy which would empower women.

Environmentalism

Another major area of criticism of development policies came from the perspective of environmentalism. The growth of the environmental movement in the North in the 1960s raised concerns about the environmental costs of economic growth. This stimulated an awareness of environmental issues at the global level, which inevitably led to a scrutiny of development policies. A major United Nations conference on the environment in 1972 generated the idea of 'ecodevelopment' (Hettne, 1990: 186). The theme of the environment continued through the 1980s and into the 1990s, expressed at the international level by the report of the World Commission on Environment and Development (1987) entitled *Our Common Future*, and by the Earth Summit in Rio in 1992. The need for an environmental dimension to development policies is now captured in the concept of 'sustainable development', which stresses not only the problem of diminishing non-renewable resources (such as oil and coal) but also the vulnerability of renewable resources (such as forests and soil).

The idea of resource scarcity and the need for conservation contradicts development thinking based on unlimited economic growth built on resource exploitation and industrialisation. Indeed, it has been argued that the current levels of resource consumption in the industrialised North could not be sustained if they were enjoyed by the world's population as a whole, as this would threaten the limits of the world's physical capacity. Thus the industrialised countries cannot provide a model of development for the South, because a global perspective on development requires that the North reduces its levels of consumption (Riddell, 1981). Furthermore, people's actual experience of environmental degradation in the South makes the environment an inescapable issue for development. Problems such as deforestation in Latin America and Asia, soil erosion and desertification in Africa, and industrial pollution in Bhopal and other cities of the South have been devastating for individuals and their livelihoods. The quality of life of many people has been badly affected by the environmental changes created by development.

Although there is an apparent consensus that environmental issues must be incorporated in development strategies, this conceals many contradictory views on what should be done. Contradictions arise essentially because the structure of the world economy since the colonial era has been based on the South supplying primary commodities of minerals and agricultural products to the North, and it is this activity which is central to the South's environmental problems. However, it is unlikely that the rich and powerful in North and South will take environmental measures that threaten their own commercial interests. Hence at the 1992 Earth Summit the International Forum of NGOs and Social Movements held an alternative summit that focused on the view that a genuine concern with environmental conservation and protection will require an alternative development paradigm. The alternative approach to environmental issues is 'people-centred' and focuses on community participation, local organisations, indigenous methods of resource management, and self-reliance. It is often opposed to urbanisation, industrial development and the centralised state (Woodhouse, 1992: 113).

Ethnoculturalism

Another critique of development theory is made from a perspective that emphasises ethnicity and indigenous culture. This critique has two dimensions. First, there are criticisms that development theory has focused on the significance of the nation-state and the need for 'nation-building' as a task of development and, in so doing, has overlooked ethnic diversity. The idea of 'national integration' has invariably meant establishing the hegemony of one ethnic group within the state, and has led to antagonism towards the cultures, religions and languages of other groups. This is evidenced, for example, in the policy of Latin American governments to assimilate indigenous populations. One outcome has been increased ethnic conflicts, as ethnic identity has been mobilised for resistance to state policies which promote cultural domination alongside political oppression and economic exploitation. The mode of action by ethnic movements has ranged from protests against local development projects, such as commercial forestry schemes in India, to full-scale civil war, as in Sri Lanka. In highlighting this problem, writers such as Stavenhagen (1986) have called for 'ethnodevelopment', an alternative approach to development which sees cultural diversity as positive, and therefore seeks to promote the identity of different ethnic groups within the national society.

Second, there is the argument that the whole conceptualisation of development is Eurocentric, because development involves the imposition on countries of the South of external models of society derived from the economic history and Judaeo-Christian values of Europe (Wiarda, 1983). The ideas and values underpinning the concepts of development promoted by the North and adopted by the dominant classes in the South are thus regarded as a manifestation of cultural imperialism, the ideological and cultural sphere of the North's economic domination. The conventional development process considers local institutions and culture an obstacle, and devalues indigenous knowledge systems, values and ways of doing things. There are many cases in which indigenous practices have been supplanted by 'modern' techniques, with negative effects. For example, some changes in areas such as farming and health have had deleterious effects on food production and health standards. This critique challenges Northern ethnocentrism in development theory and, more generally, attacks the globalising pressures towards the homogenisation of global culture.

This ethnocultural critique has been considerably strengthened since the late 1980s by the application of postmodernism to the field of development. Writers in this tradition 'deal neither with development as technical performance nor with development as class conflict, but with development as a particular cast of mind. For development is much more than a socioeconomic endeavour, it is a perception which models reality' (Sachs, 1992: 1). Thus discourse analysis is used to deconstruct the development paradigm that arose after the Second World War. The archaeology of the concept of development reveals its Enlightenment assumptions about progress (towards the model of industrialised, growth-orientated society) and its Euro-American representation of other societies as 'poor' and 'backward'. The hidden agenda of Westernisation is leading towards a monoculture in which the 'Other' disappears.

Postmodernism highlights the practical failures of development, such as social polarisation and ecological disaster, as well as the loss of cultural diversity. But its analysis seeks primarily to undermine the conceptual basis of developmentalism as a 'regime of representation' whose hegemony has stifled alternative ways of thinking about society. In so doing, it seeks to enable the imagining of an era of 'post-development'. Here people of non-Western cultures will recover local spaces to regenerate indigenous knowledge and practices through ethnocultural struggles and grassroots movements (Escobar, 1995). The affirmation of cultural difference and alternative modes of knowledge is at the heart of the postmodern critique, with grassroots organisations providing the basis for a different kind of society.

The populist model

This discussion has sketched three of the main theoretical trends which have contributed to the populist model of development. The commonalities in these trends converge in their alternative model of development, centred on an opposition to development conceived as economic growth based on industrialisation and production for the world market, carried out at the initiative of the state. This conception of development is regarded as Eurocentric, top-down, damaging to the environment, and destructive of rural society. In practice it is seen as having failed to meet the needs of the majority, who remain poor and powerless. The populist alternative therefore stresses peasant agriculture and small-scale commodity production, with a focus on meeting the needs of the poor through self-reliant, localised economic activity using labour-intensive methods and appropriate technology. It proposes decentralised, bottom-up, people-centred planning which will mobilise and empower local communities through participation in decision-making, especially in grassroots social movements and non-governmental organisations. It particularly emphasises the importance of indigenous culture and the environment.

The essence of the populist model is succinctly expressed by Trainer:

> These alternatives constitute a Third Way. They involve the rejection of the capitalist way with its emphasis on limitless increases in con-

sumption and waste, its disregard for the poor, and its indifference to any concept of appropriate development. They just as emphatically reject the big-state socialist/communist way with its typically centralised, non-democratic, authoritarian and equally affluence-and-growthobsessed approach to development. The Third Way is about simple material living standards, local self-sufficiency, grassroots participation and 'village' democracy, living in harmony with the environment, cooperation and zero economic growth. It is also about development defined more in terms of personal, ecological, community and cultural welfare and progress then in terms of the mere accumulation of economic wealth. (Trainer, 1989: 6)

Populism and adult education

The populist model of development has had a significant influence on adult education, resonating with the tradition of adult education as a popular movement for social change. The idea of 'people-centred development' necessarily puts great value on engendering the consciousness and abilities that are required for people to form and manage their own organisations. This gives prominence to forms of adult education that are highly accessible, especially to groups that are normally excluded, and very responsive to the needs and interests of the participants. Since the early 1980s the themes of participation, empowerment and popular organisation have been very prominent within the theory and practice of adult education for development.

As was the case with adult education and basic human needs, an international conference of the International Council for Adult Education (ICAE) has symbolic significance in the emergence of this trend.[2] In 1982, at a time of recession and the beginning of the Third World debt crisis, the ICAE held a conference on the theme 'Towards an Authentic Development'. The Report of the conference recorded 'basic agreements on the need for an alternative model of development and of the key role of adult education in this process' (Hall, 1982: 6). The nature of the new model had not crystallised in the Report, but it was clearly evolving from existing concerns in the field of adult education with basic human needs, derived from modernisation theory, and with self-reliance, derived from dependency theory. The new dimension was twofold. First, there was opposition to the concept of development based on industrialisation, modern technology and consumerism, and advocacy of the view that 'development is for people' (Barrow, 1982: 49). Second, there was scepticism about the centrality of the state in the development process: 'The most important factor for the development of an authentic adult education is the specific role of non-governmental and voluntary associations' (Dumazedier, 1982: 56). The emergent language on the goals, processes and organisational forms of adult education thus began to coincide with the conceptualisations characteristic of the populist approach to development.

The elaboration of the role of adult education in the populist model has continued since the early 1980s, albeit in a piecemeal fashion. As yet, this distinctive paradigm of adult education and development does not seem to have been systematically articulated in a book-length work. For example, *Adult Education in Development: Methods and Approaches from Changing Societies* (McGivenny and Murray, 1991) provides a series of case studies of community-based non-formal adult education activities, but does not attempt to analyse the examples or theorise the relationship between adult education and development. The brief preface and concluding observations simply assert the need for 'encouraging citizens' participation in planning for development' (McGivenny and Murray, 1991: 11), and the importance of non-governmental organisations for mobilising community effort. The lack of a coherent, in-depth explanation of the populist philosophy and approach, and analysis of its strengths and weaknesses in theory and practice, is surprising given its undoubted impact on adult education practice in the South.

This impact can be traced clearly in the grey literature of conference papers and reports, in the journal literature and in occasional book chapters. For example, Wangoola presents a typical argument from an African context stressing the need to 'go back to the people' and stating that 'people's culture, science, technology, skills, and value systems should be the very basis of adult education' (Wangoola, 1996: 329). The important contributory influences in adult education have been the same ones that shaped the populist model: feminism, environmentalism, ethnoculturalism and the non-governmental organisation movement. Only occasionally is a unified approach based on these elements applied comprehensively to an issue within adult education. One example is Parajuli's article 'Politics of Knowledge, Models of Development and Literacy' (1990). Parajuli argues that, 'While the minimal goal of achieving functional literacy is still far away, there are now needs for ecological literacy, gender literacy and cultural literacy' (Parajuli, 1990: 289). He contends that the concept of literacy has to be redefined by revising notions of knowledge, the state and development, as the literacy programmes of the 'developmentalist state' have served to 'delegitimize the knowledge of marginalized people ... those betrayed by the development dream' (Parajuli, 1990: 289–90). He challenges the dominant ideology of development and its concomitant role for the state, and argues that grass-roots agrarian, women's, ecological and ethnic movements are now resisting the developmentalist world-view, concluding: 'Any viable programme of literacy in the 1990s will have to recognize these knowledge claims from the bottom' (Parajuli, 1990: 291). Thus the article uses the philosophy and language of the populist model to argue for new forms of adult literacy programme.

It can be concluded that the populist approach to development has an important influence on the conception and practice of adult education. However, although adult education programmes based on these ideas have expanded dramatically, it would appear that they are concentrated in small-scale local projects, and are hence relatively restricted from a national perspective. Nevertheless, the themes of empowerment, participation and grassroots organisation have been widely adopted.

Political Economy

From the late 1960s onwards a number of studies of development issues appeared under the title of 'the political economy of development'. However, as Staniland makes clear in his book *What is Political Economy?* (1985), different writers have different conceptions of the term 'political economy'. In a general way, the term denotes a concern with explaining the relationship between political processes and economic processes, but the conceptualisation of this relationship varies enormously, and ultimately derives from an underlying theoretical paradigm. For one group of writers the label refers to their efforts to introduce a political dimension to the paradigm of neoclassical economics in order to embrace analytically the role of governments in economies, particularly through the mechanism of public budgets. This approach emerged in the late 1960s and was called 'the new political economy'. It focused on the public choices inherent in economic decision-making by governments, and sought to identify those policy choices which would interfere least with market forces, and would promote private-sector development. It was quickly applied to development economics because of its clear relevance to the role of the state in development planning. A characteristic early volume was Uphoff and Ilchman's *The Political Economy of Development* (1972), which included theoretical discussion and practical analysis. Uphoff and Ilchman defined 'the new political economy' as 'an integrated social science of public choice' (Uphoff and Ilchman, 1972: 1). This approach has maintained its appeal, and Bates's later collection *Toward a Political Economy of Development* (1988) has the subtitle 'A Rational Choice Perspective'. In his introductory sections Bates clearly explains the book's approach, which focuses on how governments interact with markets, and how and why public policies are chosen. Because of its concern with markets and the state, the 'new political economy' approach has become an element in neoliberal development policy. For example, the *World Development Report 1991* by the World Bank (1991b) has a section on 'the political economy of development' in a chapter concerned with the state's role in ensuring that markets work effectively.

But the label 'political economy' is often devoid of any clear content and the author's approach is left undefined, lacking an explicit theoretical reference point. For example, Faaland and Parkinson's *The Political Economy of Development* (1986) contains the following assertion in the Preface:

> The reason for the introduction of the term political economy into the title of the book is obvious. The practice of economics cannot be conducted in isolation and has always to be related to the political and social setting of the countries with which it is concerned. In such circumstances many issues are matters for debate and political consideration which extend far beyond economic organisation. (Faaland and Parkinson, 1986: ix)

This is the only explanation for the choice of the term, and fails completely to address the authors' understanding of how the economic and the political are related. Faaland and Parkinson provide no theoretical consideration of the issue or of its methodological implications for their study, which in fact appears to be written within the modernisation paradigm. Indeed, in too many studies which use the term there is no clear reason why it has been adopted or what relevance it has for the nature of the study. This is exemplified by a recent collection on Botswana edited by Stedman, which bears the title *Botswana: The Political Economy of Democratic Development* (1993). There is no indication whatsoever in the editor's Introduction why this heterogeneous collection of papers should have been brought together under such a title.

Many writers who adopt a political economy approach to development, however, do so explicitly from within the Marxist tradition. Marx's central focus, as we have seen, was the development of the capitalist mode of production in terms of its historical emergence in Western Europe from pre-capitalist society and in terms of the dynamics which generate its expansion (and ultimate supersession). The question of socioeconomic change is therefore at the heart of Marxist social theory. Although – as Carver has emphasised – Marx did not provide a coherent account of non-European societies, his work did indicate a relevant 'research programme' (Carver, 1985: 44) on the need to investigate modes of production other than capitalism; transitions from one mode to another; the impact of capitalism on pre-capitalist society; and the development of capitalism itself through global expansion and the creation of a world market. It is not surprising, therefore, that the Marxist tradition has been an intellectual resource for the contemporary study of development.

The first major initiatives within this 'research programme' were undertaken between 1900 and 1920 on the topic of the global expansion of capitalism. In this period the concept of 'imperialism' was elaborated by Hilferding, Bukharin and Lenin, producing what Brewer (1980: 79) has called the 'classical Marxist theories of imperialism'. These writers sought to analyse new trends in the emergent capitalist world economy marked by the growth of monopoly capitalism based on large-scale production. They identified the dynamic of this stage of capitalist development as the export of capital (rather than goods) and the search for the most profit-able areas of investment. This search involved a struggle for domi-nance (economic, political and even military) over geographical areas, a process entailing not only the subordination of less devel-oped economies by more advanced ones but also rivalry between advanced countries (as in the 1914–18 War). The concept of im-perialism therefore denoted the process of capital accumulation in the period of monopoly capitalism, and was integral to the Marxist theorisation of the continuing development of the world capitalist market. It was predicted that the export of capital would generate economic development in the backward areas.

The classical Marxist theory of imperialism laid a basis for considering the internationalisation of capital, the international division of labour, the geographical expansion of capitalist relations of production, relations between nation-states, and other aspects of the global political economy. Its main conclusion was that the development of the world capitalist system is essentially an *uneven* development as capital moves internationally to the areas in which the highest profits can be made. This means that vari-ations occur both historically and geographically in the compara-tive levels of economic development of different countries, and there are concomitant patterns of international inequality. This conclusion would find unsurprising the post-1945 pattern of the international economy which has seen such developments as the rise of Japan and the decline of Britain on the one hand, and the increasing differentiation among the countries of the South on the other.

The first specific application of Marxist ideas within develop-ment studies as it emerged after 1945, however, was in dependency theory. As noted above, dependency theory has been character-ised as 'neo-Marxist' because of its departure from earlier Marxist positions. The main difference is that whereas classical Marxist theorists saw imperialism as essentially progressive in terms of creating economic development in backward areas, dependency theory regarded development in the core capitalist countries as having underdeveloped the Third World and blocked its possibili-ties for development. This alternative approach led to an extended debate in the 1970s and a strong critique from within Marxism (Chilcote, 1982).

Marxist writers made a number of criticisms. Dependency theory was criticised for its erroneous characterisation of capitalism because of its focus on relations of exchange rather than relations of production. Thus Frank, for example, regarded capitalism as dominant in Latin America from the sixteenth century, when in fact many pre-capitalist relations of production remained, even though areas were increasingly drawn into trade within the money economy. The theory was criticised for its overemphasis on the role of external forces and for insufficient analysis of the processes by which capitalism interacted with pre-capitalist modes of production. Indeed, a major critique was made of the external focus of dependency theory, which tended to concentrate on a nation's relations within the world economic system at the expense of analysis of internal class relationships and how they shape development, including their role in the mediation of external influences.

The central critique took issue with the main thesis of dependency theory: that capitalist development in the Third World was a distorted form of development which would not develop the forces of production ('the development of underdevelopment'). This thesis was seen as misconceiving the nature of capitalism, whose development has always been 'uneven', with certain areas experiencing greater economic growth than others. The 'stagnationist' thesis of dependency was severely weakened during the 1970s by the rapid economic transformation of Brazil, South Korea and other 'newly industrialising countries' in Latin America and Asia. In fact, the very notion of 'dependency' was questioned because the opposite, 'autocentric development', did not seem a satisfactory representation of the advanced economies, in which external trade and investment play a significant role. This argument also brought into question the theory's policy logic of disengagement from the world capitalist economy as unrealistic, and even more likely to retard economic growth and technological development. Finally, there were criticisms at the political level. The dependency theorists were criticised for implying that it is nations which exploit other nations rather than recognising class as the basis of exploitation. It was also argued that they had a utopian view of socialism, and did not articulate a political strategy that related to the realities of class struggle. Often, they appeared to support a nationalist goal of autonomy rather than a socialist goal of changed class relations.

Despite these critiques, the significance of dependency theory (around which there were a lot of polemics on the Left in the 1970s) is that it not only exposed the limitations of modernisation theory but also revitalised Marxist scholarship on the world economy and the issue of development. It stimulated Marxist theory to focus on the specific dynamics of Third World countries and not to see them, as the classic writers on imperialism had done, mainly from the vantage point of the advanced capitalist countries. Indeed, a lot of the debate over dependency theory took place within the Third World, particularly in Latin America, the Caribbean and Africa. An important outcome has been a greater concern within Marxism to address the specificities of peripheral capitalism. This could be seen during the 1970s in approaches which focused on the internal characteristics of Third World countries, and considered the historical processes by which the capitalist mode of production penetrated into existing pre-capitalist modes. This analysis considered the impact of capitalism and how it had related to the existing mode of economic organisation in terms of reinforcing, changing and finally displacing it.

The study of the articulation of the modes of production (Wolpe, 1980) sought to explain how the externally introduced capitalist mode of production interacted with the internal pre-capitalist modes to generate the distinctive social formations of the different countries of the Third World. Studies focused on the processes by which old modes of production were dissolved over time and on the impact of this on class formation and class conflict – for example, in rural areas with the establishment of private property in land and the creation of a landless proletariat. Clearly, this approach provided a counterbalance to the perceived overemphasis of dependency theory on the external constraints on development. It also attempted a more country-specific analysis compared to the tendency to overgeneralisation within dependency theory, with its focus on capitalism at the level of a world system.

Sklair (1988) has argued persuasively that the existence of different Marxist theories of development is evidence not of a problem but of the fruitfulness of historical materialism as a 'meta-theory' which has generated a variety of theoretical explanations and empirical research programmes on issues of development. It is certainly true that there is now a rich source of Marxist analysis to provide a political economy of development that applies the theoretical framework adopted in Chapter 3, as I will show in subsequent chapters.

The key theoretical text for the political economy approach used in this study is the Preface to the English edition of Cardoso and Faletto's *Dependency and Development in Latin America* (1979: vii–xxv). Cardoso and Faletto argue that capitalism in the periphery does lead to a development of the productive forces and economic growth. However, this development is uneven, reaching different levels in different countries and in different regions within countries. Furthermore, it contains the contradictions and inequalities that are inherent in the capitalist mode of production. To analyse peripheral capitalism, they adopt a political economy approach in the Marxist tradition:

> We attempt to reestablish the intellectual tradition based on a comprehensive social science. We seek a global and dynamic understanding of social structures instead of looking only at specific dimensions of the social process ... we stress the sociopolitical nature of the economic relations of production, thus following the nineteenth century tradition of treating economy as political economy. This methodological approach, which found its highest expression in Marx, assumes that the hierarchy that exists in society is the result of established ways of organizing the production of material and spiritual life. This hierarchy also serves to assure the unequal appropriation of nature and the results of human work by social classes and groups. So we attempt to analyze domination in its connection with economic expansion. (Cardoso and Faletto, 1979: ix)

Their Marxist political economy of development has the following central elements:

- A recognition of both 'the structural conditioning of social life' and 'the historical transformation of structures' through social conflict.
- A focus on class exploitation and 'the mechanisms and processes of domination' that maintain existing structures.
- An analysis of classes and the contradictions that create 'possibilities for social movements and ideologies of change'.

- A recognition of the significance of political struggles and 'political capacity' based on 'organisation, will and ideologies'.
- A conception of 'the relationship between internal and external forces as forming a complex whole whose structural links are not based on mere external forms of exploitation and coercion, but are rooted in coincidences of interest between local dominant classes and international ones, and, on the other side, are challenged by local dominated groups and classes'.
- A concern with the capitalist world system and the need 'to explain the interrelationships of classes and nation-states at the level of the international scene as well at the level internal to each country' in terms of both compatibilities and contradictions.

Cardoso and Faletto put forward an approach which applies concepts such as capital, imperialism, class and state from the general Marxist theory of capitalism. They do so in order to provide concrete analysis of societies in the economic periphery in a way that will account for the specificity of these societies not only in relation to advanced capitalist countries but also in relation to each other:

> The very existence of an economic 'periphery' cannot be understood without reference to the economic drive of advanced capitalist economies, which were responsible for the formation of a capitalist periphery and for the integration of traditional non-capitalist economies into the world market. Yet, the expansion of capitalism in Bolivia and Venezuela, in Mexico or Peru, in Brazil and Argentina, in spite of having been submitted to the same global dynamic of international capitalism, did not have the same history or consequences. The differences are rooted not only in the diversity of natural resources, nor just in the different periods in which these economies have been incorporated into the international system (although these factors have played some role). The explanation must also lie in the different moments at which sectors of local classes allied or clashed with foreign interests, organized different forms of state, sustained distinct ideologies, or tried to implement various policies or defined alternative strategies to cope with imperialist strategies in diverse moments of history. (Cardoso and Faletto, 1979: xvii)

Cardoso and Faletto's theoretical position outlines, in the context of peripheral capitalism, a political economy approach congruent with the framework presented in Chapter 3. It encompasses all the eight elements in that framework, with the exception of social inequalities other than class. I therefore conclude that the theoretical framework established in Chapter 3 provides a valid and relevant basis for the analysis of adult education and development in the countries of the South.

Notes

1. This usage of 'populism' is different to the Latin American usage, which refers to an authoritarian political style based on an appeal to the masses, in the manner of Peron in Argentina and Vargas in Brazil.

2. Since its inception in 1973 the ICAE has been dominated by the social reform tradition within adult education; therefore it does not articulate the perspectives of other groups, such as the company training officers who are central to neoliberal conceptions of adult education.

CHAPTER 5

Imperialism, Aid and Adult Education

The focus of this book is the political economy of adult education in peripheral capitalist countries. Such countries, by definition, are on the edges of the core centres of capitalism in the USA, Europe and Japan. The historical expansion of capitalism from its origins in Western Europe has involved the steady incorporation of the pre-capitalist areas of the world into a global economic system. It is this process of incorporation, impelled by external forces, which has given the peripheral capitalist countries their specific characteristics. The theoretical framework established in Chapter 3 posited that:

- The dominance of the capitalist mode of production at the world level means that socioeconomic development in peripheral capitalist countries of the South must be located within the context of the global political economy. It is assumed that the dynamics of imperialism have an impact on the policies and practices of adult education.

The most important feature of the global political economy today is its structural inequality and the relative weakness of the countries of the South. External factors, therefore, have a significant role in the development of these countries, affecting not only the nature of their economies but also their politics and social forms. This chapter accordingly seeks to analyse the nature of external influences and their impact on adult education. Although the emphasis is on external influences, this does not ignore the theoretical position adopted in Chapter 3: that the relationship between external forces and internal forces must be seen as a complex whole, because external forces intersect with internal patterns of inequality, domination and resistance, and are mediated by the class structure and the state. The external influences in the periphery are discussed in this chapter in terms of the concept of imperialism. The specific impact of imperialism on adult education is considered in relation to the aid provided by the North to the South.

The Nature of Imperialism

By the late nineteenth century the expansion of capitalist trade had created a world market. Within this world market, distinct areas of influence had been established by the different capitalist countries, typified by the agreement on the division of Africa made by the European colonial powers at the 1884 Berlin Conference. The final quarter of the century saw the development of large-scale productive enterprises in Europe and the USA, based on the concentration and centralisation of capital. This represented a new stage in the evolution of the capitalist mode of production, as these monopoly companies came to play a central economic role. The enlarged capacity of these monopolies to generate surplus value led to increasingly available capital, and the large banks and monopoly companies joined forces to invest capital in productive activities outside their national boundaries. Thus capitalist accumulation took on the new form of a world-level process, which Marxist political economy defines as imperialism. This new stage was characterised by the export of capital, where previously the export of manufactured goods had been dominant. Thus, in the twentieth-century era of monopoly capitalism, the peripheral areas became not only a source of raw materials and a market for finished goods but also places for profitable investment.

Imperialism is essentially an economic process, denoting the expansion of the capitalist mode of production to all parts of the world. However, it has important political consequences as the advanced capitalist countries seek to promote their economic interests. The political dimension of imperialism consists of varieties of direct and indirect external influence over the underdeveloped

countries, and international rivalry among the industrialised nations to extend their areas of influence in the periphery. Thus the
state in the advanced capitalist countries, under the influence of
dominant capitalist classes, plays an important part in helping to
secure the conditions that will ensure the worldwide reproduction
of capital, and promote the interests of its corporations.

The character of imperialism has evolved during the twentieth
century, particularly since the war between the imperialist powers
in 1939–45, which led to a shift in the balance of economic and
political power and the emergence of the USA as the dominant
capitalist country. Since 1945 the internationalisation of capital
has increased, and the global economy has become more integrated. From the late 1940s onwards, the amount of foreign direct
investment in production by US corporations increased rapidly as
they invested in the weakened European economies and in the
underdeveloped countries. The USA quickly displaced Britain as
the most important investor in Latin America, and its advocacy of
decolonisation in Africa and Asia was motivated by its desire to
open up previously protected markets in the European colonies.
In fact, the advent of the concept of 'development' can best be
understood in terms of US capital's search for expanded economic
opportunities and the role of the US state in protecting corporate
interests against nationalist or socialist regimes that would nation-
alise and curtail foreign investment.

The main institutional form of imperialism since 1945 has been
the transnational corporation (TNC), a large capitalist firm operating in more than one country – that is, across national boundaries. The significance of TNCs grew enormously after the 1940s,
and from the 1960s onwards European and Japanese TNCs arose
alongside those of the USA. Their importance can be gauged by
the fact that by 1980, 350 TNCs controlled 25,000 subsidiaries
and produced 28 per cent of the GDP of the capitalist world
(Jenkins, 1987: 8). In some industries a small group of companies
came to dominate production – by 1983, for example, three companies controlled 70 per cent of world tobacco, nine companies
produced 80 per cent of the world's cars and seven companies 66
per cent of the world's oil (United Nations Centre on Transnational
Corporations, 1983). The TNCs continue to grow steadily. Their
size can be illustrated by the US garment producer Levi Strauss,

which had 700 plants in sixty countries in 1993 (*New Internationalist*, 1998: 19).

The early focus of the TNCs in the underdeveloped countries was on the production of raw materials from agriculture and the extraction of minerals and fuel, involving companies such as the United Fruit Company and Exxon. But from the 1960s there was a shift into manufacturing investment in the periphery. This took two forms. One form was investment in underdeveloped countries for production to meet the demand in their domestic markets – for example, in Latin America. The second form was the development of export-orientated manufacture to produce goods for markets in the advanced capitalist countries themselves. This was the case in Asia, particularly in Export Processing Zones which offered special incentives to TNCs, and low wages based on feminised and casualised labour.

The development of manufacturing in the underdeveloped countries led to a shift in the international division of labour and a certain degree of restructuring in the global economy. But this process was very selective, as only a small number of countries in Latin America and Asia experienced significant industrialisation: the so-called 'newly industrialised countries' (NICs) of Brazil, Mexico, Argentina, South Korea, Taiwan, Hong Kong and Singapore. In 1983, for example, Brazil and Mexico accounted for a quarter of the entire stock of foreign direct investment by advanced capitalist countries (Jenkins, 1987: 13). The TNCs invested largely in middle-income rather than low-income countries so that the overall effect of economic development in the peripheral countries was very uneven, leading to increased differentiation between them. This became clear in the economic crisis of the 1980s, when external debt and negative rates of economic growth led to deteriorating living standards in much of Latin America and sub-Saharan Africa. In terms of the economic criteria of income and industrialisation levels, the South came to be divided into two main categories:

1. The industrialising economies of Asia and Latin America, including not only the original group of NICs but latecomers to increased manufacturing, mainly countries in Asia such as China, India, Indonesia, Malaysia and Thailand. The category

also includes the high-income oil-exporting countries, mainly in the Middle East and North Africa.

2. The low-income exporters of primary agricultural and mineral products, mainly clustered in sub-Saharan Africa, Central America and the Caribbean, and increasingly marginalised in the world economy.

Despite the differences between these groups of countries, however, their experience is essentially a similar one of dependent capitalist development. They rely on the advanced capitalist countries for capital, technology, research and development, and markets. Their economic structures involve high levels of exports and manufactured imports, but they have little control over the terms of trade. They are subject to direct and indirect political influence by the advanced capitalist countries (including military intervention) to ensure that they provide access to resources and markets, and guarantee the conditions for profitable private investment.

Globalisation

The imperialism of the 1990s is commonly labelled 'globalisation', a label which draws attention to the intensification in the historical trends of global capitalist accumulation that took place over the last decade. Globalisation refers to the large increase in cross-border economic activity as a consequence of a number of factors. These include major technological innovations in transport and telecommunications and, especially, microprocessor applications. These innovations strengthened the economic activity of the transnational corporations, banks and finance houses. Their increased economic power is reflected in the global political dominance of the corporate agenda (Korten, 1995) and in the neoliberal policies promoted worldwide by the advanced capitalist countries through international organisations like the World Bank and the IMF.

The globalisation process can be seen in the spheres of manufacture, trade and finance. In manufacture, the changes in transport, communication and production technologies have enabled TNCs increasingly to move certain productive activities to low-wage countries, and to disperse the elements of production across different countries. The globalisation of production means that separate components (of a car or television, for example) are made in different countries and finally assembled in another country. The increase in foreign direct investment in manufacturing has created a more integrated global economy, with TNCs taking decisions to locate production in different countries according to calculations of profitability involving criteria such as wage levels, the nature of laws on unions and environmental protection, taxation and investment policies, and political stability.

In trade, there has been a significant growth in international trade accompanying neoliberal free-market policies of trade liberalisation. This was consolidated in 1995 by the establishment of the World Trade Organisation (WTO), which introduced new rules to govern international trade. These strengthened the rights of corporations to operate freely around the world without restrictions imposed by national governments, such as tariffs. The interests of global investors will be further promoted by the proposed WTO Multilateral Agreement on Investment, which will overrule restrictive national legislation and give corporations the right to sue governments that do not comply. In financial markets, there have been hugely expanded international capital flows by banks and finance houses trading in stocks, bonds, currencies and financial instruments such as derivatives. The accelerated mobility of capital follows deregulation policies by national governments which have abolished restrictions such as currency controls. The internationalisation of finance capital as it crosses and recrosses borders to find maximum returns is one of the most prominent features of globalisation. These worldwide speculative activities have been made possible by information technology which allows capital to be moved at a keystroke.

The essence of globalisation is therefore cross-border economic activity and the decreased significance of national boundaries. Thus airline bookings for London are processed in Mumbai; an aeroplane constructed in Seattle contains parts from twelve different countries; a law firm in Boston has its typing done in Beijing; clothes are designed in Germany and tailored in Morocco for sale in Europe; CNN is broadcast from Atlanta to 210 countries and territories; half of the Sony workforce is outside Japan; McDonald's has 18,000 standardised restaurants worldwide. The bottom line is capital's search for maximum returns on its investment. In this globalised economy, the political sovereignty of nation-states is being eroded, especially in the South, and social and cultural realities are being transformed by the universalisation of Western capitalist values and practices.

The use of the label 'globalisation' accurately denotes a new period in the development of the world capitalist economy. However, the fundamental dynamics of imperialism as capitalist accumulation on a world scale remain the same, as monopoly capital expands and intensifies its worldwide activity in order to control access to raw materials, enlarge its markets and find the most profitable areas for investment. The basic structure of the international division of labour, with core and peripheral capitalist countries, remains the defining characteristic of the global political economy: 'some countries are globalisers, the rest are globalised'.[1]

Aid as Imperialism

The increasing integration of the world capitalist economy since 1945 has been supported by aid – that is, the transfer of public financial and technical resources from the industrialised countries to the peripheral countries. Aid is an integral part of international political and economic relations, and it reflects the rich/poor division within the global economy. Indeed, the concept of the Third World has been defined in terms of those countries which are recipients of aid (Wood, 1986: 5). For the countries of the South, aid represents their relative weakness within the international political economy, and provides a channel for external influence over their development policies and programmes. Viewed from a global perspective, the varied activities of the state in the advanced capitalist countries carried out under the rubric of aid have a systemic role in developing and maintaining the conditions for capitalist accumulation on a world scale. The Marxist political economy approach therefore regards aid as a dimension of imperialism (Hayter, 1971).

The provision of aid is undertaken primarily in the self-interest of the providing countries. Its ostensible purpose is to promote development, but although the language of aid suggests a disinterested and benevolent helpfulness, the reality is different. The provision of aid does in some instances represent a humanitarian response to poverty or disaster, a sense of charity or a moral commitment to redress the unjust balance between rich and poor nations. But more often aid is one dimension of foreign policy, and supports a country's strategic interests and ideological alliances. This has been most clear in the case of the USA, whose aid has been used to support allies, such as South Vietnam in the 1960s, and withheld from countries whose policies it opposed, such as Chile in 1970–73 and Zimbabwe in 1983. But to a greater or lesser extent, the aid of other countries also reflects their strategic and diplomatic alignments, as evidenced by the orientation of British and French aid to their former colonies. The dominant function of aid for the countries of the North, however, is to advance their economic interests through encouraging domestic purchases, expanding foreign markets for exports, and increasing access to raw materials and areas for investment.

What is aid? Aid constitutes a transfer of resources in the form of either capital assistance (investment finance comprising loans and grants) or technical assistance (comprising experts, training and technology). It is defined in two dimensions. First, it is 'official', in that the state in the industrialised countries uses public expenditure for the international transfer of resources. In fact, aid is often labelled 'official development assistance'. Second, it is 'concessional' in so far as these transfers are provided more cheaply than market rates. Thus an official loan may be over a longer period and at a lower interest rate than a loan from a commercial bank. The extent to which aid departs from market rates defines its 'hardness' or 'softness'. Aid providers expect recipients to 'graduate' from greater to lesser degrees of concessionality (i.e. from soft to hard) as they become more creditworthy and as their income level rises. Although the concessional concept is important definitionally, it must be noted that a lot of aid is provided through development banks in the form of loans, and therefore constitutes a debt which becomes a component of a country's overall debt obligations. Furthermore, although many countries, in their directly provided aid, make outright grants which do not have to be repaid, this concession is weakened by the stipulation that the recipient has to buy goods and services from the providing country. The practice of 'tied' aid benefits the providing country in terms of stimulating its own economy and encouraging continued commercial relations, for instance for spare parts. But it reduces the real value of the aid to the recipient, who could purchase more cheaply on the open market. Indeed, although aid is defined as a transfer of resources to the South, the effect of having to service official loans and make tied purchases has been to create large reverse flows of capital to the North. In the light of this,

> the imagery of gift giving embedded in most discussions of aid becomes questionable. Donors may receive more than they give, and recipients may repay more than they receive.... The donor–recipient terminology reflects a basic asymmetry of power and status that lies at the core of the aid process. (Wood, 1986: 14)

It is important to demystify the concept of aid as a gift in order to clarify its role within the world economy, and identify it as a powerful external influence on development strategies in the South.

Aid is channelled to the South through a wide variety of different organisations. These organisations can be grouped into three types (Browne, 1990):

(a) *Bilateral*   The bilateral agency is a state agency, such as the United States Agency for International Development (USAID), which channels aid from the provider country directly to the recipient. Such agencies closely reflect national interests and the political complexion of particular governments. There are approximately twenty-five bilateral donors, of which eighteen are the advanced capitalist countries grouped in the Development Assistance Committee of the Organisation of Economic Cooperation and Development (OECD/DAC). In 1996 the four largest donors were Japan, the USA, France and Germany (Organisation for Economic Cooperation and Development, 1997).

(b) *Multilateral*   There are two types of multilateral organisation which disburse aid that has been contributed by member governments. The first are the organisations within the United Nations system, such as the United Nations Development Programme (UNDP) and the United Nations Children's Fund (UNICEF). Here, member governments have equal votes within the governing bodies, so that recipient countries have a voice in their operations. These bodies mostly provide grants for technical assistance rather than capital loans.

The second type of multilateral organisation are the multilateral banks. The main bank is the World Bank group. This comprises the International Bank for Reconstruction and Development (IBRD), which provides long-term loans at rates slightly lower than commercial rates; the International Development Association, which provides soft loans to the low-income category of poor countries; the International Finance Corporation, which provides loans to promote private-sector growth; and the Multilateral Investment Guarantee Agency, which provides insurance for private investment in underdeveloped countries. These entities are controlled by governing bodies on which all member countries are represented but in which voting rights are weighted according to shareholding. Thus the USA, which is the largest shareholder, has around 21 per cent of the vote in the IBRD, while the USA, UK, Germany, France and Japan together hold 44 per cent. There are three regional banks, such as the African Development Bank, which operate similarly to the World Bank. Membership of the World Bank is conditional upon being a member of the International Monetary Fund (IMF), and the IBRD and IMF share a common board of governors. The IMF was established to promote international trade and monetary stability, and it provides short-term loans to countries with balance-of-payments and foreign-exchange problems. Although much of the IMF's lending is not concessional, and cannot be classified as aid, IMF approval of domestic economic policies has become increasingly necessary for countries to get access to concessional sources. It must therefore be regarded as part of the aid system.

(c) *Private*   The third type of aid organisation is the private non-profit-making body such as non-governmental organisations like OXFAM and private foundations like the Ford Foundation. There are approximately two thousand non-governmental development organisations in the industrialised countries, and they are increasingly important channels of aid. It has been calculated (Browne, 1990: 82) that by the end of the 1980s these bodies disbursed aid equivalent to about 8 per cent of the aid from the OECD/DAC countries. Whereas in the past private organisations depended on charitable contributions, they have become more reliant on government funding, and many have thus become part of official development assistance. Their funding is channelled not only to governments in recipient countries but also directly to non-governmental organisations, often at the community level.

The practice of aid arose alongside the practice of development, and also had its origins in the process of reconstructing the world economy after the Depression of the 1930s and the 1939–45 war. Aid policies reflect the changing economic and political contexts that influenced the evolution of development theories. Indeed, ideas on the role of aid have a distinctive place within each theory. The origins of aid are to be found in the institutions established in the mid-1940s under the leadership of the USA, which exerted its new dominance in the world economy to promote an international economic order based on the free flows of private capital for trade and investment. The institutional framework comprised the IMF and IBRD, established at Bretton Woods in 1944, and the General Agreement on Tariffs and Trade (GATT), established in 1947. The IMF was to provide international monetary stability, the IBRD capital for investment, and the GATT regulations for international trade. The initial focus of the IMF and IBRD, which were under US control from the beginning, was on postwar reconstruction in Europe, but they subsequently became a source of aid as the underdeveloped countries became more integrated into the world economy and involved in the geopolitics of the Cold War. Alongside these economic institutions, a number of specialised United Nations agencies were established in the 1940s, such as the United Nations Educational, Scientific and Cultural Organisation (UNESCO) and the Food and Agriculture Organisation (FAO), which later became important development agencies.

But the main impetus for aid as concessional finance from strong economies to weak ones came from the USA's Marshall Plan, which provided large amounts of capital to Western Europe between 1948 and 1952. The Plan was significant less for its contribution to the economic recovery and political stability of Western Europe than for its role in establishing concessional external

finance as a key element in the new US-dominated world order
(Wood, 1986). In 1952 the programme of aid to Europe was merged
into the Mutual Security Program, which was the vehicle for the
USA's bilateral aid to underdeveloped countries as part of its policy
of communist containment. During the 1950s the number of
countries with bilateral aid programmes grew, but the US programme remained the largest. The provision of aid came to have
a significant place within the modernisation theory of development, which saw economies as backward because they lacked
resources. Within this theory, aid was regarded as a source of
capital for investment to promote economic growth, and of technical assistance to help overcome constraints of skill and knowledge.

The increase in the number of independent countries as decolonisation progressed led to greater prominence for the idea of
development and enlarged requirements for aid. At the end of the
1950s the underdeveloped countries, through the United Nations
(UN), pressed for a UN institution that would provide capital
assistance and over which they would have control, unlike the
IBRD. However, the idea of the Special United Nations Fund for
Economic Development was resisted by the USA and the IBRD;
instead, a new soft loan facility, the International Development
Association, was established within the World Bank in 1960. This
is an important indicator of the USA's concern to retain a dominant role within the aid system. Multilateral lending increased in
scale during the 1960s, and in 1970 the World Bank overtook
USAID as the largest provider of aid. The number of bilateral
donors also grew during the 1960s, and this contributed to the
diversification of sources of aid available to particular countries,
especially the former colonies of Africa and Asia.

The concern with poverty and inequality that arose in the 1970s
after the UN's First Development Decade was reflected in aid
policies, which were influenced by the 'basic needs' trend within
development theory. These ideas had an impact on the World
Bank, although its public pronouncements on poverty alleviation
proved to be largely rhetorical in terms of its fundamental policies
and actual disbursements (Hayter and Watson, 1985). The ideas
were more influential with respect to the bilateral aid policies of
social democratic governments, resonating with the views of the
Nordic countries, for example. The commitment of Denmark,

Finland, Norway, Sweden, the Netherlands and Canada to providing high levels of aid with an egalitarian focus on poverty and
a concern for recipient participation led them to be labelled the
'like-minded group' of donors, and they exhibited a distinctive
approach within the OECD/DAC countries until the 1990s.

The impact of dependency theory on official policies during
the 1970s was negligible; however, it did for the first time provide
a critique of aid from the Left. This critique was typified by *The
Debt Trap* (Payer, 1974), a study of the IMF and the Third World.
Payer argued that the IMF, under the influence of its most powerful member, the USA, used its leverage to support capitalist Third
World governments and ensure that they pursued policies which
were favourable to foreign trade and investment. But she broadened her argument to a wider criticism of aid dependency, contending that 'large-scale aid would be a pernicious influence on
development even if no conditions whatsoever were imposed as a
quid pro quo' (Payer, 1974: 211). Her conclusion was that reliance
on aid was a symptom of economic dependency on the capitalist
centre, and that underdeveloped countries should adopt socialist
policies of economic self-sufficiency, like China and North Korea.

The most important development during the 1970s was in fact
the huge increase in commercial lending to the underdeveloped
countries by private banks, which had excess liquidity in the form
of 'petrodollars' after the oil price rise of 1973. The greater use of
non-concessional funding made some countries less dependent on
aid for a while. But a combination of factors in the late 1970s,
including increased oil prices, lower commodity prices, recession
in the industrialised countries and a rise in interest rates, led to
the debt crisis in the South that became visible with Mexico's
announcement in 1982 that it could not meet its debt obligations.

The debt problems of the underdeveloped countries made them
vulnerable to the macroeconomic policy prescriptions of the IMF
and the World Bank. From the early 1980s onwards these two
institutions came to work more closely together, and to adopt a
common approach to lending that sought not only to stabilise
economies in the South in relation to balance-of-payments problems, but also to change their structure. The IMF had always
espoused monetarist policies, and its approach was reinforced after
1979 by the accession to power of neoliberal governments in the

North, which dominated the IMF/World Bank board of governors. Neoliberal thinking was antagonistic to aid, seeing it as a
form of Keynesian state interference in the marketplace. This view
was well articulated by Krauss in *Development Without Aid* (1983).
He argued that aid was a product of the welfare state ideology of
American liberals and European social democrats, as typified in
the 1980 report of the Brandt Commission, which called for greater
transfers from North to South. Krauss contended that the role of
the state must be not to redistribute income but to secure the
conditions for the growth of the private sector. He argued that
poverty can be overcome only by economic growth, and that the
effect of aid had been negative, as it had supported governments
following bad policies, and crowded out private capital. The proper
role of aid should be to induce recipients to follow appropriate
polices that would free the private sector and open their economies
to foreign trade and investment. Neoliberal theorists such as Krauss
articulated the arguments for the policy-orientated lending that
was to dominate aid from the early 1980s.

The IMF and World Bank became central to aid policies,
imposing conditions on access to aid which affected not only their
own funds but also those of other multilateral and bilateral sources.
Furthermore, agreement to their conditions also became a pre-
requisite for access to capital from private banks. The conditions
for aid were that recipient governments should adopt a standard
set of neoliberal macroeconomic policies known as a 'structural
adjustment programme'. This programme comprised: currency
devaluation to boost exports and limit imports; cuts in government expenditure on social services; reduction in public-sector
employment; privatisation of government enterprises; removal of
state subsidies on consumption items and to producers; restraints
on wages; raised interest rates and limits on credit expansion;
dismantling of price controls; removal of barriers to foreign investment and of import protection; and raised agricultural prices to
encourage production for export. These measures were intended
to stabilise the economy, promote the private sector and create
the growth that would generate the foreign exchange needed to
pay foreign debts. These policy prescriptions became hegemonic,
and a means for the imposition of 'global monetarism' (Cypher,
1988). In 1992, for example, fifty countries in the South received

adjustment loans on these terms from the World Bank (1992: 20) and/or the International Monetary Fund (1992: 97–8).

Structural adjustment programmes represented a decisive step in the integration of aid policies. But the enlarged role of the IMF and the World Bank (and the conversion of GATT into the World Trade Organisation in 1995) also signified a new stage in the management of the world economy. The co-operation among the advanced capitalist countries in the Group of Seven[2] was operationalised through the IMF and World Bank, and through aid-coordinating fora such as the OECD/DAC and the 'Paris Club' of creditor nations. This co-ordination of economic policy and aid policy has raised the degree of external influence of the advanced capitalist countries over the South to a new level as adjustment lending 'conditionality' imposes policy changes: 'Policy reforms cut into the sovereignty of recipient governments, place foremost emphasis on economic criteria and in some instances even countermand the policy mandates of elected governments' (Browne, 1990: 126). While the World Bank and the IMF argue that structural adjustment programmes are necessary for greater economic prosperity, critics such as the Nigerian scholar Bade Onimode (1988, 288–9) counter that the extent of their influence over national governments in the South constitutes a process of 'recolonisation' that intensifies the global influence of imperialism.

The populist approach to development that arose in the 1980s is sceptical of aid. This reflects its antagonism to the state and its recognition that the dominant growth-focused development strategies have been heavily supported by aid agencies. Its view of aid is therefore that it should be channelled to community-level non-governmental organisations, and should be the result of partnerships between non-governmental organisations in the South and the North, with recipients having control over its nature and use. A typical attack on aid from a populist perspective is made by Linear (1985) in a book with the revealing title *Zapping the Third World: The Disaster of Development Aid*. He gives concrete examples of aid schemes such as large dams which have had damaging ecological consequences and describes as an alternative the work of a Dutch farmer living in a village in Ghana and using modified local methods to demonstrate how to increase agricultural productivity in a sustainable way. Other advocates of the populist model, such as Millwood and Gazelius in *Good Aid* (1986), elaborate arguments for non-governmental organisations providing appropriate and useful aid to small projects which help to improve people's lives and their ability to control their situation.

As noted above, the role of non-governmental organisations in aid did expand greatly during the 1980s. However, this was due less to the influence of populism than to neoliberalism's opposition to 'big government', and its desire to reduce the state's role in economic and social development. The USA, for example, established the African Development Foundation in 1986 in order to channel funds to small-scale community projects sponsored by non-governmental organisations. In fact, non-governmental organisations in both North and South became increasingly dependent on official development assistance. The language of the populist model of development (participation, people-centred planning, environmentalism, self-reliance, and so forth) was co-opted by the aid providers. The World Bank, for instance, suggested that statism in Africa was an alien tradition, and that non-state voluntary associations represented indigenous values. After 1987, the World Bank increasingly involved non-governmental organisations in its projects (Gibbon, 1993).

The changes that took place in aid policies in the 1980s have placed the IMF and the World Bank at the centre of an increasingly homogeneous system. The World Bank – and to a lesser degree the UNDP – co-ordinates aid programmes to specific countries, while the IMF's seal of approval provides a 'cross-conditionality' whereby other aid agencies link their funding to IMF agreements. The impact of this common approach led by the IMF and the World Bank is multiplied because the acceptance of their policy prescriptions is also a condition of access to commercial loans from private banks, and influences investment decisions by transnational corporations. With the inclusion within this system of China from 1980 and Eastern Europe from 1989, the scope of aid within the world economy has attained a new dimension. Aid has become a stronger mechanism for guaranteeing a world order in which there are free flows of private capital for investment, trade and speculation. Furthermore, aid conditionality since 1989 has extended from the economic sphere to the political, embracing the concepts of human rights, democracy and good governance. The promotion of liberal democracy and efficient government is being used to strengthen the legitimacy of the market economy and the capitalist state in the periphery. It is the role of aid in reproducing and legitimating the conditions for capitalist expansion on a world scale that is the basis for regarding it as an important dimension of imperialism.

The impact of aid is economic, political, social and ideological, and it shapes the nature of development strategies. The prescriptions of the aid providers enforce dependent capitalist development and prevent self-reliant development strategies. The external influences of aid reinforce the unequal structural location of the peripheral countries in the global economy by continuing to define their role as exporters of raw materials, markets for manufactured goods and areas of profitable investment. This international inequality is shown by the fact that since 1983 there has been a net outflow of official and private capital from the South to the North. Aid also serves to reinforce internal power structures within underdeveloped countries. The provision of aid promotes an alliance between the dominant classes and the state in the advanced capitalist countries on the one hand, and the dominant classes and the state in the periphery on the other. For example, the role of structural adjustment loans in promoting a 'favourable investment climate' is not neutral, as the dismantling of wage controls and the imposition of restrictions on unions have a negative effect on the working class.

It is important to note, however, that these external influences are not always unopposed. In the 1960s and 1970s, some Third World governments followed a strategy of economic nationalism which sought to gain greater control over their economies through the nationalisation of foreign corporations (as in Chile in 1970–73) or by the repudiation of foreign debts (as in Cuba in 1960). In the 1980s and 1990s, subordinated classes resisted the imposition of structural adjustment measures – for example, through militant demonstrations in Latin America and by grassroots self-reliance strategies in Africa (Cheru, 1989). Thus although imperialism and aid are backed by state power, their influence does not always go uncontested.

The concept of imperialism provides a general theoretical framework for the analysis of aid, which is itself a form of capital export. This in turn provides the background for analysing the aid provided to particular social sectors, such as adult education, and for examining its economic, political, social and ideological consequences in particular national circumstances.

Aid and Adult Education

Education is assigned an important role in the development process by all development theories. Thus, despite changes in the conceptions of development and in rationales for providing aid, education has always been a target of aid provision. The focus of educational aid has shifted over the years in line with changing thinking. Under modernisation theory in the 1960s, ideas about 'manpower' development to meet high-level skill gaps led to aid to secondary and higher education. The reformist trends in modernisation theory in the 1970s brought a concern with non-formal education for rural development. The impact of the debt crisis and structural adjustment policies on basic services in the 1980s was so severe that there was a new focus on primary education, to address the worsening situation of the poor. Many of the trends in educational aid have been associated with the World Bank, whose research has provided intellectual leadership and whose weight among the aid agencies has encouraged common approaches (Jones, 1992; Samoff, 1992). The World Bank is the largest single agency, providing 15 per cent of total international aid to education in 1990 (Gordon-Brown, 1991: 290). The promotion of the common approach was symbolised by the World Conference on Education for All in Jomtien, Thailand in 1990, convened by the World Bank and three United Nations agencies (UNESCO, UNDP and UNICEF) in a joint effort to mobilise aid for a new concern with primary education for all.

However, the bilateral agencies also have distinct interests and philosophies. Germany's educational aid, for example, has always given a high priority to technical and vocational education, while Sweden has focused on basic education. Thus the pattern of aid to education has varied over time and between agencies. The proportion of aid given to education within overall aid budgets also varies significantly. In 1990 education comprised 7.2 per cent of the World Bank's aid and 9.8 per cent of the total aid of the OECD/DAC agencies. But within the OECD group the proportion differed considerably. For instance, the proportion of their total aid given to education by the four major bilateral providers was as follows: USA 2.2 per cent, Japan 6.9 per cent, Germany 14.2 per cent and France 28.1 per cent (Organisation for Economic Cooperation and Development, 1992: A-40/41).

The provision of aid to education in the countries of the South has been a noticeable factor in the development of their education systems. Even where the amount of aid has been relatively small in relation to the national budget, this input has often been of strategic significance in influencing policy and practice. For example, full-time foreign advisers have been placed in the planning divisions of Ministries of Education, and foreign staff appointed to teacher training colleges. The aid-and-education relationship has therefore attracted some degree of analysis. An early work in this field, Cerych's *Problems of Aid in Education in Developing Countries* (1965), was based on modernisation theory. It assumed the net effect of aid to be highly beneficial to the recipient, but identified practical problems in its provision and utilisation. It addressed questions like the issues arising from different kinds of aid (such as the supply of foreign teachers, scholarships for study abroad and new educational technologies) and the relationship between different aid agencies. Its frame of reference was how to achieve greater efficiency and effectiveness in the utilisation of educational aid.

A more critical stance towards educational aid emerged during the 1970s as the ideas of dependency theory gained currency. Analysts gave greater prominence to the degree to which aid involved external interference in the internal affairs of the underdeveloped countries, and was a symptom of their dependency on the industrialised countries. Thompson, for example (1977: 155), asked: 'How free are developing countries to develop systems of education tailored to their own individual needs?', and discussed the mechanisms through which educational aid exerts influence. His list of mechanisms included the provision of foreign personnel as teachers and experts, scholarships for overseas training, the provision of textbooks and other educational materials, cultural links which support the metropolitan language as a medium of instruction, the work of foreign researchers, international debates and trends in educational policy, and the exported model of the university. He concluded: 'the aid flow remains a potent influence upon the policies of these countries ... and it must be critically examined. In some of its forms, aid may tend to perpetuate dependency upon aid; in others it may distort patterns of development' (Thompson, 1977: 165). His conclusion indicates that the international economic order constitutes a form of neocolonialism, and aid reinforces dependency through reducing self-reliance and constraining domestic choices about appropriate development. But he does not provide a comprehensive theorisation of the nature of the world economy and the place of aid within it. Indeed, much of the writing on aid and education lacks a theoretical framework that links the processes of aid provision to the global political economy.

However, the outline of a theoretical approach based on Marxist political economy has been developed by Carnoy (1980), who maintains that an explanation of how and why aid agencies influence educational policy in the South must be rooted in an analysis of the nature of the international economic system, the state, and the interaction between states. He argues that there are different theoretical perspectives on these issues and they lead to different views on the role of the aid organisations (as shown earlier in this chapter). His discussion is important because it confirms the significance of identifying the various theoretical frameworks which underpin discussions of aid and education even when they are not made explicit. He adopts a Marxist theoretical model, as he feels that it has more explanatory power than the other theories. His model sees the international economic system as imperialist, and focuses on the role of the state, because educational aid is an element of state policy in both North and South. He views the state as the political expression of capitalist economic power, but also as an institution which reflects the conflicts and contradictions in capitalist society. Thus there are differences in the aid policies and approaches of the various capitalist countries at different times. Similarly, there are differences among the recipients in terms of the utilisation and consequences of educational aid. He concludes:

> the role of international agencies in educational change in low-income
> countries is to influence that change in certain directions consistent

with the interests of the transnational bourgeoisies of the developed countries and the bourgeoisies in the dependent countries themselves. The recommendations made and the type of financing available for education has to be consistent with the transnational capitalists' conception of the international division of labour (where things are going to be produced and how), but also acceptable to the national bourgeoisie's concept of their role in the sharing of the surplus. Both concepts are subject to the struggle for power of the dominated classes in the low-income countries and the changing conditions of power in the industrial countries.... The agencies are inserted in the struggle but they are not neutral in that insertion: they have a position to support, and they use their self-defined expertise (and funds) to do it. (Carnoy, 1980: 281–2)

The model of educational aid sketched by Carnoy is consistent with the theory of aid as imperialism presented in earlier sections of this chapter.

The literature on aid and school education is rather limited in scope and depth but there is an even greater paucity in the analysis of aid in relation to adult education. There seems to be a major gap in the research field with respect to the theoretical and empirical analysis of the significance of foreign aid for the policies, practices and consequences of adult education in the South. There is a dearth of studies which document volumes and trends in aid flows for adult education. One exception is Cassara's *Adult Education Through World Collaboration* (1995), which contains detailed information on two multilateral agencies and six bilateral agencies. Presenting data on aid to adult education is a complex task, as the conventional aid category 'education' usually focuses on formal school education, and it is difficult to disaggregate adult education from general data. Furthermore, many activities which can be classified as adult education, such as extension work in health or agriculture, fall into other data categories. King (1991), in his study of aid and education, included a chapter on adult literacy and non-formal education which gives an overview of the changing agency perspectives on aid to these forms of adult education. But he did not attempt to provide quantitative data, or to assess impact.

Very little consideration has been given to aid in the adult education literature. The work of Gelpi (1985, 1988, 1996) has drawn attention to the inequality in North–South relations, and its significance for international co-operation in adult education.

Gelpi has considered the internationalisation of the world economy, the new international division of labour, the transnational corporations and the impact of technological change in terms of the problem of dependency and the implications for adult education, which, he argues, is increasingly 'exported' from the centre to the periphery. But his discussions of adult education within the global political economy have not included an extended analysis of educational aid.

One of the few examples of writing on aid and adult education is the series of articles from an International Council for Adult Education seminar on 'The Role of International Aid in Adult Education in Developing Countries' (1986). A common position emerges from these articles because the writers share a commitment to a concept of development, and of adult education's role within it, underpinned by the philosophy of the populist approach. They see the purpose of adult education as helping to redress inequalities through empowering the oppressed to take action for social change. The non-governmental organisation is seen as the best vehicle for achieving this goal. From this perspective, they regard non-governmental organisations in the South as the most appropriate channels for aid because they are people-centred, flexible, democratic, cost-effective, and a means for international solidarity (Hall, 1986). This approach to the purposes and organisational form of development, adult education and aid provides the basis for criticising bilateral and multilateral aid agencies. Vio Grossi (1986), for example, is critical of the USA's official aid for its low volume, conditions and inefficiency, and he deplores the fact that so little OECD aid goes to non-governmental agencies. Hall (1986) points out that aid agencies tend to follow their own priorities and use the language of partnership to obscure their relative power. Although reference is made to the debt crisis (Vio Grossi, 1986), and to the emerging impact of neoliberal governments in the North on approaches to development in the mid-1980s (Duke, 1986), there is no systematic analysis of aid in terms of the international political economy and the state, so that the critique of aid remains superficial. Thus the discussion embodied in the seminar summary (Kassam, 1986) focuses on how to make aid more effective in the task of promoting bottom-up development.

The problem with these arguments is the assumption that aid agencies have a commitment to equality, poverty reduction and social change. Although poverty alleviation was on the aid agenda in the late 1970s, the commitment of bodies such as the World Bank was largely rhetorical. A partial exception was the Nordic countries, whose aid policies extended their social welfare model of capitalism to the international sphere. In this connection, Strom- quist (1986: 17) makes the important point – in relation to aid and the empowerment of women through non-formal education – that some aid agencies 'represent states where women have been able to demand and obtain greater social and economic concessions. Some bilaterals, in consequence, reflect national policies strongly committed to the advancement of women.' However, the role of the state in both the advanced capitalist countries and the periph- ery is not fully explored, and no systematic conception of aid as state policy emerges from these articles. The writers do raise some important questions about the scope and impact of aid, but these are not pursued in depth, nor at a theoretical level. In the final analysis, the writers' practical commitment to promoting adult education for development within the populist perspective meant that they adopted too narrow a frame of reference to address the full complexity of the aid-and-adult-education relationship.

Cassara's recent edited volume *Adult Education Through World Collaboration* (1995) suffers from similar limitations. Two-thirds of the book is devoted to aid for adult education. The chapters are largely descriptive of the policies and programmes of the agencies, and provide little analysis of the impact of aid and how it is linked to the global economic and political context. Thus the chapter on the World Bank uses the Bank's own technical language, presenting the Bank and the IMF uncritically 'as partners in pro- moting global economic prosperity' (Holden and Dorland, 1995: 26). There is no contextualisation of the Bank's operations or discussion of the controversies over its concept of development and its expression in structural adjustment programmes. The superficiality of the presentation is exemplified in the description of the Bank's governance, which makes no reference to the fact that 5 advanced capitalist countries out of the 167 members control 44 per cent of the vote, and the President of the Bank is appointed by the President of the USA. Thus the structure of

North–South inequality at the heart of the Bank's operations is not exposed.

Most of the chapters assume a positive role for adult education in development in terms of social change and poverty alleviation. They are permeated with the language of aid altruism and the concept of aid as a form of North–South partnership. They present aid as apolitical and restrict their criticisms to the amount of aid provided, problems of sustainability and the lack of priority given to adult education by some agencies. The only departure from this view of aid to adult education as beneficial to development is provided by the Ugandan adult educator Paul Wangoola. In his chapter, 'The Political Economy of Nongovernment Organisations', he analyses the situation of the South in terms of neocolonialism and the domination of market forces promoted by the World Bank and the IMF. He draws a picture of exploitation, debt and impoverishment in the South, with people reacting to the dismantling of social services by reverting to traditional self-help forms of organisation. In this context, he identifies aid-providing nongovernmental organisations as motivated by the economic and political interests of the North:

> In the present-day world order ... NGOs are one of the instruments for the continued conquest and occupation of the South. They join in the marginalisation of Third World governments and indigenous NGOs and leadership, so as to directly rule the people at the grass roots. This way, the North's latest conquest would be complete: the World Bank/ IMF, big powers and transnationals rule from above, while NGOs govern from below.... Needless to say, all of this is usually done in the name of empowering the grass roots. (Wangoola, 1995: 68)

This chapter is the only one in the book to provide a critique of the role of aid in adult education and development.

One full-length empirical study of development aid to adult education utilising a political economy approach has been undertaken by Unsicker (1987). The theme of the study is the impact of international aid on the development of adult education in Tanzania, with specific reference to the folk development colleges. Unsicker does not provide an extended theorisation of aid through a systematic discussion of imperialism and the state, but his overall perspective identifies aid with the world capitalist system and the external influences that shape the dynamics of dependent development. The importance of his study for the literature on adult education is its empirical account of how foreign aid affects state activity in the adult education sector.

The study provides a nuanced analysis of the interactions between aid agencies and state bureaucracies, involving at various points co-operation, conflict and manipulation by both sides. His main focus is on the impact of the Swedish International Development Authority, but he also provides some information on the role of the World Bank, USAID and UNESCO. He shows how empire-building within the state bureaucracy was linked to access to foreign aid. In a struggle between various ministries over residential training facilities, for example, the Ministry of National Education gained control of most of them through Swedish aid given to promote the Swedish concept of 'folk education', although the Ministry of Agriculture managed to retain control of some centres because of a World Bank-funded programme. The complexity of the relations between the aid agencies and the state is illustrated by Tanzania's involvement in the UN's Experimental World Literacy Programme, an international programme initiated in 1963 by the advanced capitalist countries to counter the model of Cuba's successful literacy campaign in 1961. UNESCO rejected Tanzania's proposal for general support to national literacy efforts, and insisted on a selective, small-scale demonstration project. Tanzania, in turn, refused to choose just one or two villages but selected regions around Lake Victoria in order 'to increase foreign exchange income through increasing cotton production and to quell anti-TANU [the ruling party] sentiments among the Sukuma people who would be the primary beneficiaries of the project'. (Unsicker, 1987: 181). Thus the state, while it was unable to meet its original objectives, sought to turn the project to its own economic and political advantage. Unsicker's account of aid in practice shows how the multiple interactions of aid agency officials, foreign personnel and state bureaucrats which took place in the context of evolving state and aid agency policies contributed to the directions and forms of Tanzania's adult education.

The main value of the study lies in the way it reveals how the macro-level of imperialism impacts on the micro-level of adult education activities through the processes of aid. Unsicker shows how Tanzania's peripheral status in the world capitalist economy created the material and ideological conditions which shaped the individual behaviour of those involved in the aid relationship. Thus he concludes that while the motivations and actions of individual foreigners and state officials varied considerably, seen in structural terms their participation in aid programmes ultimately promoted the interests of international capital. However, the study does not attempt an in-depth analysis of the economic, political, social and ideological consequences of the programmes which received aid. The value of analysing aid in terms of a political economy approach encompassing its wider consequences can be illustrated by the examples of agricultural extension and trade-union education.

Agricultural extension is an important form of adult education in many countries of the South. It originated in the late nineteenth century, when the USA was undergoing the transition from an agrarian society to an industrialised economy. Agricultural extension services were institutionalised by the US state in the 1914 Smith–Lever Act. The aim of agricultural extension was to promote independent capitalist farmers with the productivity to feed the growing urban industrial workforce. The agricultural extension model spread internationally – for example, to Africa, where it was introduced initially by missionaries and foreign companies like the East African Tobacco Company, but subsequently by the colonial state influenced by the reports on African education by the US Phelps–Stokes Foundation in the early 1920s. Agricultural extension as a means of management advice and technology transfer became part of the colonial process of transforming the economy so that African peasants produced cash crops for the market (particularly for export) rather than for household subsistence (Yudelman, 1975).

After 1945, as decolonisation began and the USA started to exert its dominance within the world economy, it was the US state which was instrumental in diffusing agricultural extension in the South through its aid programmes:

> Administrators, researchers and extension agents were assigned to implement these technical assistance programmes in countries around the world. Three major types of assistance were made available by the United States:

- commodities, including books, lab facilities, printing and teaching equipment and supplies, research and field tools, equipment and vehicles;
- assignment of research, teaching and extension personnel to institutions and government ministries around the world;
- scholarships for researchers, teachers and extension workers to pursue on-the-job training or study for advanced degrees at US universities and colleges.

These technical assistance activities were massive. More than 20,000 men and women from 100 countries received some training in extension education in the United States alone between 1944 and 1966. (Prawl, Medlin and Gross, 1984: 148)

Although the USA took the lead, the multilateral aid agencies have also been extensively involved. The UN's Food and Agriculture Organisation has had a key role (Maalouf, 1987), and the World Bank has been influential in providing loans. For example, the Bank promoted the training-and-visit system of agricultural extension in over forty countries between the mid-1970s and mid-1980s (Benor, 1987). Thus the direct influence exerted by the colonial state at an earlier stage – in Africa, for example – was followed after 1945 by the indirect influences transmitted worldwide through bilateral and multilateral aid. The main beneficiaries in the North have been the transnational corporations specialising in the marketing and processing of agricultural products, while in the South, agricultural extension has tended to increase social inequality in the rural areas by favouring those with productive assets. The provision of aid to agricultural extension shows how the economic process of commercialising agricultural production in the South and integrating it into the world capitalist economy has involved the introduction of adult education activities designed to change the attitudes and practices of peasant farmers.

The second example of aid and adult education is that of trade-union education in the South which has been supported by American aid. By the end of the 1939–45 war the unions in the USA had been incorporated into tripartite arrangements including business and the state, and had come to conceive their role in the narrow terms of lobbying for economic benefits within an agreement on the overall political-economic system of capitalism.

After the war, the international affairs division of the American Federation of Labor–Congress of Industrial Organisations (AFL–CIO) became an extension of the USA's foreign policy of communist containment (Thomson and Larson, 1977). It promoted the ideology of economistic trade unionism in other countries, and in international organisations such as the UN's International Labour Organisation. The AFL–CIO, funded by the US state through the Central Intelligence Agency (Agee, 1975) and USAID, and by US transnational corporations, has taken an active role in encouraging trade-union education in the South.

Godfried (1987) discusses the activities of the African American Labor Center (AALC), established by the AFL–CIO in 1964, which sought to build up national labour federations and their leaders in order to curb labour militancy and radicalism. The AALC funded national union centres with an educational role – for instance, in Ghana and Nigeria. It organised educational seminars for African trade-union leaders, provided American teaching staff and advisers, produced publications and supported research, funded study visits by leaders to the USA, and gave scholarships for participation in industrial relations courses in American universities. The education supported by the AALC focused on the acquisition of technical skills in areas such as collective bargaining and leadership, and promoted a pro-capitalist ideology of union co-operation with business and the state. Its purpose was to create a compliant union leadership, and very little training was given to the rank and file. This example highlights the role of American aid.

However, the effort to restrict workers' organisations to a non-political role within capitalist structures through a narrow focus on education in technical trade-union skills, rather than a broader form of workers' education to develop class consciousness and commitment to social change, has also been undertaken by other aid agencies. Mudariki (1996), for example, shows that in Zimbabwe in the 1980s there were ten foreign organisations providing technical assistance to the Zimbabwe Congress of Trade Unions, whose education programme failed to challenge the hegemony of capitalism. The provision of aid to trade-union education in the countries of the South can therefore be seen as an ideological element of imperialism. It has sought to promote a pro-capitalist ideology within the working class in the periphery, and to restrict the formation of a radical and politicised proletariat that might challenge capitalist development strategies. This form of adult education is part of political subordination, and mediates the ideological legitimation of the capitalist world order.

My discussion has revealed the centrality of the concept of imperialism for a political economy approach to development. It has also argued that the phenomenon of aid must be located within the concept of imperialism. Thus I have established a theoretical framework for considering the economic, political, social and ideological significance of foreign aid to adult education. The critical analysis of aid has been largely neglected in the study of adult education, and the next section suggests an appropriate research agenda that can help adult educators to examine the impact of aid in specific national contexts.

A Research Agenda on Aid and Adult Education

The theoretical position elaborated above is that aid is not neutral. Foreign aid agencies are inserted in the dynamics of a particular national political economy, and advance a certain set of interests within that context. The task for research on aid derived from these theoretical assumptions is to identify the economic, political, social and ideological consequences of aid to the adult education sector, and to clarify the processes which produce these consequences. The aim of this task is to contribute to the overall goal of the political economy approach to adult education, which is to determine who gains and who loses from adult education policies and practices. The analysis of aid being proposed is therefore significantly different from technical evaluations of aid which are intended to meet the decision-making needs of aid agencies. It is not concerned with standard evaluation questions such as the economic rate of return on capital assistance or the effectiveness of project implementation. It has a different focus as it seeks to relate the provision of aid to the wider dynamics of peripheral capitalist society, and to understand how the external influences mediated by adult education interact with these dynamics.

Previous sections of this chapter have provided generalisations about the world economy and the role of aid, but it is clear that national experiences vary considerably. It is therefore important to undertake national studies which analyse the impact of aid in particular contexts. It is suggested that the research agenda for analysing foreign aid to adult education in the countries of peripheral capitalism should have four components.

1. *Analysis of the national aid situation*

The specific issues of aid to adult education have to be contextualised within the wider national aid situation. The analysis of this situation has to take into account the country's location within the international division of labour, and its overall economic characteristics as well as its geopolitical significance. It must then trace the pattern of aid in terms of data on providers, sectoral allocations, overall flows and balance between capital assistance and technical assistance. Relevant data include the amount of official development assistance (ODA) *per capita*, ODA as a proportion of GNP and of development expenditure, the country's debt burden as indicated by its debt service ratio and foreign reserves, and the employment of foreign citizens in the public sector. This information provides aggregate data on the extent of a country's reliance on aid. The state's policy towards aid, both explicit and inferred, must be considered, as well as the stated and unstated policies of the aid providers. The aim of providing a national picture is to show the degree of aid dependency, and to indicate the overall impact of foreign aid. The national situation should be portrayed in a historical perspective, as patterns of aid change over time.

2. *Analysis of aid to the adult education sector*

The national context provides the setting for considering aid provision at the level of the adult education sector. It must be recognised that adult education is not considered a 'sector' in terms of aid data; it cuts across categories such as human resource development, agriculture, social development and health. However, the analysis must seek to identify the pattern of aid to activities defined as adult education in terms of providers, areas of allocation, and overall flows and their composition. Information should be gathered on the explicit and implicit policies of the providers in this field, and their particular conditions, procedures and approaches. The influence of trends in the international debates on adult education and development should be shown. Data should be provided on the kinds of adult education activities that have received aid, tracing changes over time, and on the state's perspectives of the purposes of aid in this sector.

3. *Analysis of aid projects in the adult education sector*

The sectoral analysis provides the context for considering aid provision at the level of particular aid projects that provide assistance to some aspect of adult education. Analysis at this level includes more detailed questions on the nature of the provider(s) and the pattern of aid provision over time, especially as this relates to policy changes in both provider and recipient countries. This should include the extent of joint financing by different providers, the degree to which this affects the institutional specificity of the aid's origins, and the operational impact of a group of varied providers. The volume of aid and the extent of counterpart funding should be identified. Analysis should explain how the project originated and the respective role of provider(s) and recipient in its identification and design, as well as the influence of international debates in the particular field. The implications of the provider's monitoring and evaluation requirements should be discussed. The role of the country representative(s) of the provider(s) should be analysed. This micro-level of analysis should focus on the mechanisms of aid activity in relation to:

(i) Capital assistance in terms of loans and grants.
(ii) Technical assistance, which has three main forms:
- personnel in the form of foreign experts as consultants, advisers, teachers, administrators and researchers;
- commodities in the form of equipment (such as vehicles and educational technology) and materials (such as books and curriculum materials); and
- training in terms of on-the-job training, local courses and scholarships for study abroad.

The aim of analysis at this level is to examine the mechanisms whereby aid in practice has an influence on a given aspect of adult education.

4. *Analysis of the consequences of aid to adult education*

The final level of analysis seeks to relate the processes of aid provision to the wider society. The consequences should be considered in terms of four dimensions:

(i) Economic consequences judged in terms of the effect of the aid project on the economic situation of the recipients with respect to their location within the national and international economy.

(ii) Political consequences analysed in terms of the effect of the aid project on power relations with respect to the location of the recipients in local and national political contexts, and to the legitimation of the state.

(iii) Social consequences considered with regard to the extent to which patterns of class, gender and ethnic/racial relations are constructed and/or reproduced by the aid project.

(iv) Ideological consequences with respect to the extent to which overt or latent ideologies embodied in the content and process of the aided adult education activities are adopted by the recipients.

An important aspect of this level of analysis, which focuses on the way the external influences interact with the internal political economy, is the consideration of whether recipients resisted (actively or passively) the impact of the aid given so that the consequences did not match the outcomes intended by the aid providers and the local decision-makers.

The research agenda proposed above is designed to help adult educators to analyse how the processes of imperialism are embodied in the provision of aid to peripheral capitalist countries, and to examine the implications of this aid for adult education policies and programmes. In the next section I illustrate the application of this research agenda with a country case study on Botswana.

Country Case Study:
Aid and Adult Education in Botswana, 1966–91

At Independence in 1966, Botswana was one of the ten poorest countries in the world; it was dependent on British aid for half of its recurrent expenditure and the majority of its development

Table 5.1   Official development assistance (ODA) to Botswana

	1966	1991
GNP per capita (US$)	75	2,530
World Bank income category	low	upper middle
Total ODA ($US million)	8.3	135
ODA *per capita* ($US)	15	102.5
Rank in World Bank list of ODA *per capita*	–	7th
ODA as % of GNP	–	3.7
ODA as % of development expenditure	100	21.0
Public foreign debt as % of GDP	10.1	12.0
Debt service ratio (%)	–	5.0
Foreign reserves (months of import coverage)	–	18
Non-citizens in public-sector jobs (%)	73.0	3.1

Sources: Bank of Botswana, 1993: 39; Colclough and McCarthy, 1980: 95, 100; Hartland-Thunberg, 1978: 11; Harvey and Lewis, 1990: 21; Murray and Parsons, 1990: 159; Republic of Botswana, 1991a: 59; Republic of Botswana, 1991c: 19; World Bank, 1993: 277.

expenditure. From the beginning, the state adopted the policy of seeking high levels of external aid to promote its development strategy; hence the national aid situation in the period 1966–91 showed a significant inflow of official development assistance. Although the state was careful to control its level of foreign debt, and to keep high levels of foreign reserves, aid constituted a significant element of the development budget, and the *per capita* level of aid was one of the highest in the world. The salient data are shown in Table 5.1.

The state entered into agreements with a large number of providers. By 1990, there were 12 UN organisations, 6 multilateral agencies, 16 bilateral agencies and 11 non-governmental organisations – a total of 45 providers. The bilateral agencies provided 72.7 per cent of the total aid in 1991. The four largest providers were Norway (22 per cent), Germany (18 per cent), Sweden (16 per cent) and Britain (15 per cent). The bilateral agencies and UN organisations generally provided grants, whilst loans were obtained from the multilateral banks, especially the World Bank and the African Development Bank. The increased role of non-governmental organisations was a feature of the 1980s; by 1989 their contribution reached 20.6 per cent of total aid.

There was a reasonable degree of consistency in the policies of the major providers over the years, and they showed clear sectoral preferences. The former colonial power, Britain, retained a high degree of involvement both bilaterally and through the European Community, and in 1991 it allocated 73 per cent of its aid to the human resources development sector. Sweden and Norway were consistent in providing a high level of aid, and in their focus on particular sectors and commitment to the rural poor. In some cases, however, changes in provider polices were reflected in the nature of their aid. For example, the change in the aid policy of the USA in the early 1980s to a more explicit promotion of private enterprise led to a new strategy in Botswana which focused on private-sector support, channelled particularly through the employers' organisation. General policy trends, such as the increased interest in the role of non-governmental organisations in the 1980s, also affected the pattern of aid provision.

The level of aid to Botswana clearly had an impact on its political economy. On the whole, aid was not linked specifically to foreign business interests – as was much of the USA's aid to Latin America, for example. The most significant impact of aid was to support the state in its policies of capitalist development and liberal democracy. Aid enabled a scale of public investment in development projects which would not otherwise have been achievable, particularly before the economic boom of the 1980s. It thus served to legitimate the state, and to sustain the ruling Botswana Democratic Party in power. For example, aid played an important role in the Accelerated Rural Development Programme of 1973–76, which helped to generate political support for the ruling party during the 1974 general election. The most explicitly political aid intervention was the funding given by the German Friedrich Ebert Foundation to the political education programme of the Botswana Democratic Party, and to two non-governmental organisations in the opposition stronghold of Kanye: the Rural Industries Innovation Centre and the Southern Rural Development Association. Aid also supported the processes of class formation fostered by the state, exemplified by the World Bank's funding of the Livestock Development Projects designed to develop capitalist cattle ranching.

At the practical level, the most important impact of aid came through the widespread use of technical assistance. Foreign personnel played an influential part in the state bureaucracy throughout the period, and the influence of foreigners 'on policy formulation and the development agenda has been overwhelming' (Molutsi, 1993: 58). In sum, the external influences of aid converged with the interests of the dominant classes within Botswana, so that aid played an integral part in economic and political development. This is the national context within which aid was provided specifically to the adult education sector.

Aid to the adult education sector

Aid to adult education between 1966 and 1991 was extensive. In 1991, according to the UNDP country report (UNDP, 1993), there were over 250 aid projects, of which about 35 were related to adult education. It is clear that the provision of aid was linked to provider policies and their areas of preference. Aid to adult education from the USA, for example, went largely to the area of agricultural extension, a traditional focus of USAID support. In fact, for a number of years after Independence, British aid continued to go to agricultural extension, which had been the main area of adult education in the colonial era. Until the late 1970s there were British advisers to agricultural extension in the Ministry of Agriculture, and a British principal of the Botswana Agricultural College (BAC), the training centre for extension cadres. But increasingly, US aid supplanted British involvement, providing capital assistance for developing the BAC buildings, scholarships for training BAC and Ministry staff, and advisers and lecturers. This is an example of aid diversification, and of the USA extending its sphere of influence and displacing the former colonial power. Neoliberal changes in USAID's own policies in the 1980s, emphasising greater support to private enterprise, were reflected in increased funding for the promotion of training in the private sector. In 1986, for example, USAID committed US$27 million to a new phase of a technical assistance project called the Botswana Workforce and Skills Training (BWAST) project. BWAST involved the provision of US experts, and overseas and in-country training for Batswana. By 1991, 200 participants had received long-term training in the USA, 52 had completed short-term studies, and 1,354 had received in-country training (USAID, 1991).

Another major provider to adult education was the Swedish International Development Agency (SIDA). Swedish development aid has always included a strong commitment to adult education, influenced by its domestic experience of the role of non-formal adult education and popular movements in the 'transformation of Sweden from a backward and poor agrarian society to a modern, industrialised society' (Edstrom, 1986: 196). Swedish educational aid policy has therefore consistently centred on non-formal education, literacy and post-literacy programmes, making it distinctive among aid providers to education. This approach was reflected in a SIDA survey of education and training in 1972, soon after SIDA had entered a bilateral agreement with the Government of Botswana. The mission found that 60–65 per cent of aid to the education sector was directed to higher education, and stated: 'A notable feature of the aid situation is that the only assistance given to adult education is in the field of agriculture and that these contributions are very small' (SIDA, 1972: 19). The report concluded: 'non formal education in Botswana is still in its infancy', but 'in order to succeed in its programme of rural development, Botswana will have to give considerable emphasis to non formal education and information' (SIDA, 1972: 83). It therefore recommended long-term support to non-formal education. SIDA subsequently directed its educational aid to basic education, including adult education. In effect, it made funds available to an area which had not hitherto been given priority by the state. One of the first programmes to receive SIDA support was a radio learning group campaign to popularise the third National Development Plan, run by the University's adult education section (Colclough and Crowley, 1974).

Substantial assistance, however, did not begin until after the promulgation in 1977 of the new *National Policy on Education* (Republic of Botswana, 1977a), which supported non-formal education. Swedish aid mainly took the form of capital rather than technical assistance (Agrell, Fagerlind and Gustafsson, 1982). The major focus of support was to the public library system and the National Literacy Programme. SIDA also gave significant budgetary support to the Ministry of Home Affairs' Women's Affairs

Unit, which had been established in 1981 with a role that included the dissemination of information through adult education activities, especially by women's voluntary organisations. The commitment of the Swedish state to women's equality led SIDA again to give more priority to its own area of concern than to that of the Botswana state. A SIDA-commissioned evaluation of its aid to education in Botswana between 1981 and 1986 concluded:

> We suspect that SIDA is a good deal more committed to singling women out as a special target group than what seems reasonable to the Government of Botswana and most of its officials. In such a situation, other government agencies may resent a widened role which the Unit through strong Swedish funding would acquire *vis-à-vis* other units of government. (Lauglo and Marope, 1987: 30)

This indicates the general trend of aid to the adult education sector: agencies provided aid largely in terms of their own policies and priorities. The non-governmental sector provides a final example. Canadian University Service Overseas (CUSO) is a large non-governmental organisation involved in over thirty countries. It runs a technical assistance programme staffed by volunteers, and disburses small capital grants. A significant proportion of its funds comes from the Canadian state through the Canadian International Development Authority (CIDA). CUSO commenced operations in Botswana in the early 1970s and a number of its volunteers worked as operational personnel in the field of adult education – for example, in the University's adult education section in the early 1970s and in the Ministry of Education's Department of Non Formal Education in the late 1970s. CUSO espoused a concept of development influenced by the basic needs approach, and populism. In adult education it supported extension in appropriate technology (at the Rural Industries Innovation Centre in Kanye), grassroots community projects (such as the Odi weaving factory), cultural action (such as the Cultural Development Project of the University's Institute of Adult Education [IAE] from 1979 to 1982) and women's programmes (such as the IAE's Women's Programme Development Project from 1983 to 1989).

The composition of aid to the adult education sector included both capital and technical assistance. In terms of capital assistance, aid was provided for both programme activities, such as

SIDA's support to the Women's Affairs Unit, and physical infra-structure, such as the World Bank loan for the headquarters of the Department of Non Formal Education. But the majority of aid went to technical assistance. Particularly in the period up to 1982, a significant number of foreign personnel were involved in the adult education sector as advisers (in areas as various as ag-ricultural extension, the training of community development staff and health education), as operational personnel (for example, in the Botswana Extension College and the Department of Non Formal Education) and as lecturers (for example, in the IAE and the BAC). One reflection of this foreign dominance was shown in the research and publications on adult education in Botswana. A bibliography of publications between 1960 and 1980 (Youngman, 1981: xii) showed that more than 80 per cent of the publications listed were by foreign authors.

During the 1980s, however, the number of technical assistance personnel diminished, although a large number of short-term consultancies were undertaken by aid-funded foreigners. The reduction in foreign personnel was largely the result of training programmes in adult education, which led to a process of locali-sation. Overseas training was a particular focus of British aid throughout the 1966–91 period, and many adult education personnel received training in the UK. This was part of an inter-national trend in British aid to Africa – Mutangira and Fordham (1989) record that between 1966 and 1983, more than 200 adult educators did postgraduate studies in the UK from a sample of four Anglophone African countries: Ghana, Kenya, Sierra Leone and Tanzania. The exposure to foreign attitudes and practices in adult education through overseas study clearly had an impact on the recipients. The motivations of the scholarship providers were influenced by political and commercial considerations. In talks at the University of Botswana in 1989, for example, the Director General of the British Council made it clear that through scholar-ships Britain hoped to cultivate relationships with current and future leaders in order to facilitate political contacts and trade development. Similarly, a USAID document stated that those who study in the USA 'tend to go home preferring U.S. goods and services. They also have a better understanding of our values' (USAID, 1982: 8).

I conclude that the aid given to the adult education sector reflected the wider trends in the national aid situation. These trends included the influence of provider policies and preferences, the influence of aid on the nature of policies and programmes, and the use of aid by the state to further its own interests. These generalisations are examined below in a study of aid at the project level.

The National Literacy Programme (1978–87)

I now move on to consider the role of aid during the initial years of the National Literacy Programme, from its conception in 1978 to the resolution of its first funding crisis in 1987. Adult literacy in the years after Independence was not given priority by the state. A number of small-scale activities were undertaken by the government's Department of Community Development, the University and some non-governmental organisations, but in 1972 the government rejected a proposal by a UNESCO consultant (Brooks, 1972) for a nationwide literacy programme. However, a major government policy paper on education in 1977 (Republic of Botswana, 1977a: 12) stated an intention to consider literacy programmes. This encouraged the Ministry of Education's adult education section, the Botswana Extension College (BEC), to undertake two pilot literacy projects (1977 and 1978), which revealed the social demand for adult literacy tuition, and provided experience in running literacy activities (Botswana Extension College, 1978a). In 1977 the US Ford Foundation, which had provided significant funding to the BEC since its establishment in 1973, commissioned an evaluation of the College. The evaluation report recommended that the College should be incorporated into a new Department of Non Formal Education within the Ministry of Education, with an expanded role in adult education beyond the BEC's original focus on distance education (Townsend-Coles, 1978). In 1978 the Ministry of Education, acting on these recommendations, established the Department of Non Formal Education (DNFE), and appointed as its Chief Education Officer the same foreign consultant who had undertaken the evaluation.

The Chief Education Officer was a British consultant with special expertise in adult literacy and extensive experience as a

UNESCO field officer. His position was funded by UNESCO. Immediately after his appointment he produced a proposal for a national literacy initiative, and in 1979 the Ministry of Education agreed a project which aimed to eliminate illiteracy in the six-year period 1980/1 to 1985/6. The thrust of this project coincided with the rural development focus of the new national development plan. The proposed project was to have an experimental year in 1980/1, then extend literacy tuition nationwide to reach 50,000 new participants in each of the following five years (Republic of Botswana, 1980b). The local government districts were to be the main units of administration, with co-ordination undertaken by a District Adult Education Officer, who was a permanent member of DNFE's staff. Each district would be divided into areas in which ten to twenty literacy groups would be supervised by a Literacy Assistant engaged on a temporary full-time basis. Literacy groups consisting of fifteen participants would be taught by a Literacy Group Leader, who was to be a volunteer paid an honorarium. It was assumed that one year of tuition plus one year of access to follow-on literature would provide basic literacy and numeracy skills. The DNFE headquarters would produce teaching and support materials, undertake staff training, and provide technical support and supervision.

The National Literacy Programme was included in the *National Development Plan 1979–1985* (Republic of Botswana, 1980a: 330–31) as a project with a capital budget to cover materials, vehicles, travel costs, and honoraria and training costs for group leaders. Although many of the costs were in effect recurrent expenditure, because the project was finite it was agreed that it should be funded through development (capital) funds (Ministry of Education, 1979). It was envisaged that the costs of using DNFE permanent staff on the project would be met through the regular annual budget, while aid funding would be sought for the direct expenditure required. The estimated capital cost of the project for the period 1980/1 to 1985/6 was 6,011,000 pula (Republic of Botswana, 1980b). The scale of the project is shown by comparison with the total recurrent budget for DNFE in 1979/80 of P212,000 (Republic of Botswana, 1980b: 128).

At this point in Botswana's development, external aid was sought for any new education project on this scale; accordingly, a

Project Memorandum (Republic of Botswana, 1980b) was drawn up by the Ministry of Education's Planning Unit as the basis for seeking aid funds to cover materials (such as paper and printing supplies), vehicles (including trucks and motorcycles), honoraria for literacy group leaders, salaries for literacy assistants, staff training and transport (i.e. petrol and maintenance). The identification and design of the project were undertaken entirely by Botswana government officials. However, a significant role in this process was taken by foreign personnel working in various parts of the state bureaucracy. The impetus for the project, for example, had come from the newly appointed Chief Education Officer. Furthermore, at the inter-ministry meeting in March 1979 which agreed on the project in principle, 19 of the 33 people who attended the full meeting were foreigners (Department of Non Formal Education, 1979). The reality of the situation in the late 1970s was that there were few nationals in senior positions in adult education, although they did occupy the highest policy positions. It can be concluded that although no aid agency was formally involved in the initiation and design of the National Literacy Programme, foreign personnel, funded by a variety of aid sources, played a significant role at the planning stage.

The search for aid funding for the project was made at a propitious time, as the Chief Education Officer was well aware from his international experience (Townsend-Coles, 1988: 36–7). The establishment of a department with the title 'non formal education' reflected current international trends, and it was not surprising that the new headquarters building was funded by a loan from the World Bank. Aid policies since the mid-1970s had expressed some concern with basic needs and a focus on non-formal education; consequently, aid funding was secured very easily. Within a month of the government's adoption of the project, the Swedish International Development Authority indicated willingness for its funds to be used in the project (Townsend-Coles, 1988: 50). In 1980 the German government – through its agency the Reconstruction Loan Corporation (KFW) – began to provide commodity aid for the purchase of materials. Other agencies followed as soon as their next cycle of aid programming took effect: in 1981 the Dutch and Swedish governments began to provide grants, and in 1982 UNICEF and the German Agency for Tech-

Table 5.2 Sources of development funds for the National
Literacy Programme 1980/81–1985/86 (in pula, 1986 prices)

Funding source	Six-year totals	Distribution by source (%)
SIDA	2,246,320	42.5
GTZ	1,923,128	36.4
Netherlands	272,729	5.2
KFW	253,561	4.8
UNICEF	107,291	2.0
Domestic Development Fund	452,499	8.6
Total	5,255,528	100.0

Source: Gaborone, Mutanyatta and Youngman, 1987: 93.

nical Co-operation (GTZ) commenced their funding. The ease of
securing aid can be attributed to a number of factors. First, the
national aid situation meant a ready availability of funds for
education, especially at a time when international attention was
being given to poverty alleviation and non-formal education.
Second, major aid providers to Botswana, such as the Netherlands and Sweden, had explicitly egalitarian policies, and a literacy
programme for the mass of the adult population fitted in well.
Third, there were close personal contacts between the foreign
personnel working for the Botswana state and the staff of the aid
agencies. For example, one of the officers in the Ministry of Education Planning Unit was a SIDA-funded Swede in close touch
with the local SIDA office. The volume of aid provided to the
project in the first six years is shown in Table 5.2.

Table 5.2 shows that the five aid agencies provided about 91
per cent of the direct expenditure on the project during the first
six years, the remainder coming from the Botswana government's
own resources through the Domestic Development Fund. If the
counterpart contribution to the costs of the project in the form of
a proportion of DNFE salaries and other recurrent expenditure
devoted to literacy work is taken into account, it is estimated that
aid provided 72 per cent of the total costs in the period (Gaborone,

Mutanyatta and Youngman, 1987: 92). It should be noted that small aid contributions were also made by other agencies in the form of short-term consultancies – for example, by UNESCO (to improve the literacy newspaper) and the German Foundation for International Development (for a mid-term evaluation and for materials writing).

Table 5.2 reveals that the proportion contributed by the various agencies differed considerably, with SIDA (42.5 per cent) and GTZ (36.4 per cent) being the major providers. The nature of the aid also varied according to the provider. SIDA provided capital assistance to literacy through its overall support to the education sector. Sectoral funds were granted on a biennial basis, and were subject to a joint annual review by SIDA and the government of Botswana. SIDA provided general funding used in all areas of the project. The Ministry of Education was given a high degree of discretion on fund allocation; consequently, its officials regarded SIDA as flexible and co-operative in its approach. The annual review procedure provided occasions on which SIDA discussed detailed progress reports. Minutes of the meetings (for example, Republic of Botswana and SIDA, 1983, 1984) indicate that SIDA personnel regularly made recommendations on programme development, showing a consistent concern with the issue of post-literacy activities and materials for instance. Such recommendations, however, appear to have been given in the spirit of professional advice rather than as requirements for future support.

GTZ, in contrast, provided a technical assistance package involving funds linked to the provision of a German expert to the programme. The funds took the form of a grant to all areas of expenditure (except vehicles), made on the expectation of a counterpart contribution of 10 per cent, and with a stipulation of progress reports every three to six months. The first expert provided was to take the position of Literacy Co-ordinator for the period mid-1982 to mid-1985. The person appointed, who had no practical experience in adult literacy, was the key operational manager of the programme. Besides holding a senior organisational position, he had considerable power because of his influence with one of the major aid providers, and because all GTZ experts have discretionary funds to support their work. He therefore had resources separate from the development expenditure controlled by the Ministry of Education, which enabled him to take small-scale initiatives with immediate impact, such as establishing a formal training programme for Literacy Assistants at the University of Botswana, and funding an overseas scholarship. When the position of Literacy Co-ordinator was localised in 1985, the technical assistance position was filled by an expert printer at the request of the Ministry of Education, though there was some reluctance on the part of GTZ because the post had no influence over departmental management, which GTZ regarded as weak.

The other three agencies provided only 12 per cent of total funding between them, and exerted little direct influence. KFW and the Netherlands provided earmarked funds, for materials and equipment and for staff training respectively, but made few reporting requirements and remained distant from the programme's operations. UNICEF provided grants specified for supplies (such as paper) and equipment (such as motorcycles and a printing press), as well as for the training of literacy group leaders. The organisation granted funds and made few demands in terms of reporting on how the funds were used, or in relation to the nature of the programme itself.

The end of the initial project period created a situation in which the two major aid agencies made significant interventions. The original design of the literacy project had envisaged the elimination of illiteracy by reaching the estimated quarter of a million illiterate people in a six-year period. However, the report of the mid-term evaluation published in mid-1984 (Ministry of Education, 1984) showed that the programme was unable to meet its numerical targets. The Ministry therefore recommended the continuation of the development project beyond 1985/6, and proposed that literacy and post-literacy activities should become a regular activity of DNFE, with the temporary literacy assistants converted into a permanent cadre of extension educators. This recommendation was included in *National Development Plan 6, 1985–1991* (Republic of Botswana, 1985: 158), although the Ministry of Finance and Development Planning sanctioned only a small proportion of the literacy assistants being made permanent, on the grounds that aid grants could be used if they remained project staff. At this stage the future of the National Literacy Programme became a concern for GTZ and SIDA.

Major concerns were expressed by GTZ, which had three reservations. First, it felt that the mid-term evaluation had failed to assess the programme's effectiveness, especially as there was no information on learner performance. Second, it was dissatisfied with operational aspects of the programme and with departmental management, in particular the role of the Chief Education Officer, who had taken over when the post was localised in 1981. Finally, it wished to use its funding primarily for technical rather than financial assistance, and queried the lack of government commitment to recurrent funding. In late 1985, GTZ indicated that it might redirect its future funding for education in Botswana from literacy to technical education. In response to this, the Permanent Secretary and Deputy Permanent Secretary of the Ministry of Education went to GTZ headquarters in Frankfurt in February 1986 and managed to persuade the agency to renew its funding to literacy for 1987/88. However, there were three consequences as a result of GTZ pressure: in February 1986 the National Literacy Committee approved an external evaluation of the programme; in October 1986 the Chief Education Officer was replaced; and in January 1987 a GTZ consultant commenced an organisational development study of DNFE.

In late 1985 SIDA also voiced concerns about the future of the programme in terms of its funding, effectiveness and management, making it clear at the joint annual review that it felt the programme was overreliant on aid funds for its recurrent costs: 'The Swedish team, whilst reaffirming its support to the programme, underlined that it would like an increasing proportion of the recurrent costs to be met from the recurrent budget of the Ministry of Education' (Republic of Botswana and SIDA, 1985: 4). Subsequently, an evaluation commissioned by SIDA of its aid to education to Botswana in the period 1981 to 1986 expressed apprehension over implementation problems and the lack of information on the effectiveness of the programme, recommending that it should remain an area of high priority because it coincided with SIDA's own priorities for development co-operation. The first draft of the report in November 1986 concluded: 'SIDA's long term commitment to this programme, and related facilities, may well – pending findings from the present evaluation [i.e. of the literacy programme] – be conditional on measures being taken to improve its effectiveness' (Lauglo and Marope, 1986: 8). It also suggested more selective funding rather than general budget support. These ideas introduced a more critical note into SIDA's view of the literacy programme and its own role.

In this context, the external evaluation of the programme undertaken by the University of Botswana's Institute of Adult Education became a critical factor in the politics of aid. In the event, the report of the evaluation, which was discussed by the National Literacy Committee in mid-1987, defused the funding crisis. The findings of the report (Gaborone, Mutanyatta and Youngman, 1987) were generally positive, especially in relation to the learners' performance on a literacy test in which 81.0 per cent attained scores equivalent to passing the primary school Grade Four attainment test. Furthermore, its detailed recommendations suggested that improving the programme was a manageable task, and that a concrete financial plan could be made for a transition to recurrent government funding and selective aid support. The report met the requirements of the aid agencies, and strengthened the Ministry of Education's case for recurrent funding in its dispute with the Ministry of Finance and Development Planning. In particular GTZ, although it wrote formally to the Ministry of Education objecting to two paragraphs in the report referring to GTZ positions, regarded the report as opening the way for negotiations on future funding to the programme.

This country study provides an analysis of the influence of aid at the project level in relation to a particular adult programme. I have discussed elsewhere the wider consequences of the National Literacy Programme (Youngman, 1999), showing that the programme was promoted by the state in terms of the modernisation of society and the extension of educational opportunity. Its equity dimension made it particularly attractive to aid providers. However, I argue that the programme in fact served to reproduce the class, gender and ethnic inequalities within society. Furthermore, at the political level it constituted a strategy of state legitimation by demonstrating a welfare concern for providing the rural areas with social services. Ideologically, the programme planners in 1979 adopted a narrow and conservative conception of literacy, and consciously rejected conscientisation or mobilisation approaches that might have empowered the learners: 'the political element in the [Freire] method was not seen as being appropriate to Botswana. There was also a negative response to a somewhat militant mass campaign' (Townsend-Coles, 1988: 41). The overall consequences of the National Literacy Programme, and therefore of the aid which sustained it, was to legitimate Botswana's capitalist development and social inequality.

This country study illustrates how aid significantly influenced the formulation and implementation of adult education policies, and shows the impact of aid at the project level. Further evidence of the economic, political, social and ideological consequences of aid in Botswana is provided in the country case studies in Chapters 6 and 7 below, as most of the adult education programmes discussed there received aid funding.

Notes

1. Paraphrased from a speech by Frederico Mayor, Director General of UNESCO, at the Seventh Conference of Ministers of Education of African Member States in Durban, South Africa, April 1998.

2. Russia has now joined the G7 countries but it clearly participates on a different basis from the original members (Britain, Canada, France, Germany, Italy, Japan and the USA).

CHAPTER 6

Social Inequality and Adult Education

There are a number of divisions in society that constitute a system of inequality between different social groups in which some groups benefit at the expense of others. From the perspective of political economy, the most fundamental divisions relate to the economic organisation of society. Inequality is a structural feature of capitalist society, because class differences in the ownership and control of productive resources constitute the basis of social domination and subordination. Although the social relations of production are the major determinant of social inequality, there are other significant divisions in society whose origins are independent of class, particularly those of gender, ethnicity and race. These divisions interact with those of class within the capitalist mode of production, and form a complex system of inequality.

The theoretical framework established in Chapter 3 posited that the analysis of social phenomena such as adult education must take into account the multiple effects and interactions of class, gender, ethnicity and race. Thus the political economy approach studies the impact of social inequality on the character and consequences of adult education. This was summarised as follows:

- Different classes have different interests, and conflicts arise as they pursue these interests. It is assumed that these conflicts have effects on the nature and consequences of adult education at every level, including policies, organisation and curricula.
- Besides the relations of class, there are other important social inequalities, especially those based on gender, ethnicity and race.

It is assumed that these inequalities have profound influences on adult education and its outcomes, including in ways which interact with those derived from class relations.

The aim of this chapter is therefore to analyse social inequality in peripheral capitalist society, and examine the implications for adult education. It is argued that social inequality affects the nature of adult education at every level, including policies, organisation and curricula, and that it shapes the outcomes of participation in adult education activities. From this perspective, adult education is a resource in society which benefits some social groups and disadvantages others.

Social Inequality in Peripheral Capitalism

The study of social inequality is based on asking 'who is disadvantaged, why, and with what consequences?' (Samoff, 1982: 111). The aim of analysis, therefore, is to clarify the relationships between different groups in society, to explain the causes of inequality, and to examine the mechanisms by which inequality is reproduced or resisted. In Chapters 2 and 3 I argued that there is a complex configuration of social inequality in which class, gender, ethnicity and race provide key explanatory variables for understanding inequality and social domination. Furthermore, there are interactions between these variables within the capitalist mode of production which have to be elucidated. I also argued that adult education is one of the social mechanisms that serve to reproduce or undermine the system of inequality. In this chapter I amplify this theoretical framework by considering social inequality and the role of adult education in the context of peripheral capitalism.

Class

Within the framework of Marxist political economy, class is defined in terms of the social relations of production. A class is a group of individuals in society who share the same relationship to the productive resources of the economy. The ownership and control of productive resources are a source of power and social domination. The economic exploitation of the majority by a minority within capitalist society is the basis of its social hierarchy, and of the conflicting interests of the classes within that hierarchy. The task of class analysis is to identify the nature of the different classes in society, to show the historical processes by which they were formed, to examine the conflicts and struggles between them, and to consider the consequences.

Class analysis in the study of the peripheral capitalist countries must take account of the special features that derive from the historical processes by which these societies were incorporated into the world capitalist economy, including the articulation of the capitalist mode of production with pre-capitalist modes of production, the role of the colonial state, and the uneven and dependent nature of their development (Alavi, 1982a; Keith and Keith, 1988). The class structure of peripheral societies is complex and evolving, because the penetration of capitalism is a relatively recent phenomenon. The transformation of the pre-capitalist class structure and the formation of new classes are taking place rapidly and extensively, as they did in Europe in the transition from feudalism to capitalism. The two basic classes of capitalism, the bourgeoisie and the proletariat, are less developed than they are in advanced capitalism. This means that the petty bourgeoisie has greater significance, while the incomplete transformation of pre-capitalist modes of production makes the peasantry a significant element of the class structure. Hence there are differences in relation to advanced capitalism. But there are also significant differences within the peripheral areas themselves – for example, between Latin America and Africa.[1] The brief conceptual overview that follows is derived from discussions of class analysis in Africa in order to illustrate this approach to social inequality.

It is generally agreed that there are four main classes in Africa: the bourgeoisie (or capitalist class), the petty bourgeoisie (or middle class), the proletariat (or working class) and the peasantry. With respect to the bourgeoisie or capitalist class, a distinguishing feature (as elsewhere in the periphery) is that an important fraction of that class is foreign, usually in the form of transnational corporate capital. The nature of the bourgeoisie has been the subject of extensive discussion, particularly in relation to the character of its domestic fraction. The main issue has been whether indigenous capitalists constitute a 'comprador bourgeoisie' that serves the interests of the foreign capital on which it depends for its own reproduction, or whether they form a 'national bourgeoisie' that owns productive property autonomous from foreign control, and seeks to generate independent capitalist accumulation. However, the debate failed to understand imperialism as a global system of capitalist accumulation. It was based on two misconceptions: (a) that imperialism is opposed to capitalist development in the periphery; and (b) that an autonomous form of capitalist development is possible. This led to a preoccupation with a false dichotomy between international and domestic capital rather than the recognition of two fractions of the bourgeoisie which, while sometimes in competition, share the same overall interest in the expansion of capitalist accumulation. The main point of significance for the configuration of class forces in most African countries is the relative weakness of the domestic capitalist class (Berman and Leys, 1994).

The petty bourgeoisie or middle class has two major fractions, with different locations in the system of production relations. One fraction owns economic property on a small scale and engages in small-business activities as traders, shop owners, building contractors, workshop proprietors, bus owners, and so forth. The other fraction uses its assets of knowledge and skill as salaried managers of either capitalist businesses or the state. In particular, it occupies the middle and upper levels of the state bureaucracy in the civil service, parastatal enterprises and the military. Because of the significance of the state in establishing the conditions for capitalist development in the initial post-colonial period, the senior members of the state bureaucracy played a dominant role in the political economy. The importance of the bureaucratic petty bourgeoisie has been a characteristic feature of the class structure in the periphery. In Africa this class used its control of the state not only to advance the interests of capital in general but also to promote its own efforts to accumulate and rise up the class hierarchy. However, the restructuring of the state and reduction of the public sector under structural adjustment programmes have weakened this fraction of the middle class.

The penetration of the capitalist mode of production is marked by the increasing incorporation of rural dwellers into wage labour, and their separation from the land and other agricultural means of production. This process of proletarianisation, often originating in migrant labour in the colonial era, is ongoing and incomplete, but a permanent urban working class has emerged. In many countries of Africa the urban proletariat is still a relatively small proportion of the population. It is steadily growing, however, as capitalist relations of production expand, evidenced by industrialisation and urbanisation (Simon, 1992). As part of this process of class formation, there is a significant fraction of the urban working class which is unemployed or in casual employment, engaged in a variety of informal cash-earning activities such as car washing, street vending, backstreet mechanics, piece jobs in gardens, and prostitution. A rural proletariat is also in the process of formation, as many rural dwellers are increasingly dependent for their livelihood on the sale of their labour-power – for example, as farm workers. The urban and rural working class is an expanding component of the class structure.

The most distinctive class in peripheral capitalism is the peasantry, which is engaged in agricultural production based mainly on family labour. The peasant class emerged from pre-capitalist modes of production in which the rural household was the main economic unit, largely self-sufficient in its production and consumption. With the penetration of capitalism, however, these households became drawn into production for sale in the market as well as for subsistence. It is characteristic of contemporary rural class structures in Africa that they are not yet dominated by capitalist farmers employing landless labourers, because the market for land is restricted by pre-capitalist forms of communal land tenure – hence the rural economy is still based mainly on production by a peasant class. This class has marked internal inequalities, and there is a continuum of rural producer relations embracing rich, middle and poor peasants (see, for example, Mamdani's analysis [1992] of a village in Uganda). At one end of the continuum is a comparatively small group of rich peasants who have significant means of production (land, animals, implements), hire labour as well as using family labour, and generate large surpluses for sale. Members of this group often have small businesses also. At the other end there is the majority of the peasant class, who lack adequate means of production. They are unable to survive only on farming, and have to sell their labour and engage in other income-earning activities such as craft production and beer brewing in order to secure a livelihood. Some of these poor peasants engage in migrant labour, entering into the process of proletarianisation in an initial stage in which they are partly workers and partly peasants. Very few rural households are engaged solely in subsistence production. We should note that the processes of rural class formation have a gendered character, as the rural poor are disproportionately women, especially female headed households.

The class structure of peripheral capitalism is a system of inequality. Class differences underlie economic inequalities of wealth and income, political inequalities of participation in decision-making, and social inequalities of status and access to services such as health, education and housing. The class structure is inherently conflictual, and classes pursue their own interests in society. Their success in doing so depends on the extent of self-awareness and organisation within the class, its capacity to act for itself. The dominant capitalist, petty-bourgeois and rich peasant classes have the political as well as the economic and social power to advance their own interests, especially through control over the state. They seek to contain their contradictions with the subordinated classes through a range of coercive and non-coercive measures, from police enforcement of restrictions on trade unions to the inclusion of capitalist values like entrepreneurship in school curricula.

At the same time, however, the subordinated classes struggle to protect and advance their own interests in various ways. In the urban areas, the working class opposes domination and inequality not only through overt and organised means, such as strikes, unionisation and political demonstrations, but also in silent, unorganised and covert protests, such as absenteeism, slow working, sabotage and theft. Similarly, in the countryside, while poor peasants and rural workers sometimes form themselves into collective organisations for change (such as peasant associations in Latin America), very often their resistance to domination by the wealthy and powerful takes more informal and disguised forms. Scott (1989) refers to these modes of rural class struggle as 'everyday forms of resistance', which take the form of activities such as poaching, pilfering, arson, squatting, and cultural expressions against the ideology of privilege. It is important analytically to recognise that the inequalities inherent in the class structure do not go unchallenged by those who are disadvantaged.

Thus the process by which classes are formed and reproduced in peripheral capitalist societies is one of conflict and struggle. There are also complex processes of contradiction and alliance between classes and between fractions within classes, which shape the changes in society and give development policies and practices a class character. Hence the trends in development reflect the configuration of class forces at any given time. The implications of the social hierarchy of class for adult education policies, practices and outcomes must therefore be examined in the specific circumstances of particular situations.

Gender

The second form of social inequality is that of gender relations and the subordination of women to men. The concept of gender refers to the socially constructed differences between females and males, who are physically distinguishable by their sex. While there is a biological distinction between women and men in women's capability to bear children, the character of feminine and masculine identity, and the expectations of the roles and interactions of the sexes, are socially determined rather than natural. Gender relations have varied widely between cultures and historical periods. Nevertheless, although they have taken different forms, the sexual division of labour and the social inequality of women have been constant dimensions of the interrelationship of women and men. Thus in all spheres of social activity there are institutions, practices and ideologies which maintain women's subordination, and distribute the benefits of society unequally between women and men.

The patterns of gender inequality within society have been extensively analysed by feminist scholars. Although there are many feminisms and different ways of categorising them (Lengermann and Niebrugge-Brantley, 1992), it is relevant here to consider four trends in feminist thought which have sought to theorise the reasons for the subordination of women: (i) liberal feminism; (ii) radical feminism; (iii) Marxist and socialist feminisms; and (iv) postmodernist and Third World feminisms. The first trend, liberal feminism, is largely articulated within the framework of function-alist sociology, and portrays sex discrimination as the product of outmoded values, a cultural aberration within a modern economy and liberal democracy. It tends to isolate gender inequality from other social divisions. From the viewpoint of liberal feminism, equality can be achieved through legislative action for equal rights and action for attitudinal changes against sexism – for example, in education. This trend is reformist, and seeks equality of oppor-tunity within the status quo of capitalist society.

The second trend, radical feminism, sees men as a group domi-nating women and benefiting from their subordination, a system of unequal relations it calls patriarchy. It believes that the system of patriarchy is universal throughout history and is independent of class relations, because all men gain from the oppression of all women. This fundamental structure of inequality has its basis in men's control over women's reproduction and sexuality (a control which is backed up by male violence) and over the labour-power of women in the household. Radical feminism regards change as being brought about by a separate struggle of women against men for autonomy and freedom from male control.

The third trend is influenced by Marxist theory. Within this trend, Marxist feminism regards gender inequality as derivative from the class relations inherent in capitalism, with women's sub-ordination serving the interests of capitalist accumulation. In this perspective, the abolition of classes within the socialist mode of production will provide the conditions for gender equality by ending the source of exploitation. Marxist feminists have resisted the notion of male domination as an autonomous system of inequality. They have therefore been critical of the concept of patriarchy for its failure to acknowledge the historical significance of changing modes of production, and for portraying a false homo-geneity among women of different classes. Their analysis has focused more on the exploitation of women by capitalism than on male oppression of women. On the other hand, socialist feminism has sought to combine the concepts of patriarchy and capitalism, using historical materialism as the mode of empirical analysis. From this perspective, women's subordination has a material base in their economic exploitation, with both men and capital benefiting from the fact that women perform unpaid domestic labour for men, and receive lower wages in the labour market than men. Because women are exploited both by men and by capital, the struggle for women's equality will need to continue within socialist society. A key emphasis of socialist feminism is the interaction between different structures of social inequality, including not only class and gender but also ethnicity and race.

Finally, postmodernist thought has been critical of other feminisms for their universal theories, which fail to emphasise the differences among women. It criticises essentialism (i.e. the use of the category 'woman' to denote a unique female nature and the commonality among women) and focuses on difference by analysing the plurality of women's experiences, identities and constructions of reality, and deconstructing the discourses that create representations of gender relations. Its implications for political and social action to change gender inequality are not always clear, as the emphasis on difference undermines the idea that women share common interests. This mode of thought has synchronised with Third World feminism, which attacks much of feminist theory as ethnocentric and also highlights the fact that men and women are not homogeneous as groups. This trend stresses multiple systems of oppression, and pays particular attention to the impact of imperialism as a central feature of Third World social reality.

From this brief review of some of the trends in feminist theory, we can see that there are different approaches to explaining the inequality of women in society. The multiple causality conception of inequality in the political economy approach adopted in Chapters 2 and 3 regards the three systems of inequality (class, gender, ethnicity and race) as analytically separable, but interrelated and conditioned by the mode of production. Thus while patriarchy existed in pre-capitalist societies, its contemporary forms are shaped by capitalist relations of production and influenced by the character of ethnic and racial divisions. This is well expressed by Walby:

> I shall define patriarchy as a system of social structures and practices in which men dominate, oppress and exploit women.... Any specific empirical instance will embody the effects, not only of patriarchal structures, but also of capitalism and racism. (1990: 20)

Hence any analysis of the gender inequality in a given society must also contextualise it in relation to the class structure, and the ethnic and racial hierarchy.

The differing theoretical perspectives on gender inequality have been reflected in the debates over the nature of development and in the analysis of the impact of development on women and their social relations with men (Visvanathan, 1997). A dominant paradigm has been that of liberal feminism, which was easily accommodated within modernisation theory. The approach deriving from this position is that of 'Women in Development' (WID), which seeks to integrate women in the modernising capitalist development process, through overcoming traditional institutions and practices which constitute an obstacle to greater opportunities for women. Since the mid-1970s this approach has underpinned much of the work with respect to the situation of women by the United Nations, the aid agencies, and governments and non-governmental organisations in the South. WID strategies include practical activities such as the promotion of women's projects, particularly income-generating groups, and policy activities, such as the establishment of government departments responsible for women's affairs. These strategies have sought to improve opportunities for women but they have not challenged the prevailing definition of development and its associated political and economic structures:

> WID thinkers fully subscribe to this view [i.e. modernisation theory]. Their difference with their male counterparts lies merely in the argument that the benefits of the Western development model have accrued only to men. (Bandarage, 1984: 497)

Other trends in feminist thought, however, have also had an impact on development thinking. For example, feminism which questions the Western development model provides an important influence on populist approaches to development. At the theoretical level, this is illustrated in the radical feminist writings of Maria Mies. In *Patriarchy and Accumulation on a World Scale* (Mies, 1986) she extended the idea of patriarchy to an analysis of gender within the international division of labour and Third World development. Her argument led her to question 'growth' models of development (both capitalist and socialist), and to propose an alternative model of self-sufficient development. Adding environmentalist and

Third World feminist ideas, she elaborates this model with Vandana Shiva in *Ecofeminism* (Mies and Shiva, 1993). The model is rooted in the perspective of subsistence agrarian economy and indigenous practices, and in the example of the survival struggles of Third World grassroots movements. At the practical level these struggles derived from the deterioration of women's economic and social situation in the 1980s, particularly as the feminisation of poverty under neoliberal structural adjustment programmes (Feldman, 1992) created material conditions which demonstrated the inability of 'development' to meet the needs of women.

The political economy approach in this book is informed by feminist scholarship within the Marxist tradition, which has sought to clarify the patriarchal nature of capitalism. It therefore seeks to analyse how changes and evolutions in the mode of production affect gender relations, and to identify the forms patriarchy takes at any given time in a particular society. It focuses on a number of key sites of gender inequality in peripheral capitalist society: (a) the household and its social relations of reproduction and sexual division of labour; (b) paid work and the labour market; (c) the state and public policy; and (d) culture and ideology. This analytical approach is illustrated by an expanding literature on the nature of gender hierarchies in Africa (see, for example, Robertson and Berger, 1986; Stichter and Parpart, 1988; Meena, 1992; Gordon, 1996). The methodology suggested by this literature includes a historical perspective that seeks to show how gender divisions in pre-capitalist societies were affected by the penetration of capitalism under colonialism, and how these processes shaped post-colonial gender relations. Furthermore, it examines how the continuing expansion and changes in the capitalist mode of production condition the forms of contemporary gender inequalities.

Gender relations constitute a system of inequality that is perpetuated by male-dominated institutions and practices. Men benefit from women's inequality in material ways, in social status, and in the exercise of power in the public and private domains. The practices and ideologies upholding women's inferiority are hegemonic; however, they do not go uncontested and women resist both individually and collectively. For instance, Wieringa's book *Subversive Women* (1995) contains many examples of women's movements and organisations in the South which have strongly resisted patriarchal oppression, documenting a wide variety of ways in which women have empowered themselves and defended their interests by opposing unequal power relations and their consequences. These include campaigns for political representation in the colonial era in Trinidad and Tobago, protest movements and labour struggles in India, popular theatre in Jamaica, and mass demonstrations in Peru. The research on these movements was informed by the understanding 'that women's oppression was compounded by class and race relations, and that struggles surrounding these issues could at times have greater weight than solely women's struggles' (Wieringa, 1995: 3). This recognition coincides with the key issue from the political economy perspective that the analysis of struggles against gender inequality must clarify whether demands and modes of organisation advance the interests of women in general or only the interests of women in a dominant class or ethnic or racial group.

Gender is an important explanatory variable in analysing social inequality in peripheral capitalism and its impact on people's lives. The pattern of gender relations in a given society influences the development process and the policies of the state. As Pearson puts it in her discussion of gender and development: 'All policies, however technical or neutral they may appear to be, will have gendered implications' (1992: 292). Thus gender inequality must be considered as part of the social context of adult education, whose policies, practices and outcomes will necessarily have a gendered character.

Ethnicity and race

The third dimension of inequality is that of ethnicity and race. The hierarchies of ethnicity and race have their origins outside the material base of society but are closely articulated with the class structure. The concept of ethnicity is based on the notion that there are groups within society which are defined by cultural distinctions, such as those identified by a common language, religion, set of customs or historical place of origin. It is therefore used to designate different social groups like the English and Afrikaaners in South Africa, or the Muslims and Hindus in India. Ethnicity is an ascribed status in that people are born into a particular group and socialised within its culture. The concept of ethnic identity refers to 'the sense on the part of the individual that she or he belongs to a particular cultural community' (Hutchinson and Smith, 1996: 5) However, the salience of ethnic differences varies by time and place, definitions of ethnic identity change, and the boundaries of ethnic groups are permeable, so that some individuals move between groups – for example, by religious conversion. Ethnicity is distinguishable from the concept of race, which denotes divisions based on socially defined biological distinctions signified by differences in physical appearance. In many circumstances the two categories overlap when a group identified in racial terms also has distinct cultural attributes, such as the Chinese in Indonesia or the Asians in East Africa. For the purposes of this discussion, the focus will be on ethnicity, but the mode of analysis is also relevant to those societies in which a racial hierarchy is part of the structure of social inequality.

Ethnicity is a system of inequality, because in multi-ethnic societies there is a hierarchy of domination and subordination between ethnic groups which has been formed by particular historical processes. The inherent contradictions of inequality lead to various forms of ethnic competition and conflict. The task of social analysis is to clarify the groups within this hierarchy, to identify how they were formed and how they are maintained, to examine the conflicts between them, and to consider the economic, political and social consequences.

The concept of ethnicity within the social sciences has received renewed attention since the 1960s, initially as a result of the emergence of organised ethnic movements in the industrialised countries. In the mid-1970s Glazer and Moynihan noted the changed usage of the term 'ethnic group': there had been a 'steady expansion of the term from minority and marginal subgroups at the edges of society – groups expected to assimilate, to disappear, to continue as survivals, exotic or troublesome – to major elements of society.' (Glazer and Moynihan, 1975: 5). Analysis shifted from 'minority groups' to the total structure of ethnic relations in society, and the overall patterns of ethnic domination and subordination within the boundaries of the nation-state. There was also a reconceptualisation of the nature of ethnicity from the position that cultural identity is preordained and fixed to the view that ethnicity is situational, its definition and significance varying according to the wider economic and political context. Thus ethnic identity came to be seen as socially constructed, often through political mobilisation, and liable to shift with circumstances. In particular, it is constructed in relation to other ethnic groups.

Alavi (1989: 224–5) cites the example of Muslims in Bengal in 1947, who united with Hindus as bearers of 'Bengali' identity proposing an independent Bengal. The proposal was blocked by more powerful political forces so that in the post-Independence framework the people of West Bengal were incorporated into India, separated from the Muslims of East Bengal merged into Pakistan. Subsequently, the people of East Bengal broke away to form Bangladesh, because despite the shared Muslim religion they felt disadvantaged by Punjabi domination of the Pakistani state. When they did this, the basis of their ethnic identification stressed their regional rather than their religious attributes. This example also draws attention to the important role of the state, as the state and development policies affect differentially the economic opportunities, political participation and social status of the varying ethnic groups. Hence the mobilisation of ethnic identity is often undertaken in the context of struggles over the state and public policies.

The concept of ethnicity has always been an element within development studies. The dominant approach has been that of modernisation theory, in which ethnicity was considered an obstacle to development. Ethnic identity was seen by theorists such as Geertz (1963) as a 'primordial sentiment', a vestige of traditional society that stood in the way – psychologically and socially – of the meritocratic social mobility essential to a modern society. Furthermore, in political terms ethnicity represented an obstacle to the key task of nation-building. Modernisation theory coincided with the political experience of many post-Independence leaders who had mobilised support for the anti-colonial struggle on the basis of nationalism that appealed across ethnic differences. The rhetoric of the post-colonial state therefore sought to delegitimise and depoliticise ethnicity, stressing citizenship for all within the nation. In practice, the state's responses to ethnic diversity varied from modes of accommodation, such as balancing civil service recruitment between ethnic groups, to forms of repression, including military suppression. Efforts were made to project the neutrality of the state even when one ethnic group was dominant within the classes holding state power, but the state remained an arena of ethnic competition (Brown, 1989).

The populist approach within development theory, however, has articulated a position which is hostile to the centralised state and positive towards the mobilisation of ethnic identity. From this viewpoint, the state itself is the obstacle to development, and ethnicity is to be encouraged because it can meet societal needs and form the basis of decentralised modes of political organisation (Ronen, 1986). These ideas gained significance with the economic crisis of the 1980s, which in many cases reduced the state's ability to provide economic opportunities and social services, so that people mobilised ethnic networks as a strategy for survival. Populism therefore advocates ethno-development because it sees ethnicity in a positive light, as ethnic assertion can help dominated groups to struggle for economic, political and social justice.

These trends of theory and practice can be illustrated within the context of Africa (Doornbos, 1991). Most contemporary African nation-states lie within boundaries determined by colonial powers which demarcated territories in ways that ignored the realities of pre-colonial societies. Thus African states are generally multi-ethnic internally, with some ethnic groups (such as the Somalis) split between states. The colonial state also constructed distinctive patterns of ethnic domination and subordination. In some cases, it favoured certain ethnic groups – for instance, the Baganda in Uganda – giving them access to greater political and economic power than others. In other cases, such as Zimbabwe (Ranger, 1989), it participated in processes that created new ethnic identities. The anti-colonial nationalist movements mobilised support across ethnic divisions, appealing to the concept of the nation-state. Thus the borders defined by colonialism were accepted as sacrosanct in post-colonial Africa, and nation-building became a key goal of politics and development, typified in slogans such as 'One Zambia. One Nation'. However, although the modernising state promoted a 'national' identity – for example, through language and educational policies – in practice, struggles for control of the state and its allocation of resources were often expressed in ethnic competition, sometimes breaking out into violent conflict, as in Rwanda and Burundi.

The ideology of ethnicity in Africa is usually labelled 'tribal-ism' (Mafeje, 1971; Saul, 1979). This concept originated in the colonial era, when anthropologists and colonial officials classified the various ethnic groups as 'tribes' (Ranger, 1983), but it has persisted in the post-colonial era. Appeals to ethnic identity are usually stigmatised as 'tribalism', which is portrayed in negative terms as divisive and threatening to the integrity of the nation-state. But although tribalism is branded by the state as illegiti-mate, the notion of the tribe has been used to mobilise support for a variety of social and political purposes. The ideology of ethnicity, however, changed in content over the years (Shaw, 1986). In the period of economic growth experienced in the years imme-diately after Independence, while ethnicity was officially decried, the holders of state power used ethnic connections as forms of patronage which strengthened the state and their own economic and political position. But in the period of economic crisis which has affected Africa since the early 1980s, ethnicity has had a grass-roots appeal as a means of self-reliant survival away from the weakened and decreasingly effective state:

> ethnicity has been reinforced as people have retreated from malfunc-tioning cities to relatively self-reliant rural areas. The politics of sur-vival has meant the revival of traditional technologies, priorities and life-styles as 'modern' inputs of imported fuel, foods and goods no longer exist. In general, of course, people have returned to their particular 'ethnic' area, so reinforcing such identities and connections. (Shaw, 1986: 589)

This social and economic response has created a positive concep-tion of the ideology of ethnicity, reflected at the theoretical level by the protagonists in Africa of the populist approach to develop-ment, such as Paul Wangoola (1996). Thus the ideology and re-ality of ethnic identities and interactions change over time – an important factor in the nature of ethnicity as a dimension of in-equality in African societies.

Marxism has traditionally been opposed to social theories such as cultural pluralism, which see ethnicity and race as the main factors in social organisation and political conflict, because of its own emphasis on materialist rather than culturalist explanations. Recent Marxist modes of analysis, however, have recognised that the causal variables of ethnic inequality and domination cannot be reduced to class. It is clear that in a range of circumstances people do exhibit a strong ethnic consciousness and identification, and that ethnic constituencies are mobilised for various kinds of social and political action. There are also processes of ethnic categorisation and labelling which are used by dominant groups to rationalise and facilitate the subordination and oppression of other groups. In both cases, a collective identity is defined in cultural terms, which transcends the social divisions of class. The political economy approach used here therefore seeks to explain why people are mobilised or oppressed in terms of ethnic identities, and focuses on the contexts in which these processes occur. It argues that cultural identities are not totally independent of the material base of society; accordingly it concentrates on the inter-actions between class relations and ethnicity (Samoff, 1982: 109–11). This approach regards 'ethnicity not as a cultural imperative, but as a strategy in the struggle for resources' (Worsley, 1984: 245) – a strategy which will inevitably have a class content. Thus it asks questions such as: What is the class position of ethnic leaders? What is the class content of expressed ethnic demands? What class interests are served by ethnic ideologies? Which class benefits from ethnically based activities?

Ethnicity and race are important explanatory variables of the social inequality in peripheral capitalist societies. Ethnic and racial hierarchies have an impact in terms of differential access to eco-nomic resources, political power and social status. They are ac-companied by ethnocentric and racist ideologies which legitimate patterns of superiority and inferiority; they are influential in the composition of the state, and affect the nature of development policies. Ethnicity and race therefore have implications for adult education policies, practices and outcomes, and must be exam-ined as part of the overall analysis of the social inequalities that impact on adult education.

Social Inequality and Adult Education

In the previous sections I have considered three major determi-nants of social inequality, and suggested that the patterns of in-equality in society will affect the nature and outcomes of adult education. The question of the relationship between education and social inequality has been extensively analysed with regard to schooling in the advanced capitalist countries, and these theories have influenced the field of adult education.

One important theoretical approach is that of functionalist sociology, which sees education as an objective mechanism for social selection and the allocation of roles in adult life (Haralambos, 1985). It argues that the objective measurement of educational attainment in schools ensures that achievement is based on ability and motivation; therefore individuals progress on merit. Thus students advance as far as they are able, and their social background is rendered irrelevant because the same standards are applied to all students, irrespective of their class, gender, ethnic or racial group. This conception of education provides the basis for the view that education can redress social inequalities. If everyone has equal access to education, then all individuals have an equal opportunity to develop their ability. The logic of this position is that there should be more upward mobility for individuals within the existing hierarchical structures rather than fundamental change to those structures. The idea that education can create a more equal society, and that equality of educational opportunity can lead to a more efficient use of the nation's human resources, has had a significant impact on educational policy in the advanced capitalist countries.

From the early 1970s onwards, however, this conception of education came under sustained critique from the revived tradition of Marxist social theory in the USA and Western Europe. Bowles and Gintis (1976) developed an alternative analysis which contended that education does not diminish inequality but, in fact, serves to reproduce the class structure of capitalist society from generation to generation. The tendency to economic determinism in this approach was criticised by writers such as Apple (1982) and Giroux (1983), who contended that schools not only reproduce capitalist social hierarchies but also reproduce the contradictions inherent in those hierarchies. Thus, while education is a social institution in which the social inequalities of class, gender, ethnicity and race are indeed expressed and reinforced, there is also resistance to these forms of social domination by students and teachers. Studies based on this approach considered not only the outcomes of education – for example, in terms of occupational status – but also the processes within the school, such as the hidden curriculum, which produce differential outcomes. They also examined the ways in which students and teachers resisted dominant ideologies. Hence these perspectives encompassed social action and the possibilities for change through education.

From the mid-1980s onwards, the influence of postmodernism on social theory led to a shift away from theories of social reproduction in education. Thus questions of power in education came to be discussed in terms of discourse rather than structures of social inequality. As Morrow and Torres (1994) indicate, however, some scholars within the critical sociology of education continued to employ the concept of social reproduction. They based their analysis of schooling on 'parallelist models' of inequality which considered that class, race and gender are distinct systems in which none is reducible to the others, and class is not primary (see, for example, McCarthy and Apple, 1988). Morrow and Torres (1994: 46) themselves argue for the continuing importance in educational analysis of the issue of the social inequalities in capitalist society. They advocate a reconstructed model of social and cultural reproduction which will allow 'for an analysis of interactions, interplay, and relationships between class, gender and race in educational settings', and will be concretised by specific empirical studies.

The theories of schooling and inequality in society have had an impact on the field of adult education in the North. The liberal view that adult education can contribute to greater equality of opportunity for adults has been influential. In Britain, for example, it was exemplified in the 1970s by the policy document *Adult Education: A Plan for Development* (Department of Education and Science, 1973), which saw adult education as redressing disadvantage and providing people with a 'second chance'. This conception of adult education saw it as providing compensatory education for those who missed out as children, in order to give them an opportunity to advance their individual social and economic situation. In the 1980s, however, it was counterposed by the radical tradition, which applied the theories of reproduction and resistance to adult education (Thompson, 1980; Youngman, 1986). From this perspective, most adult education activities reinforced class and gender inequalities, but there were examples of programmes with a collective purpose which deliberately sought to overcome them through the transformation of capitalist society.

Since the mid-1980s the dominant paradigm of adult education in the North has been that of meeting the needs of business and industry, and the radical, social action tradition has been in retreat. The theoretical turn towards postmodernism has had the same impact as in the social analysis of schooling, diminishing analytical concern with the relationship between adult education and the social inequalities of capitalist society. A growing feminist literature on adult education (Hayes, 1992; Stalker, 1996) has highlighted gender inequality, but the issue is seldom contextualised within discussions of capitalist society. The issue of class inequality has received little attention. Collins and Collard (1995), for example, discuss the absence of class analysis in North American adult education research and practice. Similarly, the question of ethnic and racial inequality has been relatively neglected. Only occasionally has an attempt been made to analyse all three forms of social inequality together. A notable example is Cunningham's 'Race, Gender, Class and the Practice of Adult Education in the United States' (1996), which argues that adult education must end its complicity with these structures of inequality, and democratise knowledge and decision-making.

Although the question of social inequality has never been a major concern of mainstream research on adult education in the North, it has received some consideration, as we have seen. However, the role of adult education in reproducing and/or undermining social inequality has not been extensively researched in the context of peripheral capitalist societies. One exception was Bock and Papagiannis's *Non Formal Education and National Development* (1983), which made a start in developing such a perspective. The book included theoretical discussions on non-formal adult education and development, and presented empirical case studies drawn from several peripheral capitalist societies. Its aim was to challenge the assumption that non-formal adult education has 'considerable potential for providing an alternative channel of upward social and economic mobility for low status social groups' (Bock and Papagiannis, 1983: 8). Its theoretical basis was the centrality of power and conflict in society, and the rejection of the idea that adult education can of itself resolve problems of unequal distribution and participation. The key theme was the analysis of who really benefits from non-formal adult education programmes.

Non-formal adult education was therefore examined in terms of its social and economic consequences, such as occupational mobility. In Zambia, for example, skill training programmes for unemployed rural youth were shown to have lowered the occupational aspirations of school dropouts and prepared them for low-skill, low-paid jobs. This process of mediating the contradictions in the capitalist economy by limiting the claims for upward mobility served 'to legitimate inequalities from which only the urban elite benefit' (Bock and Papagiannis, 1983: 88). The overall conclusion of the book was that:

> As a socially created institution, non formal education, in common with schooling, serves many of the same societal functions, including socialization, recruitment, and mobility management. It acts as an agency that defines and constrains the life chances of those it processes. (Bock and Papagiannis, 1983: 21)

Thus there are ideological ('socialization'), economic ('recruitment') and social ('mobility') consequences for participants in adult education. The book is important because it demonstrates the possibilities of applying to peripheral capitalism a theoretical approach which relates adult education to the reproduction and contestation of social inequality.

Another example was provided by Ginsburg and Arias-Godinez (1984) in a study of educational radio in Mexico. They raised the theoretical issue of how non-formal education programmes for rural adults in developing countries 'may work either to reproduce or transform existing relations of domination and subordination' (Ginsburg and Arias-Godinez, 1984: 117). This issue was explored in an analysis of two contrasting radio projects. The first project, run centrally by the state, linked radio broadcasts with a tutor, and provided literacy tuition. It was individualistic in orientation, and those with a higher socioeconomic status were the most successful learners. Its child-orientated teaching materials, and traditional hierarchical relations between teacher and taught, reinforced the peasants' sense of dependency. The second project was run by priests on a community basis, involving direct interaction with the listeners. The programmes addressed the concerns of local peasants, such as land rights, and promoted issues such as the rights of women. The authors showed that the topics covered by this project challenged social inequality by stimulating critical thought and collective action by the peasants. They therefore demonstrated the relationship between different kinds of adult education and patterns of domination and subordination.

These two examples illustrate the relevance of the concept of reproduction and resistance for the analysis of the nature and outcomes of adult education programmes in peripheral capitalist countries. This relevance has not, however, been explored at length theoretically or empirically, and this is a gap which the political economy approach developed in this book seeks to fill.

The curriculum and the mediation of inequality

My discussion has revealed the relationship between adult education and social inequality. A key element of this relationship is to be found in the adult education curriculum. The link between knowledge and social interests in the framework of political economy is analysed through the concepts of ideology and hegemony (Youngman, 1986: 59–76). Although the concept of ideology is highly contested, one usage within the Marxist tradition is to denote a set of ideas, beliefs and values, such as sexism or racism, which promotes the interests of a particular class or social group (Williams, 1976). Gramsci's concept of hegemony refers to the process by which the ideology of a dominant social group is diffused throughout society, so that everyone tends to accept as 'common sense' a set of ideas and beliefs which in fact only promote the interests of the dominant group. This diffusion takes place through a number of institutions in society, particularly through education. For Gramsci, however, the dominant ideology is never totally hegemonic and uncontested. Ideology is a terrain of struggle, and subordinated groups are able to resist and challenge the dominant world-view. Adult education therefore has the potential to undermine the legitimacy of dominant ideas, and promote an alternative system of ideas and values: a counter-hegemony.

The question of ideological reproduction and resistance concentrates attention on the curriculum of adult education. These issues have been explored at length in the sociology of schooling. They were first raised in the phenomenological approaches of the so-called 'new sociology of education' initiated by Young's collection *Knowledge and Control* (1971), which focused on the sociology of knowledge in educational institutions. The fundamental premiss of the book was that 'Education is a selection and organisation from the available knowledge at a particular time which involves conscious or unconscious choices' (Young, 1971: 24). The key question, therefore, was the nature of these choices. This question generated a large body of school-based research on both the 'official' curriculum and the 'hidden' curriculum of tacitly transmitted norms and values. However, as Young and Whitty (1977: 8) pointed out, many of these analyses failed to locate the question of choices in education to the broader economic and political context. Marxist researchers therefore sought to situate school knowledge within the wider structures of inequality and social power. The concept of ideology became central to their analysis of the role of the school in the constitution and contestation of hegemony. They looked at areas such as textbooks, language, modes of assessment, teaching techniques and communication in the classroom to uncover the processes of ideology. The work of Apple (1979, 1982, 1986) was especially comprehensive in revealing how the choices of knowledge represented in the content of the official curriculum and embodied in classroom practices are the mechanisms whereby social inequality is reproduced and legitimated on the one hand, or resisted and contested on the other. In particular, he sought to explain the complex interactions between class, race and gender ideologies (Apple and Weis, 1983).

The concept of the curriculum has not been widely applied in the context of adult education. As Boshier (1985: 15) has written: 'Whereas pre-adult educators develop "curriculum" (based on a discipline or subject matter) adult educators are more inclined to plan "programs" based on the needs of individuals, organisation and communities.' Nevertheless, adult education as a form of planned learning is based on choices about aims, contents and methods. It can therefore usefully be analysed within conceptualisations of the curriculum. The first extended study to adopt this position was Griffin's *Curriculum Theory in Adult and Lifelong Education* (1983), which contended that adult education should be analysed in curriculum terms. The book argued that the practices of adult teaching and learning must be problematised with regard to knowledge, culture and power and the structural relations of society. In particular, it concluded that the adult education curriculum reproduces the patterns of class inequality in society. Griffin cited Gelpi's view that 'It is important to expose the ideological content of all learning' (Griffin, 1983: 197). However, using Gelpi's analysis of lifelong education, he also concluded that the curriculum is a site of conflict, and there is always the possibility of transformation through education. The book is significant for signposting a fruitful line of research within adult education, although – as Blundell (1992) has pointed out – it omitted a consideration of gender and, it must be added, of ethnicity and race.

However, there are very few published empirical studies on the adult education curriculum and the mediation of social inequality. Three examples illustrate the potential for undertaking such studies on the contents and processes of adult education. Coles (1977) undertook a content analysis of adult basic education readers which showed that they conveyed sexist and racist ideologies, and an endorsement of the capitalist class hierarchy. He concluded: 'in these adult basic education texts ... are political statements about the social relations in society, statements which ... are predominantly against the interests of adults who use the texts, many of whom are minorities and poor' (Coles, 1977: 52). Quigley and Holsinger (1993) followed up this study over a decade later by analysing the most widely used reading series in US literacy instruction. They found a similar framework of ideological reproduction which conveyed the message that a white-male-dominated society is normal and appropriate. They concluded: 'cultural reproduction of sexism, racism and conformity to the job market is an everyday "hidden" presence in the popular literacy reading materials of today's classrooms' (Quigley and Holsinger, 1993: 31). They noted, however, that some teachers refused to use these readers, or used the content to engage learners in critical discussions, and suggested further research on teacher resistance. These studies show how the content of adult education learning materials can be analysed to reveal hidden curricula of dominant ideologies. They also suggest the need for research on the extent to which these ideologies are accepted or resisted by learners and teachers.

Kelly (1991) reported a classroom observation study analysing linguistic interaction in a group of female and male adults on a training course. She found that the men talked considerably longer than the women, and took more turns to speak. The methods by which the men achieved this linguistic domination included impatience, interruptions, sarcasm and aggressive language. The men thus effectively silenced the women and impinged on their learning opportunities – a reproduction of gender inequality with which the tutor colluded. This ethnographic study shows how the processes of adult learning in the classroom can reproduce the wider patterns of inequality in society.

These examples of studies of the adult education curriculum are from advanced capitalist countries: the USA and Britain respectively. Research on the curriculum of adult education in peripheral capitalist societies is a neglected area, despite the fact that Freire's work raised important issues of knowledge, language, consciousness and the social relations of teaching and learning which draw attention to the processes of ideology and social domination within adult education in the South. There are examples of the gender analysis of learning materials, such as the portrayal of women in literacy materials in Bangladesh (Sharafuddin, n.d.), but from the perspective of the political economy of adult education and development much more emphasis should be given to curriculum analysis. Curriculum investigation can reveal how conscious and unconscious choices affecting the content and processes of adult education reflect the structures of inequality in the wider society. The official and hidden curricula mediate social inequality, and are thereby a vehicle of the reproduction and contestation of class, gender, ethnic and racial hierarchies.

A Research Agenda on Social Inequality and Adult Education

The theoretical position elaborated in the sections above is that social inequality shapes the character and consequences of adult education. The task for research, therefore, is to clarify the systems of inequality in a given peripheral capitalist society, and to examine their impact on adult education. It is postulated that inequality

has multiple causes. The three major systems of inequality identified above are class, gender, ethnicity and race. These three
systems need to be analysed separately, and in terms of their
interaction within the capitalist mode of production. This analysis
then has to be linked to adult education in order to determine the
processes by which adult education either reproduces or undermines the patterns of inequality. This involves considering the
effects of inequality on adult education policies, on the way adult
education is organised, and on the curriculum in terms of its topics
and the social dynamics of the teaching and learning situation. It
also involves assessing the consequences of participation in adult
education in terms of the outcomes for the learners in relation to
their economic situation, social position and ideological outlook.

In the light of these assumptions, it is proposed that a research
agenda for analysing social inequality and adult education in the
countries of peripheral capitalism should have the following five
components. The general information generated within the first
three components provides the background for the specific consideration of adult education within the last two, which focus on
reproduction and resistance.

Class

Class denotes the social inequality inherent in the social relations
of production. Class analysis begins by examining the nature of
the mode of production, which in peripheral capitalism involves
specifying how the capitalist mode of production articulates with
pre-capitalist modes of production. It must then identify the classes
and class fractions which comprise the present class structure. The
current situation should be conceived as a particular moment
within the movement of class formation, so that the historical
processes by which the various classes have been formed should
be examined, as well as their probable future trajectory. The
analysis should assess the significance of each class within the
political economy, paying attention to their degree of self-awareness
and organisation. This assessment should be linked to the relationships between classes in terms of conflict, struggle, collaboration
and alliance, in order to indicate how these factors affect the state
and public policies, and how they are leading to change in the

society. Finally, the consequences of class inequality should be elucidated.

Gender

Gender refers to the socially constructed inequalities between women and men. The analysis of gender relations begins with a study of the situation in pre-colonial society, and examines the impact of the penetration of capitalism in the colonial era. It then considers the contemporary pattern of gender relations, paying particular attention to: (a) the household and its social relations of reproduction and sexual division of labour; (b) paid work and the labour market; (c) the state and public policy; and (d) culture and ideology. Gender analysis should reveal how gender inequality is reinforced through institutions, social practices and ideologies. It should show the extent and modalities of individual and collective resistance to patriarchy. The analysis should identify how gender relations intersect with the class structure and class conflicts, and with the ethnic and racial hierarchies and their conflicts. Finally, it should show the social consequences of gender inequality.

Ethnicity and race

Ethnicity denotes the social divisions arising from cultural distinctions between different groups in society, while race denotes divisions established by socially defined distinctions based on physical characteristics. The analysis of ethnicity and race starts with an examination of the ethnic and racial hierarchies that existed in pre-colonial society. It considers the impact of colonialism in reinforcing pre-existing ethnic and racial divisions, and creating new ones. It must then investigate the current pattern of ethnic and racial domination and subordination, and the ways in which it is being reproduced or transformed. This also entails identifying the ethnic and racial tensions and conflicts that exist, and the way these are reflected in ethnic and racist ideologies and modes of organisation, in order to reveal the modalities of ethnic and racial hegemony and resistance. In particular, it should consider the influence of ethnic and racial groups on the state and public policies. The analysis should examine the class nature of ethnicity and race in society, and show how the ethnic and racial hierarchies articulate with the class structure and class conflicts. It should also examine the relation of ethnic, racial and gender inequalities. Finally, the social consequences of ethnic and racial inequality should be elucidated.

Adult education and the reproduction of inequality

Analysis here seeks to show how adult education reproduces the various forms of inequality, both separately and in interaction within the capitalist mode of production. Class analysis considers adult education policies, organisation and curricula in terms of their impact on the reproduction of existing classes and on the formation of emergent classes. It also studies the relationship of adult education to the conflict between classes in terms of how adult education assists dominant classes to contain the opposition of subordinated classes. In terms of gender, analysis examines how adult education reinforces unequal gender relations, and serves to inhibit the questioning of women's subordination. In relation to ethnicity and race, the question is: how does adult education contribute to the processes which form and maintain ethnic and racial identities as part of a hierarchy of dominant and subordinate groups? Inquiry also considers how adult education assists dominant ethnic and racial groups to contain challenges to the legitimacy of the ethnic and racial hierarchies. The final stage of analysis is to examine the extent to which adult education acts to reinforce two or three kinds of inequality in interaction.

Adult education and resistance to inequality

Here, analysis seeks to show how adult education policies, organisation and curricula enable resistance to the various forms of inequality, again both separately and in interaction. In relation to class, it examines the ways in which adult education activities enable subordinated classes to contest their unequal situation. In terms of gender, it investigates how adult education challenges patriarchy and helps to empower women. In terms of ethnicity and race, it studies how adult education enables subordinated ethnic and racial groups to question the ethnic and racial hierarchies, and assert their identity in opposing their ascribed inferiority. The final stage of analysis is to examine the extent to which adult education acts to undermine two or three kinds of inequality in interaction.

In all cases resistance must be examined in terms of how it takes place, why it is undertaken, and what the consequences are, along two dimensions. First, some forms of resistance involve the conscious design of programmes to challenge inequality through the deliberate choice of participants, forms of organisation and curricula. Such programmes often involve organised groups at both the level of planning and the level of participation. Second, there are forms of resistance which are unplanned and individualistic – for example, in the case of learners dropping out or refusing to participate because they perceive a programme as antagonistic to their interests. Such informal modes of resistance may be hard to identify; nevertheless they have a 'hidden logic' (Quigley, 1990) which research should be able to reveal.

The research agenda outlined here is marked by its complexity. On the one hand, there are the three interacting systems of inequality conditioned by the capitalist mode of production. On the other hand, there are various dimensions of adult education which have to be taken into account. The next section illustrates the potential for research on the relationship between social inequality and adult education in peripheral capitalist countries by applying the agenda in the case of Botswana.

Country Case Study: Class, Gender, Ethnicity and Adult Education in Botswana, 1966–91

Class and adult education

The research agenda identifies two dimensions of the interaction of the class structure and adult education for study. First, what is the impact of adult education on the reproduction of existing classes, and on the formation of emergent classes? Second, in what ways do adult education programmes, either deliberately or incidentally, enable subordinated classes to challenge their unequal situation? These questions are now considered in relation to the class structure of Botswana in the period 1966 to 1991.

The majority of adult education programmes were provided by the state, which was dominated by the bourgeoisie, the petty bourgeoisie and the rich peasants. In general, state-provided programmes served the interests of these classes. As in other peripheral capitalist countries, this was most evident in the case of agricultural extension, one of the largest adult education programmes. Gaborone (1986a) shows how agricultural extension services had a clear class content. The programmes introduced in the colonial era – the Co-operation Demonstration Plot Scheme (1947) and the Pupil/Master Farmer Scheme (1962) – were specifically aimed at consolidating the position of rich peasants who owned substantial agricultural resources and employed labour. These schemes involved not only cognitive benefits in terms of skills and knowledge gained, but material assistance through access to means of production, credit and marketing facilities. In 1966 there were 2,165 participants in the Pupil/Master Farmer scheme, a significant proportion of this fraction of the peasantry. In 1973, following concerns that agricultural extension was 'elitist' and reached only the wealthy, state policy moved to 'a more broadly based extension scheme' (Republic of Botswana, 1973a: 5) intended to reach all farmers rather than a select few. Gaborone argues, however, that this form of adult education continued to benefit primarily the rich and middle peasants, owing to the unequal distribution of agricultural resources. Thus, in a study of a farmer training centre in 1980, he found that even when poor peasants participated in farmer education, they lacked the necessary resources to put into practice most of what they had learnt (Gaborone, 1980).

The continuing role of agricultural extension in reproducing the rural class structure was demonstrated in the 1980s with the Arable Lands Development Programme (ALDEP). This programme, which began in 1981, was aimed at households with fewer than forty cattle – that is, the middle and poor peasants. It involved extension support linked to financial assistance to acquire draught power, implements, fencing and water tanks. The assistance included a grant covering 85 per cent of the costs, but a down payment of 15 per cent was required; this proved a major obstacle for the poor peasants. The main beneficiaries were those who already held resources, particularly the middle peasants,

though even rich peasants with more than forty cattle participated, despite the original aim (Arntzen and Silitshena, 1989).

While agricultural extension clearly brought material benefits
to particular classes, other programmes more indirectly served to
reproduce the class hierarchy. An example is the National Literacy
Programme (NLP), started in 1980 and projected by the state as
part of its strategy to 'increase educational opportunities and reduce inequalities in access to education' (Republic of Botswana,
1985: 158). Participants were drawn mainly from the poor peasants and proletariat in the rural areas, and the unskilled and unemployed working class in the urban areas. A major motivation
for the majority was that acquiring literacy and numeracy skills
would help them to obtain wage labour in the formal sector of
the economy (Gaborone, Mutanyatta and Youngman, 1987: 68).
However, the programme provided only minimal skills in Setswana
and numeracy, and very few opportunities to learn skills more
important for employment, such as English and productive skills.
In fact, participation in the programme did not lead to paid
employment for many literacy graduates. The NLP certainly provided educational opportunity to many thousands who had not
previously had access to education; it was therefore a form of
compensatory adult education. But it did not address the fundamental inequality derived from the class structure:

> It can be postulated that the social outcome of the NLP in relation to
> class was that a small proportion of literacy graduates did enter or
> consolidate their position in the working class. A small proportion of
> others were enabled to become petty producers on their own or in
> income-generating groups, while some may have advanced their situ-
> ation within the strata of the peasantry. But it seems likely that the
> overall impact of the NLP was to enable very little upward mobility
> within the existing class structure. The NLP therefore in effect repro-
> duced class divisions and even the aspirations for advancement of the
> learners were articulated within the existing class hierarchy. There is
> no evidence to suggest any activity within the programme (at the level
> of policy or practice) that called into question the class divisions within
> the social order. (Youngman, 1999: 269)

The examples of agricultural extension and the NLP show that
one consequence of the state's adult education programmes was
to reproduce the existing class divisions economically, socially and

ideologically. But whereas the class structure in the advanced capitalist countries is relatively fixed, the ongoing processes of class formation in the periphery give adult education a role not only in reproduction but also in class formation. This is illustrated by case study 1.

Case study 1: extension services for small businesses

An example of adult education specifically designed to contribute to class formation is the extension services provided for small businesses. These adult education programmes promoted the development of the business fraction of the petty bourgeoisie. The promotion of the petty bourgeoisie is a key component of the modernisation theory of development, which sees developing countries as lacking not only capital but also entrepreneurial skills and attitudes. Furthermore, modernisation theory sees the develop- ment of a strong middle class as the basis of political stability. After Independence the Botswana state, following the precepts of modernisation theory embodied in its development strategy, sought to foster a strong class of indigenous entrepreneurs. This policy reflected the interests of the ruling Botswana Democratic Party's coalition of classes, and opened up economic opportunities which had been limited by colonial restrictions on African businesses. From 1966 onwards the state had an explicit commitment to promoting indigenous small business, as stated in *National Develop- ment Plan 1970–75*: 'The encouragement of local entrepreneurial talent will continue to be a cardinal feature of Government policy' (Republic of Botswana, 1970: 64).

The growth of the business petty bourgeoisie during the 1970s influenced the new policies that followed from the *National Policy on Economic Opportunities* of 1982 (Republic of Botswana, 1982). These policies included capital assistance to enter the manufacturing sector through the Financial Assistance Policy and 'reservation' policies in industry and commerce, restricting certain kinds of business activity to citizen-owned enterprises. A significant number of citizen-owned small-scale enterprises (i.e. those with ten or fewer employees) were established in the manufacturing, trading, con- struction, service and transportation sectors of the economy. The theme of a strong small-business sector continued in the late 1980s as the ideas of neoliberal development theory led to increasing emphasis on private-sector development. It is within this overall policy context of promoting the formation and consolidation of the business fraction of the petty bourgeoisie that an explicit role for adult education was enunciated. This was made clear soon after Independence in *National Development Plan 1970–75*: 'The Government recognises the need to provide an extension service to assist new entrepreneurs' (Republic of Botswana, 1970: 60). The organisation of the state's adult education programme for small business evolved after the establishment of the Ministry of Commerce and Industry in 1973. It had two main phases: from 1974 to 1987, and from 1987 onwards.

In 1974 the Batswana Enterprises Development Programme was started with the goal 'to provide assistance for the development of enterprises owned and managed by local entrepreneurs so that citizens may play a greater part in commercial and industrial development' (Republic of Botswana, 1973b: 248). The Batswana Enterprises Development Unit (BEDU) within the Ministry of Commerce and Industry (largely funded by SIDA, NORAD and the United Nations Industrial Development Organisation, and using USA Peace Corps volunteers) aimed to provide small entrepreneurs with advice, training and access to loan capital. BEDU initially centred its attention on developing industrial estates, and providing training and finance to small businesses on these estates. By 1979 it was supporting seventy-eight businesses (Republic of Botswana, 1980a: 206). After 1980 it placed increased emphasis on extending its support beyond the estates, and its loan facilities were handed over to the National Development Bank.

Alongside BEDU's service to entrepreneurs in the manufacturing sector, in 1974 the Ministry of Commerce and Industry established the Small Traders' Extension Service for the commercial sector. In 1977 this was renamed the Business Advisory Service (BAS). At this time, a US non-governmental organisation, Partnership for Productivity (PFP), sponsored by the Botswana Development Corporation and funded by USAID, also developed extension services for the trade sector. The two bodies worked together, with BAS operating in the north of the country and PFP in the south, until 1982, after which PFP shifted its role to running a credit scheme (Swartzendruber, 1988: 12). The third component of the

state's services was established in 1980 as part of the rural development and employment creation focus of *National Development Plan
1979–1985*. This was a cadre of Rural Industrial Officers (funded
by USAID and staffed by Peace Corps) based in district centres,
with the brief to promote small-scale enterprises in the rural areas
through identifying viable activities and entrepreneurs, and organising appropriate training.

During the 1980s, as the emphasis on the private sector increased, it became clear that the three components of the small-
business extension services had begun to overlap and needed
rationalisation. In 1987 the Ministry of Commerce and Industry
therefore created the Integrated Field Services (IFS) to form a
single extension service, to which SIDA and USAID provided
significant capital and technical assistance (Integrated Field Services, 1988: 23). IFS focused on technical and management training, and on providing advice on marketing and access to finance,
especially through the Financial Assistance Policy. It developed a
network of field offices throughout the country, with the former
BEDU estates playing the role of 'industrial resource centres' for
training in areas such as construction, metalwork and garment
production. In 1990/91 it had eighteen field offices and eight
resource centres (Department of Industrial Affairs, 1991: 23).

The content of the training provided by the extension services
for small businesses remained consistent throughout the period in
terms of its objectives of providing technical and business management skills, and developing the 'entrepreneurial spirit'. The IFS
field officers were responsible for identifying the training needs of
entrepreneurs, and for co-ordinating training activities. A wide
range of short courses was offered in various places throughout
the country, taught by IFS staff and other resource personnel. In
1991, the IFS catalogue included over three hundred courses. Novice
and upgrading courses were provided in a variety of technical
skills, ranging from bakery to metalwork. Management training
included financial management (for example, book-keeping) and
business management. After 1987, a key component was a five-day
course based on 'Improve Your Business' materials, developed by
the ILO (International Labour Organisation) with SIDA support,
which focused on management and accounting. The overall aim
of management training was to convey not only specific skills but

also relevant knowledge and attitudes: 'to give an entrepreneur a full package of business ideas', so that she or he 'is better oriented about the business field' (Integrated Field Services, 1988: 11).

The adult education programmes provided by the state to develop the small-business class had comparatively wide coverage. Between 1985 and 1990, for example, the IFS provided training to 2,827 entrepreneurs (Republic of Botswana, 1991a: 167). These programmes were complemented by the work of a number of non-governmental organisations, such as the Institute of Development Management, the Botswana Confederation of Commerce, Industry and Manpower, and the Rural Industries Innovation Centre, all of which ran short courses for small-enterprise development.

This form of adult education had particular economic, social and ideological consequences. At the economic level, it is evident that these extension services provided the training and access to credit which enabled a proportion of the small enterprises to be economically viable, and therefore become a basis for accumulation by some members of the class. On the other hand, a proportion of businesses no doubt failed. By 1983, for example, a third of the businesses supported by BEDU had collapsed (Chipasula and Miti, 1987: 76), thus weaker members of the class may have slipped down the class hierarchy. At the social level, it is hypothesised that economic success increased social status. However, in small rural communities, where there were residues of pre-capitalist ideology, it may be that increased wealth disturbed social relations. In a sociological study on small enterprises in four villages in 1981, 88 per cent of those interviewed agreed with the statement 'It is often thought that when people become wealthy it creates jealousy and the person who becomes rich is not liked' (Narayan-Parker, 1983: 102–3). At the ideological level, a major goal of the programmes was to inculcate an enterprise culture, developing and reinforcing positive attitudes towards capitalism and the ideology of free enterprise (profit, competition, risk, and so forth).

Finally, we should note that within this process of class formation there was a significant gender dimension. A number of studies considered the constraints facing women small entrepreneurs (see, for example, Somolekae, 1992). A significant number of small-enterprise proprietors were women. They were largely operational in stereotyped business activities deriving from women's role in the gender division of labour within the household: crafts, garment production and food preparation. While they faced many general problems in developing and consolidating their businesses – such as competition from South African imports and high utility costs – they also faced particular problems as women. These problems included legal constraints, such as the requirement of a husband's signature for loan applications, and social constraints such as household responsibilities. This latter problem had an impact on their participation in adult education: 'Most female entrepreneurs have to divide their time between business and domestic work. As a consequence, many of them find it difficult to spare time to attend training courses' (Silitshena, 1992: 39). The constraints faced by women led to a number of proposals for designing extension programmes that should specifically address their situation, and thus facilitate their participation in the formation of the business petty bourgeoisie.

Adult education and class resistance

These examples illustrate the role of adult education programmes in class reproduction and formation. In the period under review, there is very little evidence of class resistance through adult education. The research agenda suggests two modes of resistance: specifically designed programmes and informal learner behaviour. In the first case, attention must be directed to organisations which appear to represent the interests of particular dominated classes. It might be expected, for example, that trade unions would provide education designed to strengthen the position of the working class and challenge capitalist inequalities. The programmes of the Trade Union Education Centre established in 1972, however, were restricted to narrow technical issues of running unions rather than developing a critical consciousness of capitalist hegemony (Mogalakwe, 1997).

One of the few adult education programmes designed to challenge class inequalities was the weavers' factory established in 1973 in the small village of Oodi in Kgatleng district, a major area of labour migration. It was set up by a Swedish couple with the explicit purpose of providing an alternative model of development based on co-operative rural industry. The factory workers were drawn mainly from the poor peasantry, and were unskilled with little formal education. They had previously been migrant workers in South Africa, domestic workers in Botswana towns, or engaged in agriculture in the village. The factory, which employed about fifty people, provided full-time employment and reasonable wages. From 1975 onwards it contributed 25 per cent of its profits to a special village development fund.

The factory was conceived not only as an economic institution but also as an adult education process. The intention behind it was to develop the workers' skills and awareness so that they could produce high-quality articles, manage the factory themselves, and take a role in village development. It was therefore designed to develop rural proletarians with the confidence and capability to participate in economic and social decision-making. The organisational form of the production co-operative explicitly challenged capitalist social relations of production and class subordination.

The adult education process involved both formal tuition (for example, in technical and management skills) and informal learning through the efforts required to take collective responsibility and through the creative work of producing narrative tapestries. The Swedish facilitators deliberately sought – through a Freireian pedagogy of dialogue – to develop a critical consciousness of society, discussing concepts such as migrant labour, exploitation, oppression, racial conflict, worker control, co-operation, national liberation and social commitment. Many of these socioeconomic and political issues were reflected in the tapestries (Byram, 1980a). The outcomes of the adult education activities for the factory workers were increased security and independence at the economic level, a change in status at the social level, and greater critical awareness at the ideological level.

Because such a large proportion of the poor peasantry were women, the factory also had a significant gender dimension: 70 per cent of the workers were women. While on the one hand the predominance of women may have reflected a perception that weaving was 'women's work', on the other the absence of men in the South African mines, and the poverty of many women, meant that the new economic opportunity inevitably attracted more female workers. The impact of the factory was to strengthen the economic situation of women workers, and increase their personal independence. It gave women experience in managing their own situation, and raised their awareness of their subordination and the issues of gender inequality. There was evidence of 'women's growing assertiveness and self-confidence in running their own affairs' (Byram, 1980a: 237). The factory is an isolated example of adult education explicitly designed to challenge the unequal rural class structure and gender relations.

The second form of resistance is informal learner behaviour, which might range from active contestation of a teacher's ideological viewpoint to less articulate reactions such as dropping out. The 'hidden logic' behind a variety of learner responses is difficult to identify but Gaborone provides two examples. He suggests that the high dropout rate of subordinated rural class members from the radio learning group campaign in 1976 on the new land tenure policy constituted 'voting with their feet', a spontaneous form of resistance to learning about a policy which was against their class interests (Gaborone, 1986a: 353). In his evaluation of a farmer training centre he found that one explanation for not attending the courses was the perception that they were only for 'master farmers' (i.e. rich peasants) who have sufficient resources (Gaborone, 1980: 10). Thus dropout and non-attendance in relation to adult education activities which did not represent their class interests constituted informal resistance by poor peasants.

Gender inequality

The patterns of gender inequality that were derived from precolonial society and modified under the impact of colonialism provided the historical basis of the gender relations which obtained after Independence. The nature of gender inequality between 1966 and 1991 can be considered along four dimensions.

The first dimension is that of the household. The major phenomenon in this period was the continuation of the colonial trend towards *de jure* and *de facto* female-headed households as migration for work within Botswana expanded. The marriage rate declined, and men and women were more likely to enter transient sexual relationships. By 1991, women headed about 45 per cent of households in urban areas and 50 per cent in rural areas (Central

Statistics Office, 1994: 244, 246). Such households were essentially matrifocal, often comprised of a mother, unmarried daughter and grandchildren. In these households, unmarried women were the main economic actors and decision-makers, the evidence suggesting that their ties to extended families, male relatives and reciprocal assistance networks were diminishing.

While there were obviously differentiations among female-headed households, they were disproportionately among the poorest groups in society in terms of income and productive assets. There were many constraints on their ability to be productive and self-reliant. In the rural areas, for example, such households usually held few or no cattle, managed low acreages of land, and could not produce their own food needs. Women had to undertake a variety of alternative livelihood strategies to meet their needs for cash, including casual wage labour and petty trading and services. Often state transfers, such as feeding schemes, played an important role in the domestic economy. It was calculated that in 1985, 69 per cent of urban and 73 per cent of rural female-headed households had an income below the Effective Minimal Level required to meet basic needs (Republic of Botswana and UNICEF, 1989: 60–61). Thus the poverty of female-headed households in both rural and urban areas was a significant feature of gender inequality in this period. The feminisation of poverty constituted an intersection of gender and class differentiation.

The second dimension is that of work for cash and female participation in the labour market. As capitalist relations of production came to dominate the social formation after 1966, women became increasingly involved in paid work. By the end of the period, a significant proportion were working for cash outside the household, and thus engaging in transformed socioeconomic relations. Their involvement in the labour market, however, was on unequal terms compared to that of men. In 1991, the labour-force participation rate was 50 per cent for women and 91 per cent for men (Republic of Botswana, 1994: 12), and men held two-thirds of formal-sector jobs (UNDP, Republic of Botswana and UNICEF, 1993: 21). Women tended to be in stereotyped work such as nursing, teaching and domestic service, which reflected their traditional place in the sexual division of labour. There were significant earning-power differentials between women and men in the formal sector, so that income inequality had a gendered character (CSO and SIDA, 1991: 56). Women predominated in the urban and rural informal sector and in rural public works schemes, where income was low and insecure. Furthermore – with respect to unemployment rates – in 1991, 17 per cent of women were unemployed compared to 12 per cent of men (UNDP, Republic of Botswana and UNICEF, 1993: 23). The overall picture in relation to the labour market is that women were disproportionately in low-paid, unskilled and insecure work, giving gender inequality a significant class dimension as they were clustered in the rural and urban proletariat.

The third dimension is that of the gender biases of the state and public policy. The fundamental position of the state was expressed in an early statement in *National Development Plan 1970–75* (Republic of Botswana, 1970: 12) to the effect that most women 'will assume the natural role of home-maker'. Most development policies conceived of women as home-makers, largely engaged in household production and child-rearing in families headed by men. In line with international trends, from the mid-1970s there was increased concern with 'women in development', and some policies – such as the Arable Land Development Programme and the Financial Assistance Policy – had special provisions favouring women. In 1981 a Women's Affairs Unit was established, but it remained underresourced and marginal, and its draft National Policy on Women in Development (1988) was not adopted. In some respects state activity improved the situation of women – for example, in terms of health status – but it did not confront dominant stereotypes about their role in society, or seek to alter the balance of gender relations.

Women had little success in entering the realm of political decision-making. Although after Independence they were given the right to participate in the village meeting-place, they remained peripheral in that forum, whose significance for public policy-making was in any case in decline. In political parties, leadership positions were dominated by men. In Parliament, female membership did not exceed 5 per cent of MPs, and only two women became Cabinet members. The legal status of women remained one of inequality in relation to men; at least twenty-five statutes had provisions which discriminated against them, including important areas related to marriage and property which perpetuated male control (Republic of Botswana, 1994: 31). Thus, while women did become increasingly active in public affairs, and did have some new rights in post-colonial society, in practice many constraints on their equal participation in the public domain remained.

Finally, it is important to note that cultural and ideological practices continued to reinforce the subordinate position of women in society. The processes of socialisation raised girls and boys differently, and reproduced unequal gender relations. Cultural values and social norms continued to regard women as minors dependent on men. Thus the ideology of male superiority inherited from pre-capitalist society proved resilient despite the many economic, political and social changes that took place from 1966 to 1991.

In the face of the powerful social forces reinforcing gender inequality, there was little organised resistance to male domination. At the individual level, there were undoubtedly various forms of self-assertion and efforts to reduce dependency on men and expand personal autonomy. It has been argued, for example, that many women chose to have children but not to marry, in order to retain independence from male restrictions exerted through the family structure. Thus the actual behaviour of individuals implicitly challenged patriarchal ideology. At the collective level, however, there was little action on behalf of women's rights. Most women's organisations, such as the Botswana Council of Women, supported the status quo – for example, running beauty contests to raise funds. Only the Emang Basadi Women's Association, established in 1986, had an explicitly feminist agenda: 'to mobilise for the removal of discriminatory laws that undermine the social, political and economic development of women; to undertake actions that enhance women's position to develop themselves socially, politically and economically' (NORAD, 1989: 137). In response, the male-biased state labelled the Association's activity against discriminatory laws the work of unrepresentative, frustrated women under foreign influence, and appealed to tradition for support. Women's collective action in the period did not develop the strength to alter the balance of power between men and women that was upheld by the state and by male-dominated social and economic institutions.

Gender inequality and adult education

It was in this context of female subordination and inequality that gendered forms of adult education manifested themselves between 1966 and 1991. The most striking feature of adult education is the extent to which prevailing assumptions about women's role in re-production and in the sexual division of labour permeated its policy and practice. In terms of the research agenda, the overall impact of adult education was to reproduce women's subordinate position in society. Very little adult education challenged the ideology and practices of patriarchy in an organised way, although experience at the personal level may have had contradictory outcomes.

The provision of adult education can be considered in terms of two kinds of programme: those open to all adults, and those targeted specifically at women. Programmes open to all adults usually had a gendered character, owing to the social reality of gender relations. Thus the courses offered by commercial schools in subjects such as secretarial skills attracted predominantly women students, because within the labour market secretarial work was identified as women's work. Agricultural extension provided an-other example, as the mainly male extension officers tended to work with those who owned productive assets (especially cattle), who were mostly men. Where they did work with women – as Gaborone (1986a: 392) has pointed out – these were rich women with assets, so that class differentiations were reinforced.

The case of the National Literacy Programme (NLP) also illus-trates how a programme open to all adults had particular effects in relation to gender inequality (Youngman, 1999). Almost two-thirds of the learners in the NLP during the 1980s were women – for example, the figure in 1989 was 62.1 per cent (Department of Non Formal Education, 1990: 8). The reason for this high rate of participation is to be found in the large numbers of female-headed households and the disproportionately large numbers of women among the poor, unemployed and unskilled adults who are the programme's target.

To a large extent it is apparent that participation in the NLP served to reinforce women's social position. For example, one purpose of literacy that often appeared in official statements was to learn how to read and write letters. The significance of this is that many women in the rural areas were on their own because the men had migrated in search of wage labour, so that letters were an important form of communication. Thus the NLP reinforced the status quo of migrant labour and women's marginalisation. Furthermore, there is evidence of men being reluctant to allow women to join the programme (Gaborone, Mutanyatta and Youngman, 1987: 68), and of female participants going to great lengths to conceal their participation from their partners (Gaborone, 1986b).

The implication of emancipatory possibilities suggested by the men's reluctance, however, indicates that to a certain extent the acquisition of literacy may have been a step for individual women towards exerting greater control over their own situation. Gaborone (1986b: 2) quotes one participant:

> My partner used to keep two bank accounts, one for us and the other for girlfriends. And because I was unable to read and make sense of this, he used to leave information lying about. I did not know how much he earned or his wage. But I now know and make him account for every thebe ['penny'] he spends.

It is therefore apparent that the personal effect of the NLP for some women learners was to pose a challenge to their social situation. The NLP, however, had no policy commitment to promote forms of consciousness and collective social action that would enable women to free themselves from patriarchal oppression. Thus it reproduced the gender inequalities in society, while at the same time interacting with the latent contradictions in unequal male–female relationships in ways which had the potential to bring these disparities into question.

There were various adult education programmes directed specifically to women as a target group, which reflected prevailing assumptions about their role in society. Thus many health extension activities addressed women in terms of their reproductive role, focusing on maternal and child health. The main health extension cadre, the Family Welfare Educators, were overwhelmingly women, their title and composition revealing the premiss of their work, which included talks on topics like family planning at venues such as antenatal clinics. The agenda of health education was not a radical one (say, of stressing women's control over their own bodies) but, rather, one of health measures within existing family structures. The family was seen primarily as the domain of women, and the possibility of developing new male roles in the family was ignored.

Some women's programmes sought to reach women who were otherwise excluded from adult education activities theoretically open to all. This was the case with agricultural extension between 1975 and the mid-1980s, when policies were followed which reflected international trends on women in development. In 1974, a British consultant, working as part of an advisory team on agricultural extension funded by British aid, submitted a report entitled *Women's Involvement in Agriculture in Botswana* (Bond, 1974). The report demonstrated the important role of women in crop production and small-stock rearing, but showed that the extension services, comprising mainly male officers, were 'reaching families through the men, and this favours households headed by a male' (Bond, 1974: 2). It therefore recommended a new extension service directed towards women. Although the idea of a new service was not accepted, the Ministry of Agriculture established a headquarters post of Agricultural Officer/Women's Extension in 1975, to which the consultant was appointed. The aim of the post was to ensure that more women were reached within the general agricultural extension programme. The strategy followed included special efforts to involve women in extension activities, encouraging the election of women to Farmers' Committees, working with organised and informal groups of women, and providing special women's courses at the Rural Training Centres, which were short-course residential centres for adults run by the Ministry of Agriculture (Bettles, 1980: 33).

The women's courses were intended to cover agriculture and homecraft topics, and in 1976 two Rural Home Instructors were appointed to two centres. These instructors were home economists, and they weighted the courses to homecraft skills, reinforcing the stereotype that women's courses = home economics = domestic topics, and neglecting the reality of women as farmers. In 1980/81 the courses were evaluated from a radical feminist perspective (Higgins, 1981). The evaluation concluded that separate courses for women were valuable, but that they must reflect the many responsibilities in women's lives, not just women as home-makers.

The author recommended a new title, 'Women's Farmers' Courses', and a new curriculum with four components: Home Management Education, Agricultural Education, Social and Civic Education (including literacy) and Education for Income Generating Activities (Higgins, 1981: 103–7). She felt that the new curriculum had the potential to challenge gender inequality.

Following her report, she engaged in a curriculum development project aimed at introducing the broader approach to the women's courses (Higgins, 1982). However, her subsequent analysis of the courses (Higgins, 1984) revealed that the attempt to change the curriculum had not been successful. She reached two major conclusions: first, that the danger of separate provision of programmes for women is that they can entrench women's marginality by tending towards domestic topics and exclusion from the more powerful knowledge embedded in mainstream courses (for example, information about sponge cakes rather than sources of credit). Separate courses may therefore increase social subordination rather than facilitate empowerment. Second, the tendency towards the domestic was exacerbated by the fact that the teachers' background was in home economics, and they were unable to transcend the stereotyped definitions of their subject. The nature of home economics is considered in case study 2.

Case study 2: home economics education

In 1975, the Economic Commission for Africa estimated that 50 per cent of all the non-formal adult education offered to women in Africa was in home economics (Rogers, 1980: 88). Similarly, in Botswana a significant proportion of adult education in which women participated between 1966 and 1991 was in home economics. The economic, social and ideological consequence of home economics education, however, was to reinforce female subordination. Indeed, the synonym, domestic science, provides an echo of Freire's concept of education for domestication. Rogers (1980: 78–120) discussed at length the role of home economics in Third World societies in domesticating women and perpetuating discrimination. She focused especially on the income-generating projects for women advocated by aid agencies from the mid-1970s as a means of 'integrating women in development'. She concluded that women's projects had almost exclusively involved home economics training and their overall impact had been to relegate women to marginal and stereotyped economic activity. The experience of Botswana is supportive of her conclusions.

The origins of home economics for adult women in Botswana are to be found in the work of the missionaries in the pre-colonial and colonial eras. The wives of the London Missionary Society missionaries provided sewing classes to Batswana women from as early as 1831. Subsequently, in the early colonial period, the wives and female missionaries continued to give informal housework training to young women in the Bangwato and Bakwena areas, focusing on European foods, clothes and housekeeping procedures. Mafela (1994a) argues that this adult education conveyed a sexist ideology derived from Victorian England, and served to promote a European middle-class notion of the Christian family and female domesticity.

The missionary effort to reconstruct African womanhood took a more institutionalised form in the Mochudi Homecraft Centre, founded by the Dutch Reformed Mission in 1943. The Centre offered a residential programme for young women aimed at training them to be suitable wives for educated Christian Batswana men. However, although the main thrust of the Centre's training was directed at women's role in the household, from the 1950s onwards the curriculum had a more commercial emphasis, responding to the penetration of capitalism and the perception of Batswana that domestic science could open up opportunities for cash income (Mafela, 1994b). This illustrates the duality of home economics, in that it mainly prepares women for domestic labour while also potentially equipping them for entry into wage labour. Although it prepares women to enter the capitalist labour market, it restricts them to gender-stereotyped work activities. This duality became more apparent during the 1980s.

After 1966, home economics was a significant programme of both the state's extension agencies and the voluntary women's organisations. Initially the main organisation responsible was the Department of Community Development, which ran a home economics pilot scheme from 1967 to 1969 to investigate the educational needs of women, and lay the basis of future programmes. Although the report on the scheme (Galetshoge, 1970) recommended its transfer to the Ministry of Agriculture, this was not implemented. The provision of home economics courses remained a major element of the work of community development extension throughout the period, amplified by its support to women's organisations.

During the 1970s, the adult education branch of the Ministry of Education also began a programme in home economics. In 1976 the newly established Botswana Extension College (BEC) started the Village Home Affairs Leadership programme intended to train leaders who would learn skills and then instruct other women in the villages. It appeared, however, that the participants were often elite women interested in acquiring prestige skills (such as cake making) for themselves rather than teaching the rural poor (Rogers, 1980: 92). In 1978 the programme was renamed Skills for Development; it was supported by printed materials and a weekly radio programme (Botswana Extension College, 1978b). It became part of the provision of the Department of Non Formal Education when it absorbed the BEC later in 1978.

Until the early 1980s, it can be argued that home economics education for adult women concentrated largely on their domestic role. However, the *National Development Plan, 1979–1985* (Republic of Botswana, 1980a) introduced a new emphasis on income-generating activities and the creation of rural employment opportunities. This coincided with international trends towards the establishment of income-generating projects specifically targeted at women as a means of expanding their access to cash incomes. In this context, home economics was perceived as a means of providing skills for income generation.

The new policies and projects of the 1980s were significant because they related to a central problem identified by women. Surveys suggested that 'the major need articulated by women was for a regular cash income to help them meet their basic needs' (Godt and Nkwe, 1985: vi). However, the adult education activities for women around this issue were largely unsuccessful in terms of expanding their access to income and employment, and in reducing gender inequality. A number of surveys during the period (such as Godt and Nkwe, 1985; Jones-Dube, 1990) showed that training for women was confined to production skills in 'women's activities', and failed to teach broader business skills. Many of the women's income-generating projects failed, or produced only very small cash returns inconsistent with the time and energy expended. The result was that small projects did not lead to social and economic empowerment.

This was evident in the National Literacy Programme. A major element of post-literacy provision was home economics through the Skills for Development programme, whose participants in 1988–89 were 98 per cent female (SIAPAC, 1990: 34). Most of the income-generating groups that the Department of Non Formal Education promoted amongst literacy graduates involved tradition-ally female occupations, such as knitting, sewing, weaving, basketry and baking (Department of Non Formal Education, 1990: 3–4). Thus, while women's participation in post-literacy projects some-times generated a small cash income which provided material benefits and greater personal autonomy, it simultaneously entrench-ed the individual in the lowest levels of the capitalist production system in stereotyped women's work. Post-literacy projects there-fore did not alter the status quo of gender and class inequality.

By the end of the 1980s the home economics programmes provided by state extension agencies and women's voluntary organ-isations constituted a relatively large programme of adult education activity, reaching over a thousand households in 1988/9 (SIAPAC, 1990: 50). The aspirations of participants surveyed in 1989 focused on improving their opportunities to get work (60 per cent), though many emphasised the home benefits of their training (SIAPAC, 1990: 38). These aspirations reflected the dual nature of home economics for adults. Both aspects of home economics, however, reproduced gender inequality. Home economics directed at home-making and the family accepted prevailing assumptions about women's role in domestic labour; while its extension to training for the sphere of paid work confined women to gender-stereotyped economic activity which was poorly paid and insecure. Adult home economics, taught by women to women, served to perpetuate women's marginalisation from social and economic power.

Summary

Gender inequality during the period 1966 to 1991 was marked by the poverty of many female-headed households and the weaker position of women in the labour market, and by the ideologies and practices of female subordination. The outcomes of participation in adult education by women seldom changed their social and economic situation, or raised their consciousness about the possibilities for change. The lack of adult education programmes designed to challenge the status quo can be attributed to the lack of organisations with a feminist agenda which could mobilise collective action. Only towards the end of the period, after 1986, did the Emang Basadi Women's Association arrange adult education activities on women's rights designed to empower women. Thus I conclude that the vast majority of adult education programmes in the period functioned to reproduce gender inequality.

Ethnic inequality

The colonial period was important in the historical processes of shaping ethnic identities and establishing their significance within society (Datta and Murray, 1989). The ethnic hierarchy that had been consolidated during the colonial era was reinforced at Independence. The new name of the country, Botswana, meant 'the place of the Setswana-speakers', who constituted approximately 80 per cent of the population. This confirmed symbolically the hegemony of Setswana culture. The Constitution established an upper House of Parliament, the House of Chiefs, comprised of the main groups within the Setswana-speakers. The public policies of the post-colonial state reproduced this hegemony, and its policy of nation-building identified the idea of the nation with Setswana culture (Datta and Murray, 1989: 70). For example, Setswana was declared the national language (alongside English as the official language), and the languages of other ethnic groups were prohibited in educational activities and the media. The question of ethnic identity became a taboo subject, and the state promoted strongly an ideology of national unity based on Setswana dominance rather than cultural diversity. The state labelled as 'tribalism' any activity that questioned the domination of the Setswana-speaking ethnic group.

However, there were various forms of resistance to this ethnic hegemony. Ethnicity was a dimension of opposition party politics. The Botswana Independence Party and the Botswana National

Front (BNF) mobilised support among the Bayei in Ngamiland, and the Botswana People's Party mobilised support from the Bakalanga in North East District and Francistown. All three parties, at various times, secured parliamentary and local council seats on the basis of ethnic support. The BNF had an explicit policy of equality for all ethnic groups. Within civil society there were debates around the use of languages other than Setswana. In 1982 the Society for the Promotion of Ikalanga Language was established, and in 1990 it was reported that the Bakgalagadi were in the process of establishing a society to promote their language and culture (Kebaagetse, 1990: 12). The issue of representation in the House of Chiefs by other ethnic groups was continually raised, with the Constitution being identified as an instrument of ethnic domination (see, for example, Bule, 1991: 16). In the period up to 1991, the state regarded the main threat to the legitimacy of the ethnic hierarchy as coming from the largest and strongest minority, the Bakalanga, who were perceived as trying to infiltrate key political and economic institutions. The state succeeded in containing ethnic opposition to its legitimacy, and there were no open ethnic conflicts. Nevertheless, a variety of ethnic tensions were present in the society, and inequality between ethnic groups was evident despite their formal equality before the law.

Inequality was most manifest in the relationship between ethnicity and the class structure. Setswana-speakers were distributed throughout the class hierarchy. The class situation of minority ethnic groups was largely a product of their mode of incorporation into pre-colonial Batswana polities in terms of access to the key means of production. For example, the agriculturalist Bakalanga, in the northeastern part of the country, retained access to land and other means of agricultural production; and the pastoralist Ovaherero in the northwest retained their cattle herds and grazing areas. Such groups appeared to be evenly distributed within the class structure. However, the ethnic groups incorporated as serfs in the pre-colonial era were dispossessed of their livestock and land. The Basarwa (who speak a number of San languages) were labelled pejoratively 'Bushmen', a generic term that referred to people without livestock, living by hunting and gathering and therefore considered economically inferior. In fact there is considerable evidence that they had a history of stockholding prior to the dispossession of their herds by the Batswana from the late eighteenth century onwards. Indeed, one group which managed to retain its herds, the Bateti, were not categorised as Basarwa even though they are San-speaking, showing that the ethnic category Basarwa had a clear class dimension (Wilmsen, 1989: 278, 327).

The dispossessed Basarwa were reduced to a propertyless class of serfs, alienated from the land and working as herding labour on the cattleposts of Batswana and Ovaherero and the freehold farms of white Afrikaaner settlers, or forced into foraging in the more inaccessible parts of the Kalahari Desert and forming 'a secondary labor pool, maintained at no expense to the controlling classes' (Wilmsen, 1989: 133). In the post-colonial era, the Basarwa and other marginalised ethnic groups such as the Bakgalagadi constituted the majority of the rural proletariat, working for irregular payments in cash and kind. For Basarwa women, to the subordination of ethnicity and class was added the oppression of gender, as there was evidence of sexual exploitation by Setswana-speaking males as well as physical mistreatment by Basarwa men (Mogwe, 1992: 26–9).

Ethnic inequality and adult education

The research agenda suggests two dimensions of the interaction between ethnicity and adult education for analysis. First, in what ways does adult education contribute to the reproduction of the ethnic hierarchy? Second, to what extent do adult education activities enable subordinated ethnic groups to contest their unequal situation? It is postulated that adult education which focuses on homogeneity as the basis of national integration tends to reproduce ethnic inequalities, while activities that value ethnic diversity and the recognition of difference pose a challenge to the hierarchical order.

The majority of adult education programmes were provided by the state and therefore embodied the state's position that ethnicity is a problem. Thus they reflected the dominance of Setswana culture. This can be illustrated by the National Literacy Programme where the decision was taken at the planning stage in 1979 to use Setswana as the medium of instruction despite the preference of the professionals involved for the use of mother-tongue instruction:

> It was at this juncture that political rather than educational or func-
> tional considerations carried most weight. To achieve national unity,
> there had to be the submergence of local, tribal, languages; this was
> the practice in formal education and this example had likewise to be
> followed in non-formal education despite the fact that this seemed likely
> to decrease the motivation of some of the potential learners. (Townsend-
> Coles, 1988: 40)

In practice, as the professionals had expected, language became an obstacle and a cause of dropout. Indeed, dropout may have been a passive form of resistance to Setswana hegemony, as Nganunu (1982) suggested in her study of some Bakalanga literacy participants. Nevertheless, there appeared to be little pressure from learners to change the policy, because for some minority ethnic groups learning literacy in Setswana was perceived as increasing the possibilities for participation in the society and economy. My analysis (Youngman, 1999: 270) of the relationship of the National Literacy Programme (NLP) to the ethnic hierarchy concludes as follows:

> It is suggested that participation in the NLP had contradictory out-
> comes for Botswana's subordinated ethnic groups. The acquisition of
> literacy in Setswana ... may have enabled their fuller participation in
> the mainstream of society. But the terms of that participation were
> likely to involve reduced cultural identity and greater incorporation
> into the hegemonic culture. Also, though it may have reduced the
> extremes of economic exploitation experienced by some ethnic groups,
> it was likely to provide little advancement within the overall class struc-
> ture. Thus any transition from marginality to incorporation which was
> facilitated by literacy would not have significantly altered the pattern
> of social inequality, and may indeed have served to legitimate it by
> reducing the visibility of ethnic discrimination.

A similar conclusion may be reached on a radio learning campaign on civics education (*Lesedi La Puso*) undertaken in the Kalahari in 1979 (Byram, 1980b). The campaign was carried out in Setswana, which few participants had as a mother tongue, with the aim of increasing people's knowledge about government institutions and their own role within a representative democracy. It is probable that rather than empowering the ethnic minorities in the region (mainly Basarwa and Bakgalagadi), the campaign served to integrate them further into the status quo.

Only a few programmes showed a concern with cultural diversity, and these were provided by non-governmental organisations. Some of the ethnic minorities have written languages but, in the face of official discouragement, very little adult literacy was undertaken in these languages. An exception was the Adult Education Centre run by the Lutheran Church in Sehitwa, which taught literacy in the language of the Ovaherero in 1985–86. The University of Botswana's Institute of Adult Education (IAE) ran a 'Cultural Development Project' between 1979 and 1982 which organised cultural groups and festivals amongst three different ethnic groups in the central and northeastern areas of the country. The project sought to stimulate cultural identity and assertion, and was based on the idea that national unity requires a positive recognition of cultural differences between ethnic groups (Nfila, 1985). Its cultural action, however, remained in the domain of the performing arts, and did not directly challenge economic and political structures. In fact, no adult education programme in the period attempted specifically to empower members of a subordinated group to challenge ethnic inequality. We can therefore conclude that the overwhelming effect of adult education in the period 1966 to 1991 was to reinforce the unequal ethnic hierarchy. Case study 3 illustrates this conclusion.

Case study 3: the Remote Area Development Programme and adult education

The anthropological research undertaken in the 1960s and early 1970s documented the economic and political marginalisation of the Basarwa, who were portrayed at the time as hunters and gatherers representing a pristine aboriginal way of life. In response to this publicity, the state established a Bushmen Development Programme in 1974 to integrate them gradually into the wider society. In 1976, however, the Rural Incomes Distribution Survey (Republic of Botswana, 1976) revealed extensive rural poverty affecting other ethnic groups besides Basarwa. Furthermore, the establishment of a programme targeting a particular ethnic group had been criticised within Botswana as a form of 'separate development', echoing the racially and ethnically based strategies of neighbouring South Africa. The programme was therefore broadened in concept in 1977, and renamed the Remote Area Development Programme, aimed at

> rural citizens who (a) are poor (below the poverty datum line, (b) live outside villages (or on the fringes), (c) are generally non-livestock owners, (d) depend at least partially on hunting and gathering for daily subsistence, (e) are often culturally or linguistically distinct. (Hitchcock, 1992: 7)

The programme thus came to focus on the situation of all those who lived in small communities outside recognised villages. This categorisation incorporated people from a variety of other ethnic minorities, but very few Setswana-speakers. The programme's focus on 'the poorest of the poor' in effect gave it a class basis which overlapped with those grouped at the lower end of the ethnic hierarchy. As Wilmsen pointed out, the conception of remoteness was more about economic status and ethnic distance than about geography, and it was San-speakers who 'are generally conceived to be the most remote from Setswana society even if not from settled villages' (Wilmsen, 1989: 274). Thus, despite the new name for the programme, there continued to be ambiguity as to whether it was a special programme for discriminated ethnic minorities (particularly Basarwa) or an extension of national rural development activities (see, for example, Kann, Hitchcock and Mbere, 1990: 15–17).

In 1977, the Remote Area Development Programme (RADP) was decentralised from the Ministry of Local Government and Lands to the district councils, and units with field officers were established in seven of the ten districts, serving a target population of at least fifty thousand. The programme's objectives were stated in 1978:

1. Increased awareness of rights.
2. Self reliance.
3. Access to land.
4. Extension of services to remote areas.
5. Establishment of water rights. (Ministry of Local Government and Lands, 1978: 123)

It is also clear, however, that it had assimilationist aims with respect to the hegemonic culture. The job description of the Senior Remote Area Development Officer stated the main purpose of the job as 'To work closely with the Remote Area Dwellers (RADS) communities in order to promote RADS adaption to normal life' (Republic of Botswana, n.d.).

The programme (which was funded primarily by Swedish and Norwegian aid) concentrated on the provision of social services, the extension of economic opportunities, and issues of political, legal and cultural rights. The extent to which its objectives were met was assessed in a number of evaluations.

An evaluation of the RADP in 1990 (Kann, Hitchcock and Mbere, 1990) concluded that progress had been made in relation to social services and physical infrastructure. For example, 48 primary schools and 30 health posts had been constructed under the programme, and around 20 new settlements had been established. It was judged, however, that there had been little progress in relation to economic opportunities, despite the establishment in 1989 of a special Economic Promotion Fund. The problem of poverty remained acute, and it had been mitigated only after 1982 by drought relief food and cash income from public works schemes. Unemployment and underemployment were widespread, and those working on freehold farms and on cattleposts were severely exploited, as there was no minimum wage for agricultural labourers.

An important element of the economic insecurity of the remote area dwellers, particularly the Basarwa, was the problem of access to land and natural resources. The expansion of Tribal Grazing Land Policy commercial ranches from the late 1970s carried on the process of land dispossession begun in the nineteenth century by the Batswana polities and confirmed by the colonial state – for example, in its allocation of the Ghanzi freehold farms to Boer settlers in 1899. The continued lack of land rights was rooted in the myth of the Basarwa's nomadism and lack of a land tenure system. Despite their formal equality within the national land tenure system derived from Setswana custom, in practice their access to grazing and arable land was limited. Finally, the report recorded even less progress with respect to political, legal and cultural rights. The remote area dwellers were politically marginal, and hardly represented in decision-making institutions such as district councils and Land Boards. The Basarwa felt that their culture was looked down on; this was illustrated by the lack of official concern that many children and adults did not understand Setswana, and were thus disadvantaged in situations ranging from schools to village meetings to court proceedings. The general impression given by the report was that despite the efforts of some individuals, and some achievements, there were negative attitudes to the RADP, and the programme had a low priority within the state bureaucracy. The report confirmed the conclusion reached in 1979 by the first officer in charge of the programme: that for the state, the RADP was in essence a token welfare programme rather than a vehicle for social justice (Wily, 1979: 171).

The need for an adult education component of the programme was identified at an early stage. For instance, Wily (1979: 114–15) noted that the programme had focused on primary education, and neglected the need 'to implement adult education on a wide scale' in areas such as vocational training, literacy and non-formal education. In the target population of the RADP there were low levels of spoken Setswana and English, literacy, technical skills, and citizenship knowledge. For example, Hitchcock (1978: 366), in a study of households in the western region of Central District in 1977–78, found 99 per cent illiteracy. A decade later in the same district, a study of four settlements found illiteracy levels of 100 per cent, 94 per cent, 90 per cent and 65 per cent (Mutanyatta, 1992: 67). Women had lower rates of literacy and knowledge of Setswana than men. However, despite the RADP's objective to extend educational services, there were hardly any agricultural extension and community development workers in the designated areas, and few Family Welfare Educators. The National Literacy Programme was operational in some communities, but it failed to recruit and retain many adults in the literacy groups. It was evident that the lack of adequate and appropriate adult education pro- grammes weakened the RADP's efforts to develop community institutions, agricultural projects, income-generating activities, awareness of cultural and legal rights, and political participation, all of which have a significant adult education dimension. The 1990 evaluation concluded: 'The potential of adult education re- mains very little tapped in many remote communities' (Kann, Hitchcock and Mbere, 1990: xiv). Organisational policies and practices had led to a low level of adult education provision, despite the identified needs. The failure of the state agencies to provide adult education programmes thereby contributed to the reproduction of the ethnic hierarchy. The perfunctory nature of adult education within the RADP helped to perpetuate the economic, social and ideological subordination of the Basarwa and other marginalised ethnic groups.

The RADP was the state's only development programme with an ethnic dimension. It reflected the state's concern for national integration, but embodied a tokenist approach that served the vested interests of the dominant classes and ethnic group. However, despite the state's strategy of containment, by the end of the period there were signs that the issues of ethnic discrimination were gaining greater political salience, and that non-governmental organisations were facilitating a process of strengthening the self-assertion of the Basarwa (Mogwe, 1992). In this context the possibility emerged of adult education playing a role in the empowerment of ethnic minorities and joining worldwide trends emphasising adult education for indigenous peoples.

The curriculum and inequality

I argued above that adult education between 1966 and 1991 had economic, social and ideological consequences in relation to inequality. Economic outcomes can be seen, for example, in the material benefits accompanying agricultural and small-business extension. Social outcomes can be seen in adult education's capacity both to reinforce (for example, through home economics) and to challenge (for instance, at the Oodi weaving factory) the hierarchy between men and women. The identification of ideological outcomes is harder, as they are more intangible. The political economy approach, however, contends that there is a link between inequalities in economic and social power, and the kinds of knowledge that get diffused through adult education programmes. This linkage is evident at the level of content and of processes, so that both the topics taught and what goes on in the classroom carry messages about society and the distribution of power in society. Thus materials promoting 'the entrepreneurial spirit', and teacher–learner relations which are authoritarian, both legitimate a certain kind of society. On the other hand, topics on the rights of women and forms of co-operative learning raise questions about existing social hierarchies.

During the period 1966 to 1991 the curriculum of adult education received very little analytical attention. There were a number of technical evaluations of courses, such as the curriculum of the YWCA evening classes (University of Botswana, 1989). But there are very few examples of research examining the curriculum in sociological and philosophical terms, the main exceptions being Lecha's study (1987) of the National Literacy Programme, and Higgins's studies of farmer training discussed above. Case study 4 therefore provides an example of ideology in the hidden curriculum, and illustrates the mediation of class, gender and ethnic inequalities in the classroom.

Case study 4: ideology in the adult education classroom

This case study is based on the transcript of a tape-recorded lecture included by Malikongwa (1982: 48–59) in his study of Family Welfare Educators (FWEs), a cadre of village-level health educators. The lecture was given by the Regional Public Health Nurse, a senior state official, as part of an in-service training course for fifty-nine FWEs held at an adult training centre. The tutor and all except one of the FWEs were female. The lecture took place mainly in English and was based on the job description of the FWEs. The tutor sought to identify the duties of the FWEs and discuss the problems of carrying them out. Malikongwa (1982: 58–9) commented on the authoritarian teaching style of the tutor: 'In spite of the stated plan for an open discussion, the lecture was still delivered in a didactic fashion with the FWEs parroting like small children learning a nursery rhyme.' He therefore drew attention to the social relations of the classroom and their potential influence on the FWEs, who would be likely to imitate this teaching style rather than a style based on dialogue with their adult learners. But he did not go further to analyse the ideology expressed by the tutor in her comments on issues raised by the learners. In fact, the tutor's comments during the teaching session constituted a hidden curriculum of ideological positions in relation to class, gender and ethnicity.

First, she expressed a class-based ideology in derogatory comments on the poor. One of the tasks of the FWE was to organise community meetings to discuss environmental sanitation and promote the building of toilets:

> Tutor: You want to talk to the community about toilets – that there are no toilets in the village so you call them together to tell them that....
>
> FWE: If people tell me that they cannot afford to build toilets because they haven't got the means, what do I do?
>
> Tutor: Tell them not to leave faeces everywhere like cattle.

This comment was followed a little later by another similar remark in the context of the FWE's work with family planning:

> FWE: Most of my clients tell me they have no money to pay for things like contraceptives.
>
> Tutor: That's not true. They have money, they spend it on beer drinking.

In these comments the tutor, a member of the bureaucratic petty bourgeoisie, clearly expressed an ideology of class superiority in relation to the rural poor with whom the FWEs worked. She projected a view of the poor as subhuman ('like cattle'), liars, and given to irresponsible behaviour (spending money on beer rather than contraceptives). Second, she colluded with the group in gender stereotyping, and articulated her own acceptance of sexist ideology when the only male FWE in the group commented on the topic of mothercraft classes:

> Male FWE: I managed to organise some mothercraft classes and the women came to do some knitting. [A big laugh from the group.]
>
> Tutor: Yes. As a man you shouldn't have a problem. Women would automatically be attracted to your classes.
>
> Male FWE: I'm already being accused by jealous husbands of having affairs with their wives.
>
> Tutor: Typical of African men. I wouldn't be surprised if they said that. But what else can we do?

Here the tutor explicitly supported the prevailing assumptions about relationships between men and women, and diffused the message that they cannot be changed.

Third, the tutor expressed an ideology of superiority in relation to the Basarwa (Bushmen) minority ethnic group. This arose in a discussion on using popular theatre as a means of dramatising health issues:

> FWE: People in my village are not keen on popular theatre, they find it boring.
>
> Tutor: What a pity. If your people [she names the village] get bored with popular theatre, how are they going to learn?
>
> [Three FWEs with long experience in popular theatre describe how they had used it with success in dealing with sensitive issues like sexually transmitted diseases. Before that people were shy to come to the health facilities for treatment. Now they are not.]
>
> Tutor: You see! It is only the Bushmen ... who would get bored with popular theatre.

The tutor's remarks expressed ethnic prejudice. It is interesting to note, however, that this last comment elicited the only dissenting view expressed by a participant during the session:

> FWE: It is not necessarily the Bushmen. Even some enlightened village leaders are against popular theatre. They feel it is rude to dramatise sensitive issues before a public audience.

In this statement one of the participants questions the views of the tutor, indicating that her authoritative and domineering positions were not automatically accepted by all.

The analysis of the session reveals a hidden curriculum of dominant class, gender and ethnic ideologies expressed in the tutor's spontaneous comments. It thus provides an example of how hegemony is diffused in the adult education classroom. The participants' apparent compliance with the tutor's comments does not necessarily show acceptance, and the dissent expressed by one FWE over the ethnic aspect of this hegemony shows the possibility of resistance to the dominant ideologies expressed. But overall, the hidden curriculum was a vehicle for the reproduction of class, gender and ethnic inequalities.

This discussion of aspects of adult education in Botswana in the first twenty-five years after Independence illustrates how the research agenda of the political economy approach can be used. The evidence produced indicates the role of adult education in reproducing and resisting the social inequalities of class, gender and ethnicity.

Note

1. For an example of analysis of the rural class structure of peripheral societies in different areas of the South, see the chapters by Bernstein on Latin America, India and Sub-Saharan Africa in H. Bernstein, B. Crow and H. Johnson (eds) *Rural Livelihoods* (1992).

CHAPTER 7

The State, Civil Society
and Adult Education

The perspective of Marxist political economy argues that adult education is embedded in the political processes of society. It suggests that the nature of adult education policies, programmes and practices reflects the interests and values of different social groups, and the distribution of power in society. Hence the study of adult education must include political analysis. In particular, it must address the question of the extent to which adult education serves to reinforce the existing power structure and its socio-economic order, or contributes to social change based on alternative ideas about society and its development. In peripheral capitalist societies, the state has an important role in the provision and regulation of adult education; therefore, the character of the state and of public policy related to adult education require investigation. But many adult education activities are undertaken outside the state by organisations in civil society. These are increasingly significant as structural adjustment programmes reduce public-sector provision. Thus the adult education work of village associations, religious groups, non-governmental organisations, trade unions and similar bodies must also be examined in terms of its political implications.

The theoretical framework established in Chapter 3 embodied the political considerations that have to be taken into account in the political economy of adult education. These were summarised as follows:

- The conflicts within society that arise from class differences and other social inequalities are reflected in the state, which is a significant provider of adult education. It is assumed that the formation, implementation and outcomes of public policies on adult education can be meaningfully analysed in terms of how they relate to the inequalities in society.
- Intellectual and cultural life is shaped by the capitalist mode of production and the contestation between different classes and groups in society over the legitimacy of the existing socio-economic order. It is assumed that adult education provided by the state and the organisations of civil society constitutes an area in which struggles for ideological hegemony are carried out.
- There are different views over the nature of society and how it should develop, some of which question aspects of the capitalist socioeconomic order. It is assumed that the activities of political parties and of organisations in civil society which question the status quo have an adult education dimension because they seek to change people's ideas about society.[1]

The aim of this chapter is to elaborate these political dimensions of adult education in peripheral capitalism and to show how they might be studied in specific circumstances.

The State and Civil Society in Peripheral Capitalism

Political analysis is an integral part of Marxist political economy. It seeks to elucidate such issues as the distribution of power in society, the relationship between state and society, the character of the political regime, the nature of civil society, the configuration of political forces and the agencies of social change. It has two main concerns, one material and one ideological. It is concerned, first, with the struggles over the distribution of society's resources; second, with the conflicts over definitions of 'the good society'. Political analysis therefore focuses on power, and how the exercise of power is used to advance the interests and values of different classes and social groups. Central concepts for this analysis are those of the state and civil society.

The state

The state is defined as the political institutions and agencies of government which rule over the citizens of a given territory, its authority based on codified laws and backed by control of co-ercive power (Giddens, 1989: 302–3). It comprises a complex of publicly funded bodies (state apparatuses) which include the leg-islature, the civil service bureaucracy, the courts and prisons, the police and the armed forces. These bodies enact legislation, de-cide policies, administer public resources, provide social services, maintain law and order, and manage external relations with other states. In its modern form as the sovereign nation-state, it is associ-ated with the historical development of the capitalist mode of production. A number of different political theories have sought to interpret the nature of the modern state.

Two important theoretical positions are those derived from the liberal tradition and those in the Marxist tradition. The liberal tradition stresses the importance of the private sphere independent of the state, in which individual rights are protected and the in-dividual citizen exercises freedom of choice – for example, within the capitalist market economy. The state is seen as a neutral in-stitution which guarantees the 'common good' or 'public interest', in contrast to the private interests of individuals. It therefore operates in the general interest of all citizens. A major source of difference within the liberal tradition is over the extent to which state intervention is desirable The neoliberals promote minimal state intervention and the creation of a state based on principles of private competition. In this 'competitive state', market forces are brought into state activities through strategies such as creating internal competition between branches of the state, and by charg-ing cost-recovery fees for public services (Mackintosh, 1992). Despite this difference, there is general agreement that the iden-tification of the common good and the accountability of the state are achieved through representative (liberal) democracy.

This view of the state is contested by Marxist theories, which contend that in a divided society the state, like any other social institution, cannot be neutral and stand apart from the conflicts between classes and other social groups. The state has a class character and has biases in relation to gender, ethnic and racial contradictions. Furthermore, liberal democracy, while it provides some important political and civil liberties, is viewed as an incomplete form of democracy because there is no economic democracy – people can participate as citizens, but not as producers. Marxist theorists have paid particular attention to the nature of the state in advanced capitalism since the late 1960s. What Held (1983: 31) calls Marx's 'ambiguous heritage' has enabled two different approaches to be derived from Marx's work. In the first ('instrumental') approach, the state is considered to be directly under the control of the economically dominant capitalist class, which manipulates state apparatuses as instruments to advance its own interests. The limitation of this approach is that it tends towards economic reductionism and a simplification of political phenomena.

In the second ('relative autonomy') approach, the state is regarded as having a degree of autonomy from the capitalist class, whose internal fractions are not always in agreement. However, because of its material base in the revenues generated by capitalist production, the overall thrust of state laws and policies is to sustain the capitalist mode of production. Thus although the institutions of the state have the capacity for independent action, their activity is shaped by the structural constraints of the capitalist social relations of production. The state is 'an institutional expression of class relations' (Johnson, 1985: 176). From this perspective, the state has a dual role: first to guarantee the conditions for capitalist accumulation and reproduction; and second, to organise the legitimation of the capitalist socioeconomic order. In carrying out this role, the state is a site of struggles between classes and groups in society and political outcomes reflect the configuration of forces at a given time. For example, trade-union rights and women's rights are the historical products of social struggles, but the scope of these rights changes as the balance of power between classes and groups alters. This second approach is the one used in this study, because it enables a more complex political conceptualisation of the state and its activities.

Civil society

Complementary to the idea of the state is the concept of civil society, which was revived for use in contemporary political analysis in the 1970s (Keane, 1988). Its revival was influenced by a variety of disparate factors, including the publication of Gramsci's work in English, the experience of the democratic opposition to state socialism in Eastern Europe, the trend to neoliberalism in conservative parties in the USA and Europe, and the rise of new social movements such as feminism and environmentalism. These developments refocused analytical attention on state–society relations, and especially on the nature of social life beyond the limits of the state. In general terms, civil society refers to the realm of social affairs between private life in the family on the one hand and the political sphere of the state on the other, a realm in which individuals voluntarily form associations of various kinds. Thus the organisations of civil society include professional associations, trade unions, employers' federations, religious bodies, ethnic organisations, women's groups, peace campaigns, environmental movements, and so forth. The boundaries between the state and civil society are dynamic, the balance between the two constantly shifting as the scope of state intervention expands and contracts. The space available for the operation of the organisations of civil society varies according to the nature of the political regime, and their relationship to the state may be co-operative or conflictual.

As with the state, the liberal and Marxist traditions of political theory have differing ideas about the nature and significance of civil society. Within the tradition of liberalism, the notion of civil society is consonant with the ideas of pluralist political science about the plurality of organised interest groups which exert pressure on the state. These ideas had an impact on the democratic movements of Eastern Europe, which established independent organisations that sought to mobilise public opinion and expand citizenship rights without explicitly confronting the political power of the state. The dissent generated by these organisations of civil society, such as Solidarity in Poland in the late 1970s, was conceived as 'antipolitics' because it was not expressed in political parties and was not aimed at the capture of state power. However, it was seen as integral to the processes of democratisation. From the perspective of neoliberalism, the idea of civil society is synonymous with its project of reducing the state and expanding the scope of the market and the 'private' sphere. In sum, in the tradition of liberalism, civil society is the domain in which individuals can exercise their rights as citizens and set limits to the power of the state.

Although Marx, in his early writings, discussed Hegel's concept of civil society, the term did not become a central element of his conceptual framework. The contemporary usage of the concept within the Marxist tradition derives from the work of Gramsci, who used the idea as part of his efforts to explain the defeat of the working class in Western Europe after the First World War, and the resilience of the modern capitalist state. He identified the capacity of the capitalist state to survive in its ability not only to exert coercive power but also to generate consent through exercising ideological influences both within state institutions and beyond: namely, in the sphere of civil society. He argued that the dominant class diffuses capitalist ideology through a wide range of associations and organisations, thus reinforcing its power and protecting the state. The task of socialist politics is therefore twofold: first, to counter this hegemony through working-class cultural and ideological struggles in the organisations of civil society, with the aim of undermining capitalist legitimacy; second, to develop the workers' party in order to take control of state power (Hoare and Smith, 1971: 206–7).

Gramsci's ideas about civil society introduced into Marxist political thinking a broader approach to social transformation by adding to the traditional focus on working-class parties and state power. In the 1980s an important analytical trend went beyond Gramsci to stress the anti-capitalist significance of the new social movements and other organisations in civil society while denying the leading role of the organised working class and the centrality of the state. This trend was crystallised by Laclau and Mouffe in *Hegemony and Socialist Strategy: Towards a Radical Democratic Politics* (1985), which sought to theorise a wide range of social conflicts and struggles. The book outlined a new 'post-Marxist' conception of politics, namely, 'the struggle for a radical, libertarian and plural democracy' (Laclau and Mouffe, 1985: 4) which would be broader than the struggle for socialism. Two arguments are central to this trend. First, it discounts the traditional Marxist view that the working class is the key agent of social change because the economic location of the workers means that their class interests will be met by socialism. Instead it argues that there are numerous sources of oppression in society, and social conflict arises in many areas which can lead to opposition to the capitalist status quo.

Thus all social relations are important, not just the social relations of production. Hence organisations which struggle against racism or patriarchy, for example, are agents of social change. Second, because power is exercised in a multiplicity of social contexts, struggles for change need not be focused only on the state. Hence it is important to extend the field of struggle for a new order to civil society, deepening democracy through greater equality in a variety of social relations.

In terms of the theoretical framework used in this book, civil society is seen as a fruitful concept, because it extends the analysis of social change beyond the traditional Marxist emphasis on working-class parties to a consideration of organisations outside the political contest for state power which may also be critical of capitalism and agents of social transformation. However, three points must be emphasised. First, civil society is not apart from the class structure and other social divisions; it is therefore a site of inequality and conflict. Second, as a consequence of social divisions, while the organisations of civil society may oppose exploitative and oppressive elements of the status quo, they may also promote the hegemony of dominant classes and social groups. Finally, despite the potential of the organisations of civil society to change social relations and influence the state, any vision of a post-capitalist society must address the central role of state power in upholding capitalism.

The state in peripheral capitalism

The concepts of the state and civil society which were developed in the context of advanced capitalism and state socialism have been applied in the analysis of peripheral capitalist societies. A general portrayal of the state in peripheral capitalism is possible, although specific national situations obviously vary. Marxist analysis of the state suggests that there are distinctive factors that shape the character of the state in peripheral capitalism, although its basic functions are the same as those in advanced capitalism: securing the conditions of capitalist accumulation and organising legitimation (Alavi, 1982b). An important distinctive factor is the colonial legacy, especially for the countries of Asia and Africa which emerged from colonialism after 1945.

The colonial state had a number of characteristics which had a subsequent influence on the development of the post-colonial state (Potter, 1992; Thomas, 1984). Six may be identified as particularly important. First, the colonial state was a foreign intervention, an imposition from outside which ruptured pre-colonial political institutions, introduced an external dimension to local politics, and subordinated local interests to those of the economically dominant classes in the metropolitan power. Second, the territorial definition of the nation established by the colonial state was often arbitrary, and did not coincide with pre-existing polities. Third, the colonial state was usually established by force and maintained through the coercive apparatuses of the state, which repressed all opposition. Fourth, the regime type was authoritarian, with very limited participation in decision-making. Fifth, the state played an interventionist role in the economy, spreading capitalist relations of production, developing infrastructure, establishing agencies to control the sale and export of primary products, and generally regulating production and trade. Finally, the ending of colonial rule, which resulted from the post-1945 international conjuncture and the anti-colonial struggles of the nationalist movements, was accompanied by constitutional settlements which sought to restrict the mass popular participation expressed in the movements for independence, and to secure a political and legal dispensation favourable to capitalist accumulation. In only a few instances, such as Vietnam and Mozambique, did the national liberation struggle lead to a radical break with the colonial state and the capitalist socioeconomic order.

This is the historical context from which the post-colonial state in Asia and Africa emerged in the 1950s and 1960s, and which was the main influence on its development up to the 1980s. The distinctive factors of this period of state formation include the class context, imperialism, economic underdevelopment and problems of legitimacy. The state was subject to conflicting pressures from different classes, and used by the emergent petty bourgeoisie as a basis for its own accumulation and consolidation. Because much of the economy was controlled by foreign capital, the presence of the metropolitan bourgeoisie in the class structure was also significant. Imperialism represented by foreign capitalists and the aid agencies was a major influence on the peripheral state.

Although in some circumstances the divergence of interests between domestic and foreign capital was expressed in assertions of
economic nationalism, the state upheld the fundamental pre-
requisites of the capitalist mode of production.

The emergent post-colonial state operated in a situation of
economic underdevelopment. It assumed a central role in the
economy – not only in terms of economic management and the
enforcement of controls and regulation, but also directly in the
productive sphere through state-owned enterprises. The state
became an important source of economic opportunities and the
main appropriator of economic surplus. Its intervention was extensive, and generated a large bureaucratic apparatus. State expenditure based on local surplus value and foreign borrowing
became a significant proportion of GDP. Nevertheless, in the
context of relatively low levels of production, the state had a weak
fiscal base, and was often unable to meet mass demands for improved standards of living – for example, through education and
other social services. This was one aspect of its problem of legitimacy, despite its promulgation of the ideology of 'development'.
Two other aspects were important. The ethnic heterogeneity in
the inherited colonial boundaries made it difficult to construct a
national identity, despite the ideology of 'national unity'; and
imperialism placed significant limitations on national sovereignty
which were barely masked by the ideology of nationalism.

From the 1950s to the 1980s the state in peripheral capitalism
was contested by different classes, was subject to imperialist pressures, expanded institutionally within a weak economy, and had
problems in establishing capitalist hegemony. In many countries it
was the focus of a wide range of social struggles (including coups,
armed insurrections, civil wars and separatism), and was inherently
unstable. These factors produced states which appeared strong –
for example, in the scale of the bureaucracy and the coercive
machinery. In fact, however, they were weak in terms of their
effectiveness in securing capitalist reproduction and gaining popular support and legitimacy. Indeed, in some cases, such as Uganda
and Lebanon, the state virtually collapsed as a central authority.
The nature of any given regime was a product of the particular
form of capitalist accumulation, and of the particular configuration
of political forces. On the whole, the regime types[2] were mostly

authoritarian constitutional forms (such as Kenya) or military dictatorships (such as Iraq), with very few multiparty liberal democracies (such as India).

The international and domestic economic crises and political developments of the 1980s initiated a period in which many of the peripheral capitalist states were restructured. The debt crisis in the South weakened the forces of economic nationalism, and enabled the advanced capitalist states to accelerate the process of integrating the world capitalist market. One of the political conditions for this integration was to reduce the intervention of the peripheral capitalist state in the economy, in areas such as import controls, marketing boards and publicly owned enterprises (Beckman, 1993). The state was attacked as invasive and inefficient and its role in development was redefined to give greater scope for global market forces. Hence the conditions of World Bank and IMF structural adjustment loans included restructuring the state by curbing public expenditure – for example, through cutting public-sector employment, social services and subsidies. The fiscal crisis of the peripheral capitalist state thus decreased its sovereignty and further undermined its legitimacy. The external pressures to restructure the state converged with internal social forces which opposed repression and sought to develop democratic forms of political regime. Democratisation was therefore a feature of the restructuring of the peripheral state from the early 1980s, a process responding both to popular struggles and to efforts by the foreign and domestic dominant classes to build legitimacy for globalised capitalist accumulation.

At the ideological level, the process of restructuring was heavily influenced by neoliberalism (Colclough and Manor, 1991). This draws attention to the views on the role of the state in society held by the different development theories discussed in Chapter 4 (Mackintosh, 1992). In modernisation theory, the state is assigned a key role in the development process. This theory encompasses a liberal view of the state as benevolent, and acting in the public interest. Dependency theory, on the other hand, views the state in an instrumental Marxist perspective as a tool of the metropolitan bourgeoisie and the local comprador classes. This theory's socialist development strategy emphasises the need to capture state power and use it in the interests of the working class and the peasantry.

Both theories are therefore 'statist' in that they put the state at the centre of development. Neoliberal theory, however, regards the state as an obstacle to development which must be 'rolled back'. The resultant competitive state will be more market-orientated in its own activities, and will create the space and regulations for the free operation of market forces. This view provides the ideological basis of the IMF/World Bank structural adjustment programmes. The populist approach also rejects statist models of development, advocating development 'from below' based on decentralised, self-managing and participatory forms of organisation, such as non-governmental and community-based organisations. Thus the different perspectives on development have different ideas about the role of the state.

Civil society within peripheral capitalism

The concept of civil society developed in the context of advanced capitalism and state socialism has been applied fruitfully to the South to analyse the interaction between state and society. Bratton (1989) has developed a useful typology to capture the shifting balance between the two, expressed in terms of engagement–disengagement. He uses the concept of engagement to refer to situations in which the population has close ties with the state, and disengagement to describe situations in which the population is at a distance from the state. Thus development planning is an example of state-sponsored engagement, while structural adjustment programmes are state-sponsored disengagement; efforts to influence state policy by the organisations of civil society are society-sponsored engagement, while withdrawal into indigenous community structures is society-sponsored disengagement. Within this framework it is possible to map the changing relationship between state and civil society.

The case of Africa illustrates how the relationship changes over time. In the late colonial era society-sponsored engagement occurred in the participation in the anti-colonial struggle of the organisations of civil society, such as professional associations, ethnic welfare societies, peasant movements and trade unions. Then, in the period of the repressive post-colonial state, state-sponsored engagement reduced the scope of civil society. The subsequent fiscal and legitimation crisis of the state led in some cases to society-sponsored engagement – for example, in pro-democracy movements – and in others to society-sponsored disengagement, such as increased reliance on informal credit associations and mutual aid societies. The consequent restructuring of the state has been mainly state-sponsored disengagement as the state has contracted its activities. The essential point is that the boundaries of state and civil society are not fixed. Rather, the space available for civil society is shaped by the nature of the political regime and the scope of state intervention on one hand, and by the strength and focus of the organisations of civil society on the other.

The relationship between the organisations of civil society and the peripheral capitalist state ranges on a continuum from co-operation to confrontation. Some organisations function as vehicles for the diffusion of capitalist hegemony. This function may be undertaken directly by the state itself, as in the case of state-sponsored trade unions or peasant co-operatives. Or it may reflect the power of dominant classes or groups to control independent bodies such as women's organisations or village associations. However, other organisations are oppositional and engage in activities which challenge the status quo of peripheral capitalism. This opposition has two important dimensions.

The first dimension is the role of the organisations of civil society in promoting democratisation in the South in the face of typically authoritarian and dictatorial regimes. These organisations, such as the churches in Malawi and the trade unions in Zambia, have had a key role in pro-democracy movements. Indeed, for many analysts, such as Kamrava (1993), a strong civil society is a precondition for democracy. Peripheral capitalism has been characterised by repressive states, and the organisations of civil society in theory and practice represent a source of opposition and an agent of democratic change.

The second dimension is the role of the organisations of civil society in constructing alternative models of development which meet the interests and values of subordinated classes and social groups, as opposed to state-centred development which has served the dominant classes and groups. The contraction of the state during the 1980s led to a proliferation of voluntary development organisations. Some of these organisations articulated an approach to development which explicitly challenged the development strategies of the peripheral capitalist state. Their critique focused on the failure of these strategies to meet the needs of exploited and oppressed groups, such as the rural poor. This failure was seen as rooted in the 'top-down' approaches of the state. Their practical alternative was the community-based organisation whose own procedures would be participatory and democratic, thus creating more equal social relations. These grassroots organisations were conceived as having the capacity to empower the poor and challenge existing power structures, as in the case of peasant organisations in Asia fighting for the rights of the landless. For some writers, the essence of these organisations was self-reliance and disengagement from the centralised state (Wangoola, 1990); for others, voluntary organisations had the potential to engage the state through advocacy to influence public policy (Clark, 1991). The common oppositional characteristic was to confront the socioeconomic order of peripheral capitalism with an alternative social vision, and with practical action for social change.

The struggles in civil society for greater democracy and for alternative conceptions challenged many aspects of the socioeconomic order of peripheral capitalism. However, this has not necessarily meant that they have fundamentally questioned the capitalist mode of production. The oppositional activity for democracy has usually been articulated in terms of multiparty liberal democracy and curbing the powers of the state. The advocates of the populist model of development have often portrayed it as a 'third way' which avoids the statism of both capitalism and socialism. The struggles by the organisations of civil society to change peripheral capitalist society have therefore seldom been socialist in character, and with the collapse of state socialism since 1989 the very concept of socialism has been constrained.

We can conclude that in relation to social transformation in peripheral capitalism, civil society is a contested terrain in both theory and practice. At the ideological level, this is illustrated by contrasting the ideas of populism on the role of civil society with the way neoliberalism uses the concept to justify its project of reducing state intervention in the South (Beckman, 1993). At the practical level, the contestation can be seen over the role in development of non-governmental organisations (NGOs). The populist proponents of NGOs see them as embodying an alternative vision of society and development, and as a means to empowering the poor (Sen and Grown, 1988). There is, however, increasing evidence of a concerted effort by international aid agencies (which are the main source of NGO funds) to co-opt NGOs to be dispensers of charitable social welfare services, while the state's role in the provision of social services is cut back (Fowler, 1992). Thus NGOs are being funded to play a role in neoliberalism's project of privatisation.

In summary, the concepts of the state and civil society can help in the analysis of the political dimensions of the development process, and in the identification of the material interests and ideological values that are involved nationally and internationally. The nature of the state and civil society changes over time, responding to internal and external factors. The colonial and early post-colonial periods were distinctive conjunctures in the development of state–society relations in peripheral capitalism. A new era commenced in the 1980s, when major changes in the global political economy converged with internal economic and political processes to initiate a reordering of the state and civil society. These considerations clarify the context for studying the political consequences of the role of adult education in development.

The State, Civil Society and Adult Education

The concepts of the state and civil society developed above have been elaborated in order to explore the political dimensions of adult education in peripheral capitalism. The analytical point of departure is that the nature of the state and civil society shapes the character of adult education. Thus it is suggested that public policies on adult education will reflect the dual role of the state in promoting capitalist accumulation and legitimating the socio-economic order. With respect to civil society, it is postulated that the adult education activities of some organisations reinforce the hegemony of dominant classes and social groups, while in other organisations adult learning is part of efforts to change society. The political analysis of adult education from the perspective of Marxist political economy therefore seeks to investigate how it relates to the distribution of power in society, and to the contending interests and values of different classes and social groups.

This is an area of study which has had little systematic attention in the literature on adult education. The practitioners of adult education have often been very clear about the political implications of their work, whether as proponents of the status quo or as radicals seeking social change. In the USA, for example, the organisers of 'Americanization' programmes in the public evening schools after the First World War explicitly sought to assimilate immigrants into the hegemonic culture (Knowles, 1977). In contrast, the civil rights adult education of the Highlander Center in Tennessee in the 1950s and 1960s was designed to challenge the institutionalised racism in American society (Glen, 1988). But Thomas (1991) indicates that theoretically informed political analysis of adult education started to develop only in the mid-1980s, especially in North America and Western Europe. Two full-length works have appeared in English which begin to fill the gap.

The first is a volume edited by Pöggeler, *The State and Adult Education* (1990), which brings together a range of contributions of varying scope and quality. The collection reflects state intervention in Europe during the 1980s which limited the adult education work of socially orientated voluntary organisations, and promoted adult vocational training linked to the economy. This change in the reality of adult education focused analytical attention on the state. Although the authors do not theorise the nature of the state and civil society, they do identify a number of issues with regard to the political dimensions of adult education. The most useful contribution is that of Bown (1990), who takes a historical and comparative perspective. She considers the nature and significance of state involvement in adult education in different national contexts and periods in terms of its policies, its supportive actions and its constraining influences on the work of voluntary organisations. She also considers the extent to which adult education has had an impact upon the state as illustrated by its role in working-class movements in nineteenth-century Britain, and in Guinea-Bissau's national liberation movement from 1956 to 1974. Her argument supports the hypothesis that adult education is shaped by, and influences, the shifting balance between the state and civil society. Her contribution strengthens the case for political analysis, and she regards adult education and the state as a 'neglected theme' (Bown, 1990: 445).

There is a more unified and in-depth treatment of the theme in Jarvis's *Adult Education and the State: Towards a Politics of Adult Education* (1993). Jarvis seeks to apply political theory to the education of adults in the context of contemporary Britain. The book is useful in that it highlights the political implications of adult education, criticising the emphasis in much adult education literature on a narrow concern with adult learning and teaching that is 'based on an individualistic conception of the person in which little or no consideration about the person-in-society, let alone the person-in-a-state, has been given' (Jarvis, 1993: 18). It therefore includes discussion of some central concepts of political analysis, including civil society, the state, state policy and justice, the bureaucracy, democracy and citizenship, rights, interests, civilised society and utopia. But the book is uneven in its exposition of these concepts, and does not develop a coherent theoretical perspective even within its liberal framework. A recurring theme, however, is the growing intervention of the state in civil society, and the implications for adult education. Jarvis argues that in Britain there has been a decisive shift in the nature of adult education, which has become an instrument of the state used for social control and for serving the needs of industry and commerce. Simultaneously, the state has reduced the scope for adult education in the context of interest groups and social movements, thus constricting its potential to promote citizenship, democracy and social change.

These two books begin to develop the theoretical issues and research questions which can guide analysis of the role of adult education in relation to the distribution and organisation of power in society. However, they are eclectic in terms of theoretical perspectives, and they do not, for example, illuminate political analysis within the Marxist tradition. Apart from brief considerations in Thompson (1980) and Youngman (1986), the implications of the state for a Marxist political economy of adult education were not explored in depth until the publication of Torres's *The Politics of Nonformal Education in Latin America* (1990). The particular significance of this book for this study is that it seeks to develop a consistent theory of the state, politics and adult education in the context of peripheral capitalism, and it includes theorisation of the peripheral state and adult education supported by case studies.

Torres's theoretical position is that public policy on adult education reflects the state's role in the reproduction of capitalism and its project of legitimation. Thus in the context of Latin America he explains the marginal role of state-sponsored adult education as follows:

> Why has adult education in Latin America had a marginal role in public policy formation, in terms of financial expenditure and enrolment? I suggest that adult education lacks correspondence with the model of capitalist accumulation and has little utility for the model of political domination. (Torres, 1990: 33)

To support this contention, he presents two main arguments. First, in relation to economic development, he adopts the conception of a segmented labour market in which the primary sector offers stable, well-paid, skill-dependent jobs, while the secondary sector offers unstable, low-wage, unskilled jobs. The dominant Latin American development strategy in the 1960s and 1970s – import-substitution industrialisation – relied on the primary labour market. Thus adult education programmes like on-the-job training and professional upgrading were provided to enhance the productivity of the primary sector. But few state resources were allocated to adult basic education and training for the labour force in the secondary sector, which was seen as economically marginal. Second, in relation to legitimation, the economic marginality of those in the secondary sector was a source of political weakness, so that the subordinate classes were limited in their ability to demand adult education provision by the state. Hence little was done in terms of public adult education. In some situations, however, the state's need for legitimation led to adult education as a welfare policy designed to build support, as in the case of the Brazilian mass literacy programme (MOBRAL) in the 1970s. Torres notes that such reformist state adult education programmes were not designed to enhance civic and political participation, and they were kept inexpensive so that they did not draw resources from other areas of state activity. Any meaningful development of adult education took place only when there was a change in political regime and in economic strategy, as in Cuba after 1959 and Nicaragua after 1979, where policies for greater economic and political participation were adopted.

The focus of Torres's book is on the state, and on adult education as public policy. He therefore does not provide a theorisation of civil society, although he makes it clear that the analysis of the policies of non-state institutions carrying out adult education is an important task (Torres, 1990: 129). He shows that many 'popular education' programmes in Latin America represent an alternative to state-sponsored adult education, and have an explicit emphasis on social mobilisation and political development. These programmes are run by organisations in civil society such as church groups, trade unions and social movements, some of which consciously resist the hegemonic practices of the capitalist state. He notes, however, that the state often impinges on these organisations, especially through funding, and that international aid also modifies the nature of adult education programmes initiated in civil society. Thus the struggle for hegemony in civil society is also played out within adult education.

This is an important point, because many radical discussions of adult education and popular education linked to social movements emphasise their counter-hegemonic nature, and seldom consider congruences between the ideologies of organisations in civil society and those of the state. Welton (1993), for example, discusses the new social movements as 'particularly privileged' sites for adult learning and for an emancipatory praxis of collective action to change power relations in society. But while he shows an awareness of conflicts within social movements (such as class and race biases within a women's movement dominated by white middle-class feminists), he does not problematise these movements as sites of ideological struggle. Also, as Holford (1995) points out, he does not confront the fact that some popular movements are reactionary and politically conservative. Thus, while social movements may be a context for adult education which challenges capitalist hegemony, they may also promote learning and action which seek to reinforce the established order of power.

The theoretical perspective on the relationship between the peripheral capitalist state, civil society and adult education derived from Marxist political economy can be summarised as follows. The political consequences of adult education provided by the peripheral state are the promotion of its model of capitalist accumulation and the legitimation of the capitalist socioeconomic order. In some situations, where there are strong oppositional organisations within civil society, the state provides adult education as a concession to demands from within civil society. The political consequence of adult education organised in the context of voluntary associations is either to advance capitalist hegemony or to promote an alternative vision of society that questions the socioeconomic order and existing power structure. In some cases, the alternative conception of society has an explicit socialist character.

This theoretical conclusion can be briefly illustrated by the experience of British colonial Africa. A major adult education programme sponsored by the colonial state was agricultural extension, which had the aim of transforming subsistence peasant agriculture into cash crop production, largely for export. The state's adult education activity in this case clearly served the colonial model of capitalist economic development based on the export of primary commodities. In the period from the mid-1940s, as the British sought to control the forces of nationalism, the colonial state introduced community development programmes. These programmes ostensibly sought to mobilise African participation in local decision-making and development projects, but their fundamental purpose was to contain popular dissatisfaction and reinforce the legitimacy of colonial rule. The work of voluntary associations during the colonial period often reflected the hegemony of European capitalism. For example, adult education programmes provided by missionary bodies transmitted Western conceptions of the family and of economic relations, and upheld the colonial system and capitalist values. On the other hand, many local organisations, such as the ethnic associations, sports clubs and women's unions in Nigeria, provided informal and organised modes of learning which developed nationalist consciousness and opposition to colonialism. In some cases, the adult education of these organisations of civil society had an explicitly socialist dimension, as in the workers' education undertaken within the Sudanese trade-union movement from the mid-1940s. The example of British colonial Africa indicates the potential of a political analysis of adult education in peripheral capitalism within the framework of Marxist political economy.

A Research Agenda on the State, Civil Society and Adult Education

The theoretical position put forward in this chapter is that adult education is embedded in the political processes of society expressed in the state–civil society relationship. Adult education provided by the state reflects its role in securing the conditions of capitalist accumulation and generating legitimacy in a context of social divisions. A wide variety of adult education activities are undertaken by the organisations of civil society. These organisations are a site of struggles for hegemony by the dominant classes and groups; some organisations support the status quo, while others seek social change. Thus adult education activities, whether undertaken by the state or by the organisations of civil society, have political implications, because they reinforce or undermine the existing distribution of power in society. An important task for adult educators is therefore to clarify the nature of the state and civil society in a given context, and to investigate their significance for the form and consequences of adult education policies, programmes and practices. The research agenda below provides a guide for undertaking this task.

The state

The analysis of the peripheral capitalist state starts from the idea that the character of the state changes over time. For countries which emerged from colonialism after 1945 there is a need to examine the nature of the colonial state and the Independence settlement. Then the period of the initial post-colonial era should be considered, followed by analysis of the contemporary period that started in the 1980s. Within this historical perspective, four main factors should be taken into account:

- *Social inequality.* Which domestic classes exert a dominant influence over the state, and how does the state contribute to the processes of class formation? What impact do the subordinate classes have on the state and its policies? How does the state relate to other social inequalities, particularly those of gender, race and ethnicity, and how do they affect public policy?

- *Imperialism.* What influence does foreign capital have on the state, and how is this influence mediated by the state? What degree of national sovereignty is exercised by the state, and what impact do external pressures have on public policy?
- *Economic development.* What model of economic development does the state espouse, and what pattern of capitalist accumulation is taking place? What is the level of economic development, and what fiscal resources are available to the state? What is the nature and scale of state intervention in the economy, and what is the scope of the state (indicated, for example, by its share of GDP and of formal-sector employment)? How effective is the state bureaucracy in the implementation of development policies?
- *Legitimacy.* What is the regime type, and how much political authority does the state have? How successful is the state in generating capitalist hegemony, and what strategies does it use to secure legitimacy for the socioeconomic order? What degree of popular support does the state have, and to what extent are there popular struggles over the nature of the state and public policy? What social forces challenge the legitimacy of the state?

The analysis should provide a historical account of the state, assessing how weak or strong it is at any given point, and indicating whether it is expanding or contracting in terms of its penetration of the economy and society. The assessment should elucidate how changes in the state and public policy are related to particular configurations of political forces, and identify the sources of changes that have taken place.

Civil society

The analysis of the character of the state provides the basis for examining civil society, conceived as the associational life beyond the limits of the state. The main premise with respect to civil society is that it is in a dynamic relationship with the state, so that it responds to the nature of the political regime, and to the expansion and contraction of the state. The changing balance of the state and civil society over time can be analysed in terms of Bratton's typology of engagement–disengagement. Thus the analysis requires a historical perspective which considers the evolution of civil society in relation to the changing character of the state.

The analysis should identify the number and nature of organisations in civil society, and examine their autonomy and strength in relation to state institutions. Important indicators are the sources of funding (domestic and foreign) of the particular organisations, and how indigenous they are. Given that civil society exists in a context of social inequality, the role of the different organisations in relation to the status quo must be ascertained. In particular: Which organisations serve to diffuse the hegemony of the dominant classes and social groups? Which organisations are oppositional and challenge the socioeconomic order? For those organisations which are oppositional, further analysis must be undertaken in terms of their ideology and practice, and the extent to which they may be agents of the fundamental social transformation of peripheral capitalism.

The state and adult education

Here the analysis seeks to show how the character of the state has an impact on the nature of adult education policies and practices. It questions why the state provides adult education at any given time, and addresses the central issue of which classes and groups within the structure of power in society benefit from the public resources allocated to adult education. What forms does publicly funded adult education take, and whose interests and values in society does it serve?

In particular, analytical attention focuses on two dimensions. First, it considers the way in which public adult education policies and programmes reflect the state's model of capitalist accumulation. How do the state's adult education activities relate to its economic development strategy and the reproduction needs of capital? How do state adult education programmes providing technical skills and knowledge support capitalist accumulation and prepare adults for various locations within the labour market? Second, political analysis considers the ways in which the state adult education apparatus serves to promote the legitimacy of the state and the socioeconomic order it upholds. How does the state's involvement in adult education promote its own authority among the citizenry? How do state-sponsored programmes fulfil the ideological function of socialising adults into certain values and rationales, and thus generate capitalist hegemony? In what ways does the state's adult education activity promote forms of participation in public life consonant with the nature of the political regime, and its mode of political representation and control? Finally, research should consider in what circumstances the state itself initiates adult education policies, and in what circumstances the provision of adult education is a response to demands from within civil society. What is the nature of adult education in these two sets of circumstances?

Civil society and adult education

The focus of this level of analysis is adult education undertaken outside the state. Research must study how the shifting balance between the state and civil society influences forms of adult education provided by voluntary associations. An important consideration is the extent of state engagement with independent adult education providers. Does the state seek to restrict and control their adult education activities – for example, by regulations? Does it positively encourage their adult education work – for example, by subsidies? If so, what are the political implications of state involvement? What effects do the changes in the relationship between state and civil society have on adult education outside the state? In what circumstances do organisations in civil society make demands on the state for various kinds of adult education provision?

Against this background, the research agenda has two main areas of concentration. The first area is adult education activity undertaken by organisations in civil society which serves to reinforce the hegemony of the dominant classes and social groups. What kinds of organisation provide such adult education, and what forms does it take? Whose interests and values are served, and how is their influence over adult education policies and programmes exerted? The second is the adult education within those social movements and other organisations which have the goal of changing society and its prevailing power structure. What kinds of organisation provide adult education linked to social change objectives, and what forms does it take? What ideologies and alternative conceptions of development are promoted through such adult education activities? How do their adult education practices strengthen the forces for social change?

In each area of concentration, research seeks to uncover how the conflicts generated by social inequalities have an impact on the policies, programmes and practices of adult education. How does the struggle for hegemony in civil society affect the adult education activities of both kinds of organisation: those committed to capitalist hegemony and those committed to social change? Our overall aim is to reveal the nature and political implications of adult education in civil society.

The research agenda outlined here focuses on the struggles over power in society and the politics of development in peripheral capitalism. It provides a tool for studying the impact of these struggles on adult education policies, programmes and practices, and for examining the political implications of different forms of adult education. The next section illustrates the political analysis of adult education and development within peripheral capitalism by considering the case of Botswana.

Country Case Study: The State, Civil Society and Adult Education in Botswana, 1966–91

The state and adult education

The character of the Botswana post-colonial state in the period to 1991 was one of steadily growing strength and scope, based on an expanding economy and a firm coalition of class forces. The Independence settlement established multiparty liberal democracy, and this remained in place throughout the period, with one party winning all the elections. This party was based on a coalition of the cattle-owning class and the petty bourgeoisie (supported by foreign capital), and the influence of these classes over the state was reflected in public policy. The state pursued a model of development which promoted capitalist accumulation through the encouragement of foreign investment in the productive sector (especially mining), and used foreign aid to develop infrastructure and social services. Its strategy of welfare capitalism successfully promoted the legitimacy of the state and its development model in the context of deep social inequalities. Hence the Botswana state did not suffer the fiscal and legitimation crises common within peripheral capitalism in the 1980s.

During the years 1966 to 1991, the state was the main provider of adult education. Its programmes were organised through a variety of central and local government bodies. For most of the colonial era, there had been very little publicly funded adult education with the exception of agricultural extension, which had been started in the 1930s. In the years immediately before Independence, however, the colonial state had established a number of departments with adult education responsibilities, such as those undertaking co-operative education and community development. The scope and range of state adult education programmes grew steadily after 1966 as new departments, cadres and programmes were created as part of the expansion of the state bureaucracy.

By the beginning of the 1980s, the institutional framework of state adult education was fully established. A review of provision at this time (Townsend-Coles, 1982: 46–77) indicated that eight central government ministries had a role in adult education:

- Ministry of Agriculture (agricultural extension and co-operative education);
- Ministry of Commerce and Industry (small-business and rural industries extension, and wildlife conservation education);
- Ministry of Education (non-formal and vocational education);
- Ministry of Health (health extension);
- Ministry of Home Affairs (vocational training, libraries, museums and prison education);
- Ministry of Local Government and Lands (social and community development, and remote area development);
- Office of the President (broadcasting and public information).

Also, the Ministry of Finance and Development Planning's Rural Development Unit played a key co-ordinating role through its responsibility for the Rural Extension Co-ordinating Committee comprised of central government representatives.

The review estimated that 8.8 per cent of the total recurrent budget of these ministries in 1980/81 was allocated to adult education (Townsend Coles, 1982: 66) and noted that a significant proportion of their development expenditure was allocated to adult education projects. Apart from central government provision, a number of adult education programmes were provided through local government councils, particularly for community development, remote areas and self-help housing. I have calculated (Youngman, 1983: 132) that there were around 1,700 full-time posts for adult educators in the public sector in 1982/3, compared to 6,600 in primary education and 840 in secondary education. Thus by the early 1980s the state's involvement in adult education was extensive.

The main form of publicly funded adult education between 1966 and 1991 can be characterised as extension programmes. These programmes sought to extend to adults information and techniques which would help them to improve aspects of their life, such as their health status or agricultural production. In some cases they also sought to organise adults for collective action to address problems of development in their communities. Besides the extension programmes, the largest sustained programme of adult education was the National Literacy Programme started in 1980 by the Ministry of Education's Department of Non Formal Education. The Department also offered limited distance education opportunities for the study of secondary-school qualifications. Finally, the state provided a variety of programmes for the in-service training of its own personnel – for example, through civil service training bodies like the Botswana Institute of Accounting and Commerce, the Botswana Police College and the Local Government In-service Training Unit.

In earlier sections I argued that publicly funded adult education programmes reflect the state's model of economic development and the reproduction needs of capital. Two important extension programmes illustrate how the Botswana state provided knowledge and technical skills to support its economic strategies: agricultural extension and business extension. Throughout the period, the largest extension programme was that of agricultural extension.

The rural economy was an important element of the overall economy because it provided the majority of the population with food, income and employment opportunities, and for some it was a source of significant capital accumulation. The agricultural sector had two main branches, cattle-rearing and crop production. These two branches were closely interlinked, as cattle were the main means of draught power for arable production, which meant that the large proportion of peasant households with no or few cattle also had low crop yields. At the time of Independence, about 96 per cent of the population lived in rural areas, and agriculture constituted 40 per cent of GDP. By 1991 only 67 per cent of the population was rural, and agriculture's contribution to GDP had fallen to 5.2 per cent. Despite the decline in the proportional economic significance of agriculture because of urbanisation and the growth of the mineral industry, its development was an important part of the state's economic policy throughout the period. The major focus was on improving cattle production and commercialising the livestock industry. Beef was the only major export besides minerals. After 1979, however, increased emphasis was given to arable agriculture, with improved producer prices and more subsidies, especially through the Arable Lands Development Programme started in 1981. The greater commitment to the arable sector reflected both international trends favouring smallholder production and local political and economic concerns about maintaining adequate peasant livelihoods through promoting food production, rural incomes and employment.

Agricultural policies thus sought to increase rural productivity through improving standards of animal husbandry and introducing better arable farming techniques. These policies included a variety of measures, especially extension service packages which involved not only the provision of information and advice but also access to improved technologies and subsidised inputs. The Ministry of Agriculture therefore had a large extension service based on cadres of agricultural demonstrators and veterinary assistants. It inherited from the colonial state an elitist extension approach based on the Pupil/Master Farmer and Pupil/Master Stockman schemes, which focused on a small number of peasants who had the requisite resources to modernise their production. In 1975, however, the extension services were reorganised in order to decentralise and extend coverage to a greater number of farming households. Another reorganisation in 1990 divided extension services clearly between the livestock and crop sectors.

The goals of the agricultural extension services were consistent with evolving agricultural policies. In the livestock sector, extension workers sought to improve cattle management (for example, through the use of vaccines, dehorning and better grazing practices) and to encourage a more commercial attitude that would lead to higher rates of off-take. In the arable sector, extension efforts were directed to improved techniques (such as row planting, weeding and early ploughing) in order to increase crop production for both consumption and sale. The effectiveness of agricultural extension was questioned throughout the period, with persistent criticisms of the limitations of its coverage, and of its tendency to favour the wealthier farming households and neglect the significant number of rural households with inadequate means of production (see, for example, Mayende, 1993: 69). Nevertheless, the state invested considerable resources in this branch of adult education, providing a ratio of about one extension worker to three hundred farming households from 1970 to 1991 (Republic of Botswana, 1970: 37; Republic of Botswana, 1991a: 263). The scale of the state's adult education related to agriculture reflected the sector's significance for the state's model of development.

While agricultural extension supported the state's rural development strategy, the extension services for small businesses promoted the growth of small-scale industry and commerce in both the rural and the urban areas. As I discussed in Chapter 6, these services were established in the early 1970s as part of the model of capitalist development underpinned by modernisation theory with its emphasis on local entrepreneurship. They were consolidated in 1987 as the Integrated Field Services (IFS) of the Ministry of Commerce and Industry at a time when neoliberal ideas were beginning to influence the state's development strategy, and the private sector was being identified as an 'engine of growth'. In this context, state support for local private enterprise attained greater priority; this was reflected in efforts to improve the small-business extension services.

The state also sought to meet the reproduction needs of capital through adult education. One role of the state in securing the conditions of capitalist accumulation is to take responsibility for ensuring an appropriately skilled labour force. The development of the Botswana state's involvement in adult vocational training to provide skills for the workforce in the modern sector can be seen in this light. This occurred from the mid-1980s, when the mineral-led economic boom revealed shortages of appropriately skilled workers, especially in the construction and manufacturing industries. In 1986 the Ministry of Home Affairs opened the Madirelo Training and Testing Centre, which not only managed a new apprenticeship scheme for young adults but also ran short skills-upgrading courses for existing workers seeking to take trade tests. The expanded provision of state vocational training for young adults and older workers reflected the new requirements of the rapidly growing labour market in the private sector for skilled and semi-skilled workers.

The second dimension of publicly provided adult education identified in the research agenda is its role in advancing the legitimation of the state, and the capitalist socioeconomic order the state upholds. A number of the Botswana state's adult education activities between 1966 and 1991 clearly fulfilled this legitimation function. The largest state programme in terms of coverage of adult learners was the National Literacy Programme (NLP), which began in 1980 and reached over 100,000 participants. The programme provided basic reading and writing skills in Setswana to literacy groups nationwide, and some post-literacy activities in a few areas. It was promoted by the state in terms of the extension of educational opportunity, modernisation and the enhancement of the individual's role in national development. Participants perceived it largely as an avenue to paid employment, although objectively their possibilities of formal-sector jobs were limited. It can be argued (see Youngman, 1999) that the NLP was one of a number of social welfare programmes provided by the state to generate support from the rural and urban poor in a period of increasing class divisions. The apparent equity in its role in extending access to education helped to legitimate the state as acting in the interests of all. But in practice the NLP served to reproduce the existing patterns of class, gender and ethnic inequality, so that its outcome was to fortify the position of the dominant groups and reinforce the unequal socioeconomic order. Thus through the NLP the state strengthened its own authority among the citizenry and advanced capitalist hegemony.

Another significant use of adult education as part of the state's legitimation strategies can be seen in the forms of participation in public life which the state promoted. The regime type throughout the period was that of liberal democracy, whereby the state derived authority from regular elections. However, the ideology of liberal democracy was also fostered through a rhetoric that encouraged people's participation in development. Thus in 1970, for example, the foreword to *National Development Plan 1970–75* spoke of ensuring that 'the people of Botswana participate to the greatest practicable extent in the formulation and implementation of government policy' (Republic of Botswana, 1970: n.p.). During these years the state professed commitment to participation in relation to public policy, development planning, and project identification and implementation. But the concept of participation is an ambiguous one, susceptible to differing interpretations. In the Botswana context between 1966 and 1991, participation in practice meant either information-giving or non-binding consultation. The state thus gave the impression of seeking popular involvement, while pursuing an essentially top-down and paternalistic approach to development and democracy. Forms of participation were therefore implemented to extend the legitimacy of the state and its policies, while leaving power in the hands of the dominant classes and social groups.

The state's adult education apparatuses, particularly the extension services, played an important part in these legitimation processes. Noppen (1982), in a study revealingly entitled *Consultation and Non-Commitment*, looked in detail at the evolution of the system of district-level planning based on consultation which emerged between 1976 and 1980. He showed how adult education techniques were used as tools for the consultations carried out in preparation of the district development plans. These techniques included district conferences of village representatives, discussion in village meeting-places, discussions with village groups based on printed materials and cassettes, and various forms of opinion survey. The consultation activity was carried out mainly by extension workers, especially the community development workers, and their activities were co-ordinated through Village Extension Teams and District Extension Teams. However, Noppen questioned whether the information gathered had any significant influence over decision-making. Furthermore, he noted that consultation was restricted to the area of social infrastructure and services, and did not cover economic activity and production relations (where the interests of the dominant classes would clash with those of the rural majority). He also revealed that involvement in discussions was largely confined to village elites, thus excluding the rural poor. Above all, he concluded that the state as represented by politicians and civil servants had no real commitment to participation that might alter the economic and political status quo:

> The active political commitment on the part of the Government is an essential factor in stimulating a broader involvement in decision-making by the people than is the case under the present circumstances. No indications were found to show that such commitment existed. Consequently, involvement has been limited to the planning of the social services, a sector which does not affect the economic position of the rich. (Noppen, 1982: 171)

The idea of popular participation in development planning and implementation was a recurrent theme throughout the period, and it was portrayed by the state as part of Botswana's open democratic environment. It was seen as an important task of extension work to generate such participation. Thus the Ministry of Finance and Development Planning's Rural Extension Co-ordinating Committee sponsored major workshops in 1985 (Tsiane and Youngman, 1986) and in 1990 (Republic of Botswana, 1991b) on 'The Theory and Practice of People's Participation in Rural Development'. It was evident from these workshops, however, that the forms of participation implemented were not altering the existing distribution of power or enabling the rural poor to influence decision-making. In practice, adult education activity around participation contributed to the state's legitimation strategies, and reinforced the hegemony of the dominant classes and social groups. This is illustrated in the following example of an adult education campaign.

Case study: the radio learning group campaign on the
Tribal Grazing Land Policy

Cattle were central to the rural economy, and had significant cultural as well as economic value. While small-scale holdings provided important economic and social resources, large-scale cattle-ownership was the basis of social prestige and political influence as well as wealth. The commercialisation of cattle-rearing began in the colonial era, gathering speed in the mid-1950s when beef exports for the world market became a key element of the economic development strategy. During the 1960s the dominant class of large cattle-owners used its influence over the state to enlarge the range of programmes and subsidies favouring live-stock development.

By the early 1970s, the problem of overstocking and overgrazing in the unfenced communally held areas was identified as the major constraint to the continued development of the cattle industry. The traditional modes of land tenure and cattle-rearing were seen as an obstacle to more ecologically sound and efficient produc-tion. A series of official studies and policy documents in 1972 and 1973 enunciated the state's conclusion that private land-holding by large cattle-owners would enable improved range management and productivity, while easing the pressure of cattle numbers in the communal areas. The outcome was the declaration in 1975 of a large-scale reform in land tenure, the Tribal Grazing Land Policy (TGLP).

The TGLP proposed the re-zoning of tribal land into com-munal areas, commercial areas providing exclusive leasehold rights to fenced ranches, and areas reserved for future use. The policy's overt aims of environmental conservation, greater equity and im-proved productivity did not disguise its major goal: to provide the institutional condition essential to the development of capitalist agriculture, namely the private ownership of land. The policy was thus a state project designed to meet the interests of the dominant cattle-owning class. The policy document recognised the sociocul-tural significance of the planned changes:

> Proposals are made here for implementing Government policy on grazing land development. This means changing the traditional system of land tenure in the tribal grazing areas. It will change the Botswana way of life; it will affect directly or indirectly virtually every Motswana. (Republic of Botswana, 1975: 1)

The state realised that the transformation implied in the privati-sation of a hitherto communal resource required legitimation by the co-option of the peasantry; it therefore undertook a major public relations exercise to gain public support. This exercise, announced as a process of consultation, included a large adult education component in the form of a radio learning group campaign.

The consultation process organised by the state sought to inform the public about the policy, sound out public opinion on its implementation, and defuse any criticisms. At the centre of the process was the large-scale radio learning group campaign. The radio learning group campaign model of mass adult education had been pioneered in Tanzania (Kassam, 1978: 50–60) and adopted in Botswana by the University's Division of Extra Mural Services in a campaign in 1973 on the national development plan. The model was a form of non-formal distance education which involved organising people into groups to listen to and discuss a series of radio programmes and accompanying study materials.

The nationwide campaign on the TGLP (which was funded by British aid) took place over a five-week period in mid-1976 (Republic of Botswana, 1977b). It was organised at the centre by a committee involving the responsible government ministries, with technical support from adult education specialists in the Division of Extra Mural Services and the Botswana Extension College. In the field, the responsibility for recruiting radio learning group leaders lay with the government extension workers in agriculture, health and community development assisted by primary-school headteachers. The significance the state attached to the exercise was indicated by the fact that the extension personnel were instructed to spend 50 per cent of their time on the campaign (Noppen, 1982: 83). The extension workers recruited 3,500 group leaders who were trained as facilitators to run twice-weekly group sessions. Each session involved group members listening to a radio programme with accompanying illustrative flipchart, listening to the leader read from the study guide, engaging in discussion and helping the leader to complete a report form. The report forms recorded the group's answers to the pre-set discussion questions, and noted the questions they wished the government to answer. This information provided feedback on public opinion about the policy and inputs to new radio programmes addressing questions raised by the groups. The campaign reached about 55,000 people (approximately one-sixth of the adult population), of whom about 40 per cent were illiterate. It was therefore a very large-scale adult education programme.

The nature of the radio learning group campaign and the evaluation of its success were the subject of controversy. Undoubtedly, in technical terms the campaign was an achievement in that it organised large numbers of adult citizens into a non-formal learning context in which information was conveyed and discussed. But questions arose as to the basic purpose of the campaign. The policy document was contradictory and the exact meaning of 'consultation' was an area of contestation (Picard, 1987: 246–52). While the document raised the possibility of revising the policy in the light of public opinion, its emphasis was on public information about agreed decisions, and it indicated that allocation of ranches in the new commercial areas would begin before the public consultation. On the basis of the statement that the policy might be changed as a result of consultation, the main campaign organiser claimed that the consultation was a democratic process which 'must be unusual in the history of government anywhere' (Crowley, 1977: 19). More considered opinion took the view that the consultation was essentially token, and that the campaign was primarily a public relations exercise (Cliffe and Moorsom, 1979: 51; Holm, 1982: 96–7; Molomo, 1989: 240). It represents an example of what Holm and Molutsi (1992: 83) had in mind when they said that consultation is a means whereby 'Botswana's political elite aggressively manipulates public thinking'. Thus adult education methods were used to legitimate a public policy that met the interests of a powerful minority. The radio learning group campaign exemplifies the use of adult education by the Botswana state to legitimate its policies for expanding the capitalist socioeconomic order.

Civil society and adult education

The nature of the state–society relationship during the period 1966 to 1991 was one of state-sponsored engagement, allowing little space for the development of autonomous organisations in civil society. Although the constitutional form of liberal democracy led to regular elections and the protection of human rights, the state limited popular participation in decision-making and implemented a top-down model of development. The dominant classes, through the state, exercised control over economic and political power, and sought to limit the potential for civil society to provide alternative sources of power and of influence on the state. In this context it is not surprising that the voluntary adult education sector was small and limited in scope. Nevertheless, a number of the organisations in civil society did provide adult education activities, but the majority of these served to reinforce the hegemony of the dominant classes and social groups. This can be illustrated with examples from the work of the churches, the NGO sector and the employers' association.

There were over 150 registered churches, including the denominations of the mission churches and many indigenous African Independent Churches, and most of them engaged in social welfare as well as providing religious services. The churches had a long tradition of involvement in adult education. Indeed, the first adult literacy work was done in the context of teaching congregations to read the Bible, the New Testament having been translated into Setswana by 1840. A major form of adult education provided by the churches in the period under consideration was Bible study. A number of churches also ran informal programmes of cookery, home-keeping, knitting and sewing for women members of the congregation. Churches also ran home economics centres for young women. In Serowe in the early 1970s, for example, the Catholic Ursuline Sisters started the Tlhwaafalo Training Centre, which provided a two-year domestic science course for young women with primary level education. The aim of the course was to provide practical skills to enable students to obtain employment and the syllabus included religious education.

In some church circles, such as the distance-education-based Kgolagano College of Theological Education after 1982, there was identification with the ideas of liberation and black theology that were part of the anti-apartheid struggle in South Africa. But in most churches the dominant theology was a conservative one that promoted an approach to social issues which was apolitical and orientated to charity. Thus the ideology mediated by adult education in the form of Bible study was generally supportive of the existing socioeconomic order. The ideology of home economics also served to reproduce the status quo by reinforcing the stereotypes of women and their position in society. The largely informal and uncoordinated adult education activities of the churches were therefore hegemonic in their impact.

The NGO sector included organisations which had an adult education component to their work. For example, the Botswana

Red Cross Society, with 100 groups nationwide, carried out extensive training programmes in first aid and primary healthcare, thus
providing skills in basic healthcare and preventive medicine to a
large number of volunteers. The Botswana Council of Women
(BCW) – the largest women's organisation, with over three hundred
branches – encouraged adult education among its members, for
example in homecraft. It also undertook specific projects, including the promotion of backyard gardening, the training of women's
leaders and, from 1988, health education relating to AIDS. However, it did not have an explicit concern with changing the status
of women. The impact of both organisations was to promote the
status quo. For example, a sociological survey of six rural villages
in 1980 which included consideration of the Red Cross and the
BCW concluded: 'Voluntary organisations in general appeal to
the elite, the educated and the traditionally respected families.
They are based on the middle and upper classes almost totally
excluding the poor' (Kjaer-Olsen, 1980: 41). Their adult education activities therefore served to reproduce the existing patterns
of social inequality and distribution of power. This was consistent
with the overall position of most NGOs: that they were 'development partners' of the state whose programmes should comple-
ment those of the state.

One of the most powerful organisations in civil society was the
employers' association. The Botswana Employers' Federation (BEF)
was established in 1971, and represented the interests of large
capitalist enterprises. It established itself as one of the few effective
lobby groups in civil society (Holm, 1989: 152). The BEF was
recognised by the state as a major interest group, and given
representation on important government committees such as the
National Employment Manpower and Incomes Council. With the
economic boom of the 1980s the BEF's membership grew; it also
consciously sought to encourage small-business membership. By
1989/90 it had 635 members employing more than 50,000 people
(BOCCIM, 1990: 4). Its development was heavily supported by
USAID, and from the early 1980s onwards it articulated many
neoliberal ideas on the role of private enterprise in development.

The USA's funding after 1982 gave particular encouragement
to the BEF to assist in the training of employees in private companies – for example, by giving access to scholarships in the USA.

Indeed, in 1986 the BEF took over from the state the management of the large-scale Botswana Workforce and Skills Training project, through which the USA provided funding for adult education that supported private-sector employment creation. In 1988, with US support, the BEF was reorganised as the Botswana Confederation of Commerce, Industry and Manpower (BOCCIM) with a mandate which included specific responsibility for promoting continuing education and training for the private sector. After 1988, BOCCIM's training section developed an adult education programme which included the direct provision of courses in management skills (particularly for small and medium enterprises) as well as commissioned courses by local training bodies. The adult education activities of BOCCIM show an organisation in civil society using adult education to strengthen and expand the capitalist mode of production through disseminating appropriate skills and attitudes.

The work of the churches, NGOs and the employers' association illustrate education in civil society which reinforced capitalist hegemony and the power of the dominant classes and social groups. The state sought to contain potential opposition based in civil society; therefore there are few examples of voluntary associations or social movements which had goals of social change based on alternative conceptions of the socioeconomic order. Hence very little adult education can be characterised as counter-hegemonic, and there are only a few instances of adult education which questioned the prevailing power structure.

Two NGOs established in the mid-1980s had explicit social change goals which raised questions about the status quo. In 1986 the Emang Basadi Women's Association was founded by a group of middle-class women with the aim of enhancing women's position socially, politically and economically. Its main focus initially was a response to a Law Reform Committee, and it sought to mobilise support against discriminatory laws. From 1986 to 1990 it undertook adult education on the theme of 'Women and the Law' in a series of workshops. The association quickly achieved a high profile, and raised public awareness on issues of discrimination and gender stereotyping, challenging patriarchy and the male bias of the state. However, it lacked a permanent secretariat and the organisational capacity to reach out to the working class and the peasantry, so that its adult education activities were restricted in their impact.

In 1986, Co-operation for Research Development and Education (CORDE) was established (largely with Dutch aid) to promote producer co-operatives through education and technical assistance. It started with four enterprises; by 1990 it had twenty-two member groups including furniture-making, printing, baking and pottery enterprises. The organisation espoused the aims of the populist model of development based on self-managed manufacturing and agricultural enterprises using natural resources and environmentally sound sustainable agricultural practices. Its social goals stressed participation, gender equality, the rights of ethnic minorities and community empowerment. Its adult education programmes included raising awareness about the potential of co-operative enterprises, the provision of practical production skills and training in co-operative management, as well as Leadership Development Training courses for other NGOs. CORDE championed an alternative conception of development based on employment for the poor and grassroots democracy. It saw itself as a policy advocate in relation to the state, and its basic approach to the state was not confrontational. In 1991, however, it was attacked by the state for its activities with the Basarwa minority ethnic group, so its close relationships with many state structures deteriorated (CORDE, 1993: 10). Overall, the impact of CORDE in its first five years was limited as many member groups were in a fledgling state and the organisation itself was constrained in its capacity to meet its objective adequately. Thus, while it had the aim of promoting an alternative model of development, its adult education activities to support social change remained small-scale.

A social movement which might have generated counter-hegemonic adult education was the trade-union movement. The constitution of the Botswana Federation of Trade Unions (BFTU) included a major objective 'to provide training, education, literature and other facilities for the advancement of workers and the labour movement' (Molutsi, Mogalakwe and Mufune, 1993: 67). Worker and trade-union education has the potential to advance class interests which conflict with those of the dominant classes in the capitalist mode of production. However, the work of the Botswana Trade Union Education Centre, which was established in

1972, was funded and largely staffed by aid agencies that specifically sought to contain the development of radical trade unionism
in the South, particularly the USA's African American Labor
Center and Germany's Friedrich Ebert Foundation. Through the
Centre the BFTU ran courses for both union members and leaders
which covered general topics, such as health and safety in the
workplace, and basic trade-union skills such as organising and
collective bargaining. There was an active programme of seminars,
workshops and short courses in the 1970s and early 1980s, though
this subsequently declined (Molutsi, Mogalakwe and Mufune,
1993). But the adult education work of the Centre took place within
a perspective on trade unionism which focused narrowly on the
immediate economic interests of members, and did not raise
broader questions about the capitalist mode of production. During
the period as a whole a good number of trade unionists were
reached by the Centre's programmes – for example, there were
two thousand participants between 1972 and 1974 (Simkin, 1975).
However, the impact was limited to the development of a trade-
union consciousness rather than an anti-capitalist consciousness.
Thus adult education in the context of the trade-union movement
contributed to what Mogalakwe (1997: 74) has accurately called
'ideological habituation' – namely, the acceptance of capitalist
hegemony.

Finally, there was one example of an organisation in civil society
which used adult education to promote an explicitly socialist vision.
In the mid-1960s, Patrick van Rensburg established an education-
with-production centre called the Serowe Brigades, whose main
focus was providing young school leavers with work skills. In the
late 1960s he began to develop a socialist ideology derived from
the ideas of writers such as René Dumont and Frantz Fanon, and
from the example of the Cultural Revolution in China. In 1969
Van Rensburg established Boiteko as a model rural development
project of education, training and employment for poor adults
based on self-managed production. Its conception was influenced
by the model of a socialist co-operative and by his understanding
of what was happening at the time in China, where rural development was emphasising labour-intensive methods, cheap technologies and small-scale collective production (Van Rensburg, 1994).
The model aimed to raise rural living standards, and also

(f)   To encourage co-operation and interdependence;
(g)   To encourage spontaneous capital formation and to promote the control by ordinary people of their own enterprises and capital;
(h)   To impart and to improve skills;
(i)   To broaden the horizons and increase the awareness of participants.
(Van Rensburg, 1974: 100)

The project involved both men and women, and maximised the use of local raw materials, such as lime and animal skins. By the early 1970s over one hundred adults were engaged in a variety of productive activities such as gardening, weaving, tanning and brick-making. Van Rensburg envisaged the model of the village co-operative as a context for imparting technical and management skills, and providing general education, including literacy. Above all, the co-operative would create 'a new reality in people's lives to shape ... a new consciousness' (Van Rensburg, 1974: 104). In fact, Boiteko ran into a number of problems deriving from organisational issues and the wider socioeconomic environment, and was unable to provide sufficient income to retain its members. The number of participants dwindled in the mid-1970s to fewer than twenty, all of whom were women.

Van Rensburg's socialist ideology developed in its sophistication and in its theoretical basis in Marxist analysis. By 1976 he saw the Serowe Brigades as a microcosm of alternative development that would meet the needs of the poor peasant and rural proletariat classes, which were being increasingly marginalised by state development policies that focused on urban areas, formal-sector employment and commercial cattle production. The alternative development model was underpinned by a socialist ideology that challenged neocolonialism and dependency, and was disseminated in study circles among the staff and in a development studies course for trainees. Van Rensburg saw the centre's education as a means for preparing young people from poor peasant and rural proletarian backgrounds to oppose capitalist exploitation and fight for social transformation. As part of this strategy he encouraged consciousness-raising adult education by Brigades staff among their unskilled workers (such as cooks and drivers) and among Boiteko's members (Van Rensburg, 1984: 41–3). But these activities were short-lived as the Serowe Brigades came under sustained attack by the state in 1977 and 1978 because the centre was regarded as promoting 'communism' and as a project of the main opposition party. Van Rensburg resigned in 1979, and by 1983 the Serowe Brigades had collapsed. In 1984 Boiteko was registered as an Agricultural Management Association under the Ministry of Agriculture, becoming a conventional income-generating project engaged in vegetable and poultry production. Thus the state contained the oppositional potential of the Serowe Brigades and Boiteko, and successfully limited the impact of the socialist adult education experiment.

This country study illustrates how adult education is part of the politics of development in peripheral capitalism. The nature of the adult education activities of both the state and the organisations of civil society in this period of Botswana's history clearly show the impact of the capitalist socioeconomic order and its power structure.

Notes

1. For present purposes, adult education undertaken by political parties is not discussed, as its partisan nature defines and makes clear its aims and political implications.

2. Regime types are differentiated by the modes in which political power and representation are institutionalised.

CHAPTER 8

Conclusion

My aim in this book, as stated in Chapter 1, was to develop a mode of analysis that would clarify the historical and structural influences on adult education in the South. I have sought to elaborate a theoretical framework for a political economy approach to the study of adult education and development, and to generate agendas which could guide research applying this theoretical position. In order to examine the explanatory capability of the approach, I have applied these agendas to a specific peripheral capitalist country. These case studies provided an analysis of aspects of adult education in Botswana during the first twenty-five years after Independence from British colonial rule.

Chapter 2 contained a discussion of Marxist social theory in order to establish the book's analytical approach based on Marxist political economy. It advocated an undogmatic and creative conception of Marxism that can address new realities and theoretical developments, and provided an outline of Marxist political economy which focused on a number of key concepts: historical materialism, the mode of production, class, capitalism, imperialism, social revolution, socialism, the state, the party, consciousness, ideology and hegemony. I argued that these concepts provide the basis for a distinctive type of analysis which examines the relationship between the mode of economic organisation on the one hand and social and political phenomena on the other. I then assessed six recent critiques of Marxist theory and practice. Following the discussion, I presented a summary of the political economy approach.

239

The summary furnished the basis in Chapter 3 for reviewing the literature on the political economy of adult education since the mid-1970s. The literature was found to be uneven in terms of its conceptual basis, its analytical sophistication and its coverage of the field of adult education. The review concluded that none of the previous works had achieved an integrated approach using all the key elements of the theory included in the summary. Taken together, however, they did illustrate the analytical potential of applying the political economy approach to the analysis of adult education in the South. I concluded the chapter by presenting the theoretical framework of the book.

The central argument of the book was that adult education in the countries of the South takes place in the context of theories and practices of development – that is, the idea that deliberate action can be undertaken to change society in chosen directions considered desirable. Policy-makers and practitioners set goals, establish systems, organise programmes and assess performance in terms of ideas about the relationship between adult education and development. In Chapter 4 I therefore provided a discussion of the evolution of different conceptions of development and their perspectives on adult education. I considered five schools of thought about development – modernisation theory, dependency theory, neoliberal theory, populism and political economy – and showed that each of the first four paradigms has a distinctive position on the nature of development and the means for achieving it. Consequently, they have differing ideas about the role of adult education in relation to development. Finally, I considered political economy as a theoretical approach to the analysis of development, arguing that the Marxist tradition of the political economy of development provided a fertile source of analytical concepts for the study of social phenomena in the specific context of peripheral capitalism. Hence I concluded that the theoretical framework established in Chapter 3 provided a valid and relevant basis for the study of adult education and development.

My focus in this book has been the political economy of adult education in peripheral capitalist countries. Such countries are, by definition, on the edges of the historic centre of capitalism, whose evolution involved the steady incorporation of all the pre-capitalist areas of the world into a global economic system. I have maintained that it is this process of incorporation, impelled by external forces, which gives the peripheral countries their specific characteristics. In Chapter 5 I theorised this position in terms of imperialism – that is, the process of capitalist accumulation on a world scale. Since 1945, imperialism has involved an increased integration of the world economy, leading to the present period of globalisation, but the international division of labour continues to be characterised by a high level of inequality. The peripheral countries depend on the advanced capitalist countries for capital, technology, research and development, and markets. This global political economy is supported by aid, which is the transfer of public funds by the state in industrialised countries to the South. I argued that aid provides a channel for external influences over development policies and programmes, and that it has a systemic role in developing the conditions for worldwide capitalist accumulation. I discussed the nature of the aid regime in terms of aid as imperialism, identifying the provision of aid to adult education as an important factor in the development of adult education in the South, and thus as one of the modes of mediation of imperialism. I discussed and illustrated the ways in which this mediation takes place by the examples of agricultural extension and trade-union education. In this chapter I developed a research agenda for studying aid and adult education within specific national contexts, illustrating it by a country case study of Botswana between 1966 and 1991 which showed that aid had significantly influenced the formulation and implementation of adult education policies.

The theoretical framework of the book posited that social inequality is a structural feature of capitalist society. It suggested that the analysis of social phenomena such as adult education must take into account the multiple effects and interactions of the inequalities of class, gender, ethnicity and race within the capitalist mode of production. In Chapter 6 I argued that social inequality affects the nature of adult education at every level, including policies, programmes and curricula, and that it shapes the outcomes of participation in adult education activities. From this perspective, adult education is a resource in society which benefits some social groups and disadvantages others. To explore this viewpoint, I considered social inequality in peripheral capitalism along the dimensions of class, gender, ethnicity and race. I then related inequality to the provision of adult education and its effects in either reproducing or undermining the hierarchies of the status quo. The discussion led to the presentation of a research agenda for the study of social inequality and adult education within peripheral capitalism. My agenda proposed that the specific nature of class, gender, ethnicity and race in a given country must be analysed as the basis for studying how adult education reproduces the various forms of inequality or involves resistance, either formally (for example, in the choice of curriculum contents) or informally (for example, through dropout). I noted the complexity of the agenda, as it needed to comprehend three interacting systems of inequality within capitalism. The country case study applied this agenda to Botswana in the period 1966 to 1991, and showed that the overwhelming effect of adult education was to reproduce the social inequalities of class, gender and ethnicity. There were few examples of adult education activities which sought to resist the ideologies and practices of inequality, and transform the hierarchical structures within the society.

The final element of the theoretical framework of the book was the contention that adult education is embedded in the political processes of society. I suggested that the nature of adult education reflects the interests and values of different social groups, and the distribution of power in society. Thus the study of adult education must investigate the extent to which it serves to reinforce the existing power structure and its socioeconomic order, or contributes to social change based on alternative ideas about society and its development. The key concepts identified for political analysis were the state and civil society, and in Chapter 7 I elaborated these concepts in the context of peripheral capitalism, arguing that the state has a dual role: (a) to guarantee the conditions for capitalist accumulation and reproduction; and (b) to organise the legitimation of the capitalist socioeconomic order. I defined civil society as the associational life beyond the limits of the state, and indicated that it is a domain of ideological contestation. Hence while some organisations in civil society uphold the status quo, others oppose aspects of capitalist society and propose different ideas of development, some of which embody a socialist vision of society. I suggested that these concepts provide the basis for assessing the political dimensions of adult education in peripheral capitalism. Thus the adult education provided by the state is likely to reflect its role in promoting capitalist accumulation and legitimating the socioeconomic order. Similarly, the struggle for hegemony within civil society is also played out in adult education. Some organisations of civil society provide adult education which is congruent with the ideologies of the state, while others engage in counter-hegemonic adult education activities that promote social change. I put forward a research agenda on the state, civil society and adult education designed to reveal the political nature and implications of adult education in a given national context. This was applied to Botswana, and I concluded that public adult education served the interests of the state, while there was little evidence of counter-hegemonic adult education by the organisations of civil society.

The Study of Adult Education and Development

This book had the theoretical purpose of elaborating the political economy approach to adult education and development. To illustrate the application of this theory, the country case studies provided a historical analysis of adult education in Botswana between 1966 and 1991. The results of this theory-building exercise have a number of implications for the study of adult education in the South in terms of further theoretical development and empirical research.

The development of adult education as a field of study has been hampered by the tendency for research to focus on empiricist studies, so that the building of theories embodying conceptual schemes and general propositions has been restricted. The example of this book, however, suggests that the effort to develop appropriate theoretical frameworks for the study of adult education in the South is worthwhile, as the political economy approach has provided explanations of a wide range of adult education phenomena. One implication of the study is that different theoretical frameworks based on other paradigms (such as feminism, Habermasian critical theory or postmodernism) should also be elaborated and applied in order to investigate their usefulness for understanding adult education in the South. These approaches would also be judged in terms of their ability to generate research questions, their internal consistency and their explanatory power.

I suggest that a specific area for increased theoretical awareness is that of development theory. There is a need to identify the theoretical foundations of trends in development policies, and to reveal their implications for adult education. The conscious identification of development theory will enable both a more analytical approach to adult education and the avoidance of normative discussions which leave theoretical assumptions unexamined and unexplained. Thus clear distinctions will be apparent between the model of development being studied in a particular situation and the conception of development held by the individual. Two tasks are particularly important at this time. First, there is need for an in-depth critical analysis of neoliberal development theory and its significance for adult education. Second, there is need for a comprehensive study of the populist paradigm of development, including an analysis of its strengths and weaknesses and a discussion of its implications for adult education. The fact that by the late 1990s the study of adult education had not yet comprehensively analysed the implications of these two schools of thought about development which emerged in the 1980s provides a lesson for the future: research on adult education in the South must identify trends in development theory as soon as they become discernible in practice and in the specialist literature, and immediately debate their ramifications. The emerging ideas of 'post-development' (Rahnema and Bawtree, 1997) provide a case in point.

In the light of the analysis undertaken in this book, the theoretical framework of Marxist political economy for the study of adult education and development needs to be refined and extended in a number of ways:

- Refinement of the conceptualisation of the development of the capitalist mode of production (including the concepts of peripheral capitalism and the South) in terms of the idea of uneven development, in order to encompass the increasingly varied levels of development within the South – for example, in East Asia compared to sub-Saharan Africa.
- Refinement of the analysis of imperialism with regard to the extent to which globalisation represents a new stage in worldwide capitalist accumulation. Extension of the analysis of the effects of imperialism on adult education to include (a) the

specific impacts of the transnational corporations; and (b) the
specific impacts of globalisation.

* Refinement of the analysis of social inequality in terms of the
  theorisation of the complex relationships and interactions of
  class, gender, ethnicity and race within the capitalist mode of
  production. Also refinement of the nature of ideology and
  hegemony in adult education in relation to the concepts of
  contestation, resistance and transformation. Extension of the
  scope of the analysis of social inequalities and adult education
  to include a greater consideration of race and specific areas of
  social division, such as caste in India.

* Refinement of the analysis of the state and adult education to
  encompass situations in which the state collapsed (as in Liberia
  and Somalia), and the implications of the reduced autonomy of
  the state in the international political economy. Extension of
  the area of political analysis to include political parties and
  their adult education activities.

* Refinement of the concept of socialism and analysis of its continued significance for adult education in the South, taking into
  account practical and theoretical developments since 1989–91.
  Extension of the analysis of socialism and adult education to
  include historical studies of adult education in the South in
  countries which followed a socialist model of development, such
  as China and Cuba.

* Refinement of the theoretical framework to include the political economy of the environment. Extension of the analysis to
  consideration of adult education related to ecological issues.

In general terms, the adequacy of the framework needs to be
tested in a variety of different national contexts to produce country
studies for purposes of comparison and generalisation.

The theoretical framework of this book provides the basis for
detailed empirical studies of aspects of adult education with the
following characteristics: (a) an explicit theoretical foundation; (b)
a historical perspective; and (c) an appreciation of the structural
context of adult education. The guidelines for empirical studies
within the political economy framework are presented in the research agendas in the conclusions to Chapters 5, 6 and 7:

(i) *Aid and adult education.* There have been very few empirical studies of aid and adult education; hence there is need for a variety of studies ranging from national policy studies (including statistical analyses) to micro-level studies of aid's impact on specific programmes (including ethnographic investigations). Particularly interesting would be studies designed to examine the extent to which policy-makers, practitioners and participants resisted the external influences embodied in the aid process and followed agendas of their own which diverged from those of the aid providers.

(ii) *Social inequality and adult education.* The growth of feminism has made it increasingly likely that empirical studies of gender relations and adult education will be undertaken, which is to be welcomed. But it is important that studies related to class, ethnicity and race are also carried out, so that the full scope of the research agenda is covered. A special area of attention should be the interaction between the various systems of inequality, as it poses complex problems of analysis. Overall, two lines of inquiry may be especially fruitful. The first is outcomes research which analyses over time the consequences of participation in particular forms of adult education, perhaps through tracer studies and life histories of participants. The second is research into the content and processes of the curriculum, using textual and content analysis, classroom observation and other qualitative techniques.

(iii) *The state, civil society and adult education.* The political analysis of adult education is a neglected area of research, so the field suggested by the research agenda is wide open. There is a broad variety of areas of empirical inquiry, ranging from policy studies relating to state programmes to case studies of particular organisations in civil society.

In conclusion, I hope that the tools of analysis elaborated in this book will advance the study of adult education and development in the peripheral capitalist countries of the South. In particular, the political economy approach should enable systematic inquiry into the historical and structural influences that shape adult education. On the basis of such inquiry, both the limitations on adult education and the possibilities for change should be clearer. Above all, there should be better answers to the fundamental question: what kind of adult education for what kind of development?

Bibliography

Agee, P. (1975) *Inside the Company*. Harmondsworth, Penguin.

Agrell, J.O., Fagerlind, I. and Gustafsson, I. (1982) *Education and Training in Botswana 1974–1980: The Impact of Swedish Assistance*. Stockholm, SIDA.

Alavi, H. (1982a) 'The Structure of Peripheral Capitalism', in Alavi, H. and Shanin, T. (eds) *Introduction to the Sociology of 'Developing Societies'*. London, Macmillan. pp. 222–46.

Alavi, H. (1982b) 'State and Class under Peripheral Capitalism', in Alavi, H. and Shanin, T. (eds) *Introduction to the Sociology of 'Developing Societies'*. London, Macmillan. pp. 289–307.

Alavi, H. (1989) 'Politics of Ethnicity in India and Pakistan', in Alavi, H. and Harriss, J. (eds) *South Asia*. London, Macmillan. pp. 222–46.

Altbach, P.G. and Kelly, G.P. (eds) (1986) *New Approaches to Comparative Education*. Chicago, University of Chicago.

Amin, S. (1975) 'What Education for What Development?' *Prospects*, vol. 5, no. 1, pp. 48–52.

Amin, S. (1976) 'Literacy Training and Mass Education for Development', in Bataille, L. (ed.) *A Turning Point for Literacy*. Oxford, Pergamon. pp. 79–92.

Apple, M.W. (1979) *Ideology and Curriculum*. London, Routledge & Kegan Paul.

Apple, M.W. (ed.) (1982) *Cultural and Economic Reproduction*. London, Routledge & Kegan Paul.

Apple, M.W. (1986) *Teachers and Texts: A Political Economy of Class and Gender Relations in Education*. London, Routledge & Kegan Paul.

Apple, M.W. (1988) 'Facing the Complexity of Power: For a Parallelist Position in Critical Education Studies', in Cole, M. (ed.) *Bowles and Gintis Revisited: Correspondence and Contradiction in Educational Theory*. London, Falmer. pp. 112–30.

Apple, M.W. and Weis, L. (1983) 'Ideology and Practice in Schooling: A Political and Conceptual Introduction', in Apple, M.W. and Weis, L. (eds) *Ideology and Practice in Schooling*. Philadelphia PA, Temple University Press. pp. 3–33.

Armstrong, P.F. (1988) 'The Long Search for the Working Class: Socialism and the Education of Adults, 1850–1930', in Lovett, T. (ed.) *Radical Approaches*

247

in Adult Education. London, Routledge. pp. 35–58.

Arntzen, J. and Silitshena, R. (1989) 'Access to Land and Farm Income in Botswana', in Swindell, K; Baba, J.M. and Mortimore, M.J. (eds) *Inequality and Development*. London, Macmillan. pp. 158–88.

Bandarage, A. (1984) 'Women in Development: Liberalism, Marxism and Marxist-Feminism', *Development and Change*, vol. 15, pp. 495–515.

Bank of Botswana (1993) *Annual Report 1992*. Gaborone, Bank of Botswana.

Baran, P. (1957) *The Political Economy of Growth*. New York, Monthly Review Press.

Barrow, N. (1982) 'Social Action and Development: A Liberating Power', *Convergence*, vol. XVI, no. 1, pp. 46–51.

Bates, R.H. (1988) *Toward a Political Economy of Development: A Rational Choice Perspective*. Berkeley, University of California Press.

Bataille, L. (1976) *A Turning Point for Literacy*. Oxford, Pergamon.

Bauer, P.T. (1972) *Dissent on Development*. London, Weidenfeld & Nicolson.

Beckman, B. (1993) 'The Liberation of Civil Society: Neo-Liberal Ideology and Political Theory', *Review of African Political Economy*, no. 58, pp. 20–33.

Benor, D. (1987) 'Training and Visit Extension: Back to Basics', in Rivera, W.M. and Schram, S. (eds) *Agricultural Extension Worldwide*. London, Croom Helm. pp. 32–45.

Berman, B.J. and Leys, C. (eds) (1994) *African Capitalists in African Development*. Boulder CO, Lynne Rienner.

Bernstein, H. (1983) 'Development', in Thomas, A. and Bernstein, H. *The 'Third World' and 'Development': Third World Studies: Block 1*. Milton Keynes, Open University Press. pp. 48–87.

Bernstein, H., Crow, B. and Johnson, H. (eds) (1992) *Rural Livelihoods*. Oxford, Oxford University Press.

Bettles, F. (1980) 'Women and Agricultural Development in Botswana', in Youngman, F. (ed.) *Women and Productive Activities: The Role of Adult Education*. Gaborone, Institute of Adult Education. pp. 31–9.

Blundell, S. (1992) 'Gender and the Curriculum of Adult Education', *International Journal of Lifelong Education*, vol. 11, no. 3, pp. 199–216.

BOCCIM (1990) *Annual Report 1989/1990*. Gaborone, BOCCIM.

Bock, J.C. and Papagiannis, G.J. (eds) (1983) *Non Formal Education and National Development*. New York, Praeger.

Bond, C.A. (1974) *Women's Involvement in Agriculture in Botswana*. Gaborone, Republic of Botswana.

Boshier, R. (1985) 'A Conceptual Framework for Analyzing the Training of Trainers and Adult Educators', *Convergence*, vol. XVIII, nos 3–4, pp. 3–22.

Botswana Extension College (1978a) *Go Bala Ke Tswelelopele: A Report of the First Pilot Project on Functional Literacy in Botswana*. Gaborone, Botswana Extension College.

Botswana Extension College (1978b) *Report on the Ditiro Tsa Ditlhabololo Project*. Gaborone, Botswana Extension College.

Bottomore, T. *et al.* (eds) (1983) *A Dictionary of Marxist Thought*. Oxford, Blackwell.

Bowles, S. and Gintis, H. (1976) *Schooling in Capitalist America*. London, Routledge & Kegan Paul.

Bown, L. (1990) 'The State and Adult Education: Suggested Issues for Historical and Comparative Study', in Pöggeler, F. (ed.) *The State and Adult Education*. Frankfurt, Lang. pp. 445–58.

Bratton, M. (1989) 'Beyond the State: Civil Society and Associational Life in Africa', *World Politics*, vol. 61, no. 3, pp. 407–30.

Brewer, A. (1980) *Marxist Theories of Imperialism*. London, Routledge & Kegan Paul.

Brooks, K. (1972) *Prospects for a National Work-Oriented Literacy Programme in Botswana*. Paris, UNESCO.

Brown, D. (1989) 'Ethnic Revival: Perspectives on State and Society', *Third World Quarterly*, vol. 11, no. 4, pp. 1–17.

Browne, S. (1990) *Foreign Aid in Practice*. London, Pinter.

Bule, E.J. (1991) 'An Open Letter to the President', *Mmegi*, 6–12 July, p. 16.

Byram, M.L. (1980a) 'Oodi Weavers: Material Culture, Workers' Organisation and Nonformal Education in Botswana', in Kidd, R. and Colletta, N. (eds) *Tradition for Development*. Berlin, ICAE and DSE. pp. 207–44.

Byram, M.L. (1980b) *Lesedi La Puso*. Gaborone, Ministry of Education.

Callinicos, A. (1989) *Against Postmodernism*. Cambridge, Polity.

Cardoso, F.H. and Faletto, E. (1979) *Dependency and Development in Latin America*. Berkeley, University of California Press.

Carnoy, M. (ed.) (1972) *Schooling in a Corporate Society: The Political Economy of Education in America*. New York, McKay.

Carnoy, M. (1974) *Education as Cultural Imperialism*. New York, McKay.

Carnoy, M. (1980) 'International Institutions and Educational Policy: A Review of Education-Sector Policy', *Prospects*, vol. X, no. 3, 265–83.

Carnoy, M. and Levin, H. (1985) *Schooling and Work in the Democratic State*. Stanford CA, Stanford University Press.

Carver, T. (1982) *Marx's Social Theory*. Oxford, Oxford University Press.

Carver, T. (1985) 'Marx and Non-European Development', in Banerjee, D. (ed.) *Marxian Theory in the Third World*. New Delhi, Sage. pp. 41–6.

Cassara, B.B. (ed.) (1995) *Adult Education Through World Collaboration*. Malabar, Krieger.

Central Statistics Office (1994) *Administrative / Technical Report and National Statistical Tables*. Gaborone, Central Statistics Office.

Cerych, L. (1965) *Problems of Aid in Education in Developing Countries*. New York, Praeger.

Cheru, F. (1989) *The Silent Revolution in Africa*. London, Zed Books.

Chilcote, R.H. (ed.) (1982) *Dependency and Marxism*. Boulder CO, Westview.

Chipasula, J.C. and Miti, K. (1987) *Botswana in Southern Africa: What Lies Ahead*. Delhi, Ajanta.

Clark, J. (1991) *Democratizing Development*. West Hartford CT, Kumarian Press.

Cliffe, L. and Moorsom, R. (1979) 'Rural Class Formation and Ecological Collapse in Botswana', *Review of African Political Economy*, no. 15–16, pp. 35–52.

Colclough, C. (1991) 'Who Should Learn to Pay? An Assessment of Neo-Liberal Approaches to Education Policy', in Colclough, C. and Manor, J. (eds) *States or Markets? Neo-liberalism and the Development Policy Debate*. Oxford,

Clarendon. pp. 197–213.

Colclough, C. and Manor, J. (eds) (1991) *States or Markets? Neo-liberalism and the Development Policy Debate*. Oxford, Clarendon.

Colclough, C. and McCarthy, S. (1980) *The Political Economy of Botswana*. Oxford, Oxford University Press.

Colclough, M. and Crowley, D. (1974) *Setshaba Le Togamaano: The People and the Plan*. Gaborone, University of Botswana, Lesotho and Swaziland.

Coles, G. (1977) 'Dick and Jane Grow Up: Ideology in Adult Basic Education Readers', *Urban Education*, vol. 12, pp. 37–54.

Collins, M. and Collard, S. (1995) 'Examining the Case for Class Analysis in Adult Education Research', in Collette, P; Einsiedel, B. and Hobden, S. (eds) *36th Annual Adult Education Research Conference*. Edmonton, University of Alberta. n.p.

Coombs, P.H. (1968) *The World Education Crisis*. New York, Oxford University Press.

Coombs, P.H. and Ahmed, M. (1974) *Attacking Rural Poverty: How Nonformal Education Can Help*. Baltimore MD, Johns Hopkins University Press.

CORDE (1993) *Strategic Planning Document 1994–1998*. Gaborone, CORDE.

Crowley, D. (1977) 'The Public Consultation on Botswana's National Policy on Tribal Grazing Land', in Weimer, B. (ed.) *A Policy for Rural Development: The Case of Botswana's National Policy on Tribal Grazing Land*. Gaborone, National Institute for Research. pp. 15–26.

CSO and SIDA (1991) *Women and Men in Botswana: Facts and Figures*. Gaborone, CSO and SIDA.

Cunningham, P. (1996) 'Race, Gender, Class and the Practice of Adult Education in the United States', in Wangoola, P. and Youngman, F. (eds) *Towards a Transformative Political Economy of Adult Education*. De Kalb, LEPS Press. pp. 139–59.

Cypher, J.M. (1988) 'The Crisis and the Restructuring of Capitalism in the Periphery', in Zarambeka, P. (ed.) *Research in Political Economy, Volume 11*. Greenwich, JAI. pp. 45–82.

Datta, K. and Murray, A. (1989) 'The Rights of Minorities and Subject Peoples in Botswana: A Historical Evaluation', in Holm, J. and Molutsi, P. (eds) *Democracy in Botswana*. Gaborone, Macmillan. pp. 58–73.

Department of Education and Science (1973) *Adult Education: A Plan for Development*. London, HMSO.

Department of Industrial Affairs (1991) *Annual Report 1990–1991*. Gaborone, Ministry of Commerce and Industry.

Department of Non Formal Education (1979) *Minutes of the Meeting Considering a National Approach to the Eradication of Illiteracy in Botswana*. Gaborone, Department of Non Formal Education.

Department of Non Formal Education (1990) *Annual Report on the National Literacy Programme: 1989*. Gaborone, Department of Non Formal Education.

Deshler, D. and Hagan, N. (1990) 'Adult Education Research: Issues and Directions', in Cunningham, P. and Merriam, S.B. (eds) *Handbook of Adult and Continuing Education*. San Francisco, Jossey-Bass. pp. 147–67.

Doornbos, M. (1991) 'Linking the Future to the Past: Ethnicity and Pluralism', *Review of African Political Economy*, no. 52, pp. 53–65.

Duke, C. (1986) 'Relationship between Adult Education and Poverty', *Convergence*, vol. XIX, no. 4, pp. 1–19.

Dumazedier, J. (1982) 'Questions pour les associations volontaires', *Convergence*, vol. XVI, no. 1, pp. 52–57.

Edge, W.A. and Lekorwe, M.H. (eds) (1998) *Botswana: Politics and Society*. Pretoria, Van Schaik.

Edstrom, L.-O. (1986) 'Education Yes – But Why?', in Fruhling, P. (ed.) *Swedish Development Aid in Perspective*. Stockholm, Almqvist & Wiksell. pp. 195–203.

Elias, J.L. and Merriam, S.B. (1995) *Philosophical Foundations of Adult Education*. Malabar, Krieger.

Escobar, A. (1995) *Encountering Development*. Princeton NJ, Princeton University Press.

Faaland, J. and Parkinson, J.R. (1986) *The Political Economy of Development*. London, Pinter.

Feldman, S. (1992) 'Crises, Poverty and Gender Inequality: Current Themes and Issues', in Beneria, L. and Feldman, S. (eds) *Unequal Burden*. Boulder CO, Westview Press. pp. 1–25.

Filson, G. (ed.) (1991) *A Political Economy of Adult Education in Nigeria*. Ibadan, Ibadan University Press.

Filson, G. and Green, C. (1980) *Toward a Political Economy of Adult Education in the Third World*. Toronto, International Council for Adult Education.

Foley, G. (1994) 'Adult Education and Capitalist Reorganisation', *Studies in the Education of Adults*, vol. 26, no. 2, pp. 121–43.

Foster-Carter, A. (1974) 'Neo-Marxist Approaches to Development and Underdevelopment', in de Kadt, E. and Williams, G. (eds) *Sociology and Development*. London, Tavistock. pp. 67–105.

Fowler, A. (1992) 'Distant Obligations: Speculations on NGO Funding and the Global Market', *Review of African Political Economy*, no. 55, pp. 9–29.

Frank, A.G. (1969) *Latin America: Underdevelopment or Revolution*. New York, Monthly Review Press.

Freire, P. (1972a) *Cultural Action for Freedom*. Harmondsworth, Penguin.

Freire, P. (1972b) *Pedagogy of the Oppressed*. Harmondsworth, Penguin.

Freire, P. (1974) *Education for Critical Consciousness*. London, Sheed & Ward.

Freire, P. (1978) *Pedagogy in Process*. London, Writers & Readers.

Freire, P. and Shor, I. (1987) *A Pedagogy for Liberation*. London, Macmillan.

Fukuyama, F. (1992) *The End of History and the Last Man*. London, Penguin.

Gaborone, S.S.M. (1980) *The Evaluation of Farmer Education at Impala Short Course Centre*. Gaborone, Institute of Adult Education.

Gaborone, S.S.M. (1986a) 'The Political Economy of Adult Education in Botswana with Special Reference to the Agricultural Sector'. University of Warwick. Unpublished Ph.D. thesis.

Gaborone, S.S.M. (1986b) Unpublished Notes on Fieldwork Undertaken for the Evaluation of the National Literacy Programme.

Gaborone, S.S.M., Mutanyatta, J. and Youngman, F. (1987) *An Evaluation of the*

Botswana National Literacy Programme. Gaborone, Institute of Adult Education.

Galetshoge, M.D. (1970) *Report on the Home Economics Pilot Scheme in Botswana – 1967–1969*. Gaborone, Community Development Department.

Geertz, C. (1963) 'The Integrative Revolution: Primordial Sentiments and Civil Politics in the New States', in Geertz, C. (ed.) *Old Societies and New States: The Quest for Modernity in Asia and Africa*. New York, Free Press. pp. 105–57.

Gelpi, E. (1985) *Lifelong Education and International Relations*. London, Croom Helm.

Gelpi, E. (1988) 'Education, International Relations and Cooperation', in Stephens, M.D. (ed.) *International Organisations in Education*. London, Routledge. pp. 9–15.

Gelpi, E. (1996) 'Adult Education for Export', in Wangoola, P. and Youngman, F. (eds) *Towards a Transformative Political Economy of Adult Education*. De Kalb, LEPS Press. pp. 127–35.

Gibbon, P. (1993) 'The World Bank and the New Politics of Aid', *The European Journal of Development Research*, vol. 5, no. 1, pp. 35–62.

Giddens, A. (1989) *Sociology*. Cambridge, Polity.

Ginsburg, M.B. and Arias-Godinez, B. (1984) 'Nonformal Education and Social Reproduction/Transformation: Educational Radio in Mexico', *Comparative Education Review*, vol. 28, no. 1, pp. 116–27.

Giroux, H.A. (1983) 'Theories of Reproduction and Resistance in the New Sociology of Education – A Critical Analysis', *Harvard Educational Review*, vol. 53, no. 3, pp. 257–93.

Glazer, N. and Moynihan, D. (eds) (1975) *Ethnicity: Theory and Experience*. Cambridge MA, Harvard University Press.

Glen, J.M. (1988) *Highlander: No Ordinary School 1932–1962*. Lexington, University of Kentucky Press.

Godfried, N. (1987) 'Spreading American Corporatism: Trade Union Education for Third World Labour', *Review of African Political Economy*, no. 39, pp. 51–63.

Godt, S. and Nkwe, A. (1985) *Women's Community Projects in Botswana*. Gaborone, Institute of Adult Education.

Gordon, A.A. (1996) *Transforming Capitalism and Patriarchy: Gender and Development in Africa*. Boulder CO, Lynne Rienner.

Gordon-Brown, S. (1991) *Education in the Developing World*. London, Longman.

Gottleib, R.S. (1992) *Marxism 1844–1990*. London, Routledge.

Griffin, C. (1983) *Curriculum Theory in Adult and Lifelong Education*. London, Croom Helm.

Griffin, C. (1987) *Adult Education: As Social Policy*. London, Croom Helm.

Hall, B.L. (1978) 'Continuity in Adult Education and Political Struggle', *Convergence*, vol. XI, no. 1, pp. 8–15.

Hall, B.L. (1982) 'The Paris Conference: Renewal of a Movement', *Convergence*, vol. XVI, no. 1, pp. 1–9.

Hall, B.L. (1986) 'The Role of Non Governmental Organisations in the Field of Adult Education', *Convergence*, vol. XIX, no. 4, pp. 1–20.

Hall, B.L. and Kidd, J.R. (eds) (1978) *Adult Learning: A Design for Action*. Oxford,

Pergamon.

Harala.nbos, M. (1985) *Sociology*. London, Bell & Hyman.

Harrington, W. (1987) *The Theory and Practice of Non-Formal Education: Case Studies from Papua New Guinea*. Manchester, Manchester University Press.

Hartland-Thunberg, P. (1978) *Botswana: An African Growth Economy*. Boulder CO, Westview.

Harvey, C. and Lewis, S.R. (1990) *Policy Choice and Development Performance in Botswana*. New York, St. Martin's Press.

Hayes, E. (1992) 'The Impact of Feminism on Adult Education Publications: An Analysis of British and American Journals', *International Journal of Lifelong Education*, vol. 11, no. 2, pp. 125–38.

Hayter, T. (1971) *Aid as Imperialism*. Harmondsworth, Penguin.

Hayter, T. and Watson, C. (1985) *Aid: Rhetoric and Reality*. London, Pluto.

Healey, P. (1983) 'Who Gains and Who Loses? The Political Economy of Adult Education', *Convergence*, vol. XVI, no. 4, pp. 49–55.

Held, D. (1983) 'Central Perspectives on the Modern State', in Held, D. (ed.) *States and Societies*. Oxford, Martin Robertson. pp. 1–55.

Hettne, B. (1990) *Development and the Three Worlds*. London, Longman.

Higgins, K.M. (1981) *Women Farmers and Their Training*. Gaborone, National Institute for Research.

Higgins, K.M. (1982) *Report on a Curriculum Development Project*. Gaborone, National Institute for Research.

Higgins, K.M. (1984) *Curriculum Development and Citizen Education: A Case Study of a Farmer Training Programme for Women in Botswana*. Gaborone, National Institute for Research.

Hitchcock, R.K. (1978) *Kalahari Cattle Posts*. Gaborone, Republic of Botswana.

Hitchcock, R.K. (1992) 'The Rural Population Living Outside of Recognised Villages', in Nteta, D. and Hermans, J. (eds) *Sustainable Rural Development*. Gaborone, Botswana Society. pp. 6–21.

Hoare, Q. and Smith, G.N. (eds) (1971) *Selections from the Prison Notebooks of Antonio Gramsci*. London, Lawrence & Wishart.

Holden, J.B. and Dorland, J.R. (1995) 'Adult Education and the World Bank', in Cassara, B.B. (ed.) *Adult Education Through World Collaboration*. Malabar, Krieger. pp. 23–38.

Holford, J. (1995) 'Why Social Movements Matter: Adult Education Theory, Cognitive Praxis, and the Creation of Knowledge', *Adult Education Quarterly*, vol. 45, no. 2, pp. 95–111.

Holm, J.D. (1982) 'Liberal Democracy and Rural Development in Botswana', *African Studies Review*, vol. XXV, no. 1, pp. 83–102.

Holm, J.D. (1989) 'How Effective are Interest Groups in Representing their Members?', in Holm, J. and Molutsi, P. (eds) *Democracy in Botswana*. Gaborone, Macmillan. pp. 142–53.

Holm, J.D. and Molutsi, P.P. (1992) 'State–Society Relations in Botswana: Beginning Liberalization', in Hyden, G. and Bratton, M. (eds) *Governance and Politics in Africa*. Boulder CO, Lynne Rienner. pp. 75–95.

Hunt, D. (1989) *Economic Theories of Development*. New York, Harvester.

254   *The Political Economy of Adult Education and Development*

Hutchinson, J. and Smith, A.D. (eds) (1996) *Ethnicity*. Oxford, Oxford University Press.

Inkeles, A. and Smith, D.H. (1974) *Becoming Modern: Individual Change in Six Developing Countries*. Cambridge MA, Harvard University Press.

Integrated Field Services (1988) *Annual Report 1987/88*. Gaborone, Ministry of Commerce and Industry.

International Monetary Fund (1992) *Annual Report 1992*. Washington DC, International Monetary Fund.

Jarvis, P. (1993) *Adult Education and the State: Towards a Politics of Adult Education*. London, Routledge.

Jenkins, R. (1987) *Transnational Corporations and Uneven Development*. London, Methuen.

Jenkins, R. (1992) 'Theoretical Perspectives', in Hewitt, T., Johnson, H. and Wield, D. (eds) *Industrialisation and Development*. Oxford, Oxford University Press. pp. 128–66.

Johnson, D.L. (1985) 'The State as an Expression of Class Relations', in Johnson, D.L. (ed.) *Middle Classes in Dependent Countries*. Beverly Hills CA, Sage. pp. 167–95.

Jones, P.W. (1992) *World Bank Financing of Education*. London, Routledge.

Jones-Dube, E. (1990) *Training and Educational Needs of Women in Botswana*. Mimeo submitted to the African Association for Literacy and Adult Education.

Kamrava, M. (1993) 'Conceptualising Third World Politics: The State–Society See Saw', *Third World Quarterly*, vol. 14, no. 4, pp. 703–16.

Kann, U., Hitchock, R. and Mbere, N. (1990) *Let Them Talk: A Review of the Accelerated Remote Area Development Programme*. Report Submitted to the Ministry of Local Government and Lands and to the Norwegian Agency for Development Co-operation, Gaborone.

Kassam, Y.O. (1978) *The Adult Education Revolution in Tanzania*. Nairobi, Shungwaya.

Kassam, Y.O. (1986) 'Adult Education, Development and International Aid: Some Issues and Trends', *Convergence*, vol. XIX, no. 3, pp. 1–11.

Keane, J. (1988) 'Introduction', in Keane, J. (ed.) *Civil Society and the State*. London, Verso. pp. 1–31.

Kebaagetse, K. (1990) 'Body to Promote Bakgalagadi', *Guardian*, 7 December, p. 12.

Keith, N.W. and Keith, N.Z. (eds) (1988) *New Perspectives on Social Class and Socioeconomic Development in the Periphery*. Westport CT, Greenwood Press.

Kelly, J. (1991) 'A Study of Gender Differential Linguistic Interaction in the Adult Classroom', *Gender and Education*, vol. 3, no. 2, pp. 137–43.

King, K. (1991) *Aid and Education in the Developing World*. London, Longman.

Kitching, G. (1989) *Development and Underdevelopment in Historical Perspective*. London, Routledge.

Kjaer-Olsen, P. (1980) *Environmental Sanitation and Protection Project: Report on Baseline Study*. Gaborone. Mimeo.

Knowles, M.S. (1977) *A History of the Adult Education Movement in the US*. Malabar, Krieger.

Knowles, M.S. (1978) *The Adult Learner: A Neglected Species*. Houston TX, Gulf.

Korten, D. (1995) *When Corporations Rule the World*. West Hartford CT, Kumarian.

Krauss, M.B. (1983) *Development Without Aid*. Lanham, University Press of America.

Laclau, E. and Mouffe, C. (1985) *Hegemony and Socialist Strategy: Towards a Radical Democratic Politics*. London, Verso.

Lauglo, J. and Marope, P.T.M. (1986) *Education in Botswana 1981–1986 with Swedish Support*. Gaborone. Mimeo.

Lauglo, J. and Marope, P.T.M. (1987) *Education in Botswana 1981–1986 with Swedish Support*. Stockholm, SIDA.

Lecha, M.D.N. (1987) 'A Conceptual Analysis of the Botswana National Literacy Programme Curriculum'. University of Botswana. Unpublished M.Ed. dissertation.

Lengermann, P.M. and Niebrugge-Brantley, J. (1992) 'Contemporary Feminist Theory', in Ritzer, G. (ed.) *Sociological Theory*. New York, McGraw-Hill. pp. 447–96.

Linear, M. (1985) *Zapping the Third World: The Disaster of Development Aid*. London, Pluto.

Lovett, T. (1988) *Radical Approaches in Adult Education*. London, Routledge.

Lowe, J. (ed.) (1970) *Adult Education and Nation Building*. Edinburgh, Edinburgh University Press.

Maalouf, W.D. (1987) 'The Impact of the FAO on the Planning of Extension and Adult Education in Member Countries', in Rivera, W.M. (ed.) *Planning Adult Learning: Issues, Practices and Directions*. London, Croom Helm. pp. 106–26.

McCarthy, C. and Apple, M.W. (1988) 'Race, Class and Gender in American Educational Research: Toward a Nonsynchronous Parallelist Position', in Weis, L. (ed.) *Class, Race and Gender in American Education*. Albany, State University of New York. pp. 9–39.

McGivenny, V. and Murray, F. (1991) *Adult Education in Development: Methods and Approaches from Changing Societies*. Leicester, NIACE.

Mackintosh, M. (1992) 'The State: A Crisis of Governance', in Wuyts, M., Mackintosh, M. and Hewitt, T. (eds) *Development Policy and Public Action*. Oxford, Oxford University Press. pp. 61–90.

McLaren, P. and Leonard, P. (1993) *Paulo Freire: A Critical Encounter*. London, Routledge.

McLellan, D. (1973) *Karl Marx: His Life and Thought*. London, Macmillan.

McLellan, D. (ed.) (1983) *Marx: The First 100 Years*. London, Fontana.

Mafeje, A. (1971) 'The Ideology of Tribalism', *Journal of Modern African Studies*, vol. 9, no. 2, pp. 253–61.

Mafela, L. (1994a) 'Domesticity: The Basis for Missionary Education of Batswana Women to the End of the 19th Century', *Botswana Notes and Records*, vol. 26. pp. 87–93.

Mafela, L. (1994b) 'The Mochudi Homecraft Centre: Training Batswana for a Euro-Western Type of Womanhood, 1943–1972', *Mosenodi*, vol. 2, no. 1, pp. 3–17.

Malikongwa, D.M. (1982) 'The Family Welfare Educator as an Agent of Primary Health Care in Botswana'. University of Southampton. Unpublished M.A. dissertation.

Mamdani, M. (1992) 'Class Formation and Rural Livelihoods: A Ugandan Case Study', in Bernstein, H., Crow, B. and Johnson, H. (eds) *Rural Livelihoods*. Oxford, Oxford University Press. pp. 195–216.

Marx, K. (1969) 'Preface to a Contribution to the Critique of Political Economy', in Marx, K. and Engels, F. *Selected Works. Volume 1*. London, Lawrence & Wishart. pp. 502–6.

Marx, K. and Engels, F. (1969) 'Manifesto of the Communist Party', in Marx, K. and Engels, F. *Selected Works. Volume 1*. London, Lawrence & Wishart. pp. 98–137.

Marx, K. and Engels, F. (1962) *Selected Correspondence*. Moscow, Progress Publishers.

Marx, K. and Engels, F. (1970) *The German Ideology*. ed. Arthur, C.J. London, Lawrence & Wishart.

Mayende, G. (1993) 'Bureaucrats, Peasants and Rural Development Policy in Botswana', *Africa Development*, vol. XVIII, no. 4, pp. 57–78.

Mbilinyi, M. (1980) *Towards a Methodology in Political Economy of Adult Education in Tanzania*. Toronto, International Council for Adult Education.

Meena, R. (ed.) (1992) *Gender in Southern Africa*. Harare, SAPES.

Merriam, S.B. and Simpson, E.L. (1989) *A Guide to Research for Educators and Trainers of Adults*. Malabar, Krieger.

Mies, M. (1986) *Patriarchy and Accumulation on a World Scale*. London, Zed.

Mies, M. and Shiva, V. (1993) *Ecofeminism*. London, Zed.

Miles, R. (1989) *Racism*. London, Routledge.

Millar, C. (1991) *Adult Education: Delimiting the Field*. Unpublished Paper for the National Educational Policy Initiative, South Africa.

Millwood, D. and Gazelius, H. (1986) *Good Aid*. Stockholm, SIDA.

Ministry of Education (1979) *Memorandum: E.14/2 79–80 I (2) National Initiative Against Illiteracy. 6 December 1979*. Gaborone, Ministry of Education.

Ministry of Education. (1984) *How Can We Succeed? Summary Report from the Evaluation of the National Literacy Programme*. Gaborone, Department of Non Formal Education.

Ministry of Finance and Development Plannning (1997) *Community-Based Strategy for Rural Development*. Gaborone, Ministry of Finance and Development Planning.

Ministry of Local Government and Lands (1978) *Remote Area Development Programme Workshop*. Gaborone, Ministry of Local Government and Lands.

Mogalakwe, M. (1997) *The State and Organised Labour in Botswana 1966–1990*. Aldershot, Ashgate.

Mogwe, A. (1992) *Who Was (T)Here First?* Gaborone, Botswana Council of Churches.

Molomo, M.G. (1989) 'The Bureaucracy and Democracy in Botswana', in Holm, J. and Molutsi, P. (eds) *Democracy in Botswana*. Gaborone, Macmillan. pp. 237–43.

Molutsi, P. (1993) 'International Influences on Botswana's Democracy', in Stedman, S.J. (ed.) *Botswana: The Political Economy of Democratic Development.* Boulder CO, Lynne Rienner. pp. 51–61.

Molutsi, P., Mogalakwe, M. and Mufune, P. (1993) *Report of the Study of the Trade Unions and the Botswana Federation of Trade Unions.* Gaborone, University of Botswana.

Morrow, R.A. and Torres, C.A. (1994) 'Education and the Reproduction of Class, Gender and Race: Responding to the Postmodern Challenge', *Educational Theory,* vol. 44, no. 1, pp. 43–61.

Mudariki, P.T. (1996) 'The Political Economy of Adult Education in Zimbabwe: A Case Study', in Wangoola, P. and Youngman, F. (eds) *Towards a Transformative Political Economy of Adult Education.* De Kalb, LEPS Press. pp. 223–47.

Mulenga, D. (n.d.) 'The World Bank, Structural Adjustment and Education: Implications for Adult Education in Africa'. Unpublished paper.

Murray, A. and Parsons, N. (1990) 'The Modern Economic History of Botswana', in Konczacki, Z.A., Parpart, J.L. and Shaw, T.M. *Studies in the Economic History of Southern Africa, Volume One.* London, Cass. pp. 159–99.

Mutangira, J. and Fordham, P. (1989) 'Process and Product: Researching the Advanced Training Needs of African Adult Educators', in Lichtner, M. (ed.) *Comparative Research in Adult Education.* Frascati, CEDE. pp. 199–207.

Mutanyatta, J.N.S. (1992) 'The Role of Adult Education in Assisting Sustainable Development in Remote Area Dwellers of Botswana', in Wall, D. and Owen, M. (eds) *Distance Education and Sustainable Community Development.* Athabascar, University of Athabascar Press. pp. 57–73.

Narayan-Parker, D. (1983) *Women's Interest and Involvement in Income Generating Activities: Implications for Extension Services.* Gaborone, National Institute for Research.

Nelson, C. and Grossberg, L. (eds) (1988) *Marxism and the Interpretation of Culture.* London, Macmillan.

New Internationalist (1998) 'Jeans — The Facts', no. 302, pp. 18–19.

Nfila, B. (1985). *Evaluation of the Cultural Development Project.* Gaborone. Mimeo.

Nganunu, T.E. (1982) *The Evaluation of the National Literacy Programme in Mapoka.* Gaborone, Institute of Adult Education.

Noppen, D. (1982) *Consultation and Non-Commitment.* Leiden, African Studies Centre.

NORAD (1989) *A Directory of Non-Governmental Organizations in Botswana.* Gaborone, NORAD.

Oman, G.P. and Wignaraja, G. (1991) *The Postwar Evolution of Development Thinking.* London, Macmillan.

Onimode, B. (1988) *A Political Economy of the African Crisis.* London, Zed.

Organisation for Economic Cooperation and Development (1992) *Development Cooperation. 1992 Report.* Paris, Organisation for Economic Cooperation and Development.

Organisation for Economic Cooperation and Development (1997) *Development Cooperation. 1997 Report.* Paris, Organisation for Economic Cooperation and

Development.

Parajuli, P. (1990) 'Politics of Knowledge, Models of Development and Literacy', *Prospects*, vol. XX, no. 3, pp. 289–98.

Paulston, R.G. and Altenbaugh, R.J. (1988) 'Adult Education in Radical US Social and Ethnic Movements: From Case Studies to Typology to Explanation', in Lovett, T. (ed.) *Radical Approaches in Adult Education*. London, Routledge. pp. 114–37.

Payer, C. (1974) *The Debt Trap*. New York, Monthly Review Press.

Pearson, R. (1992) 'Gender Matters in Development', in Allen, T. and Thomas, A. (eds) *Poverty and Development in the 1990s*. Oxford, Oxford University Press. pp. 291–312.

Picard, L.A. (1987) *The Politics of Development in Botswana*. Boulder CO, Lynne Rienner.

Pillay, G.F. (1992) *Skills Development Framework in Singapore*. Paper presented to the World Bank/IFC/MIGA Seminar on Vocationalisation of School Curriculum, Johannesburg, South Africa, January.

Poggeler, F. (ed.) (1990) *The State and Adult Education*. Frankfurt, Lang.

Pomata, G. (1986) 'A Common Heritage: The Historical Memory of Populism in Europe and the United States', in Boyte, H. and Riessman, F. (eds) *The New Populism*. Philadelphia PA, Temple University Press. pp. 30–50.

Potter, D. (1992) 'The Democratisation of Third World States', in Allen, T. and Thomas, A. (eds) *Poverty and Development in the 1990s*. Oxford, Oxford University Press. pp. 273–90.

Prawl, W., Medlin, R. and Gross, J. (1984) *Adult and Continuing Education Through the Cooperative Extension Service*. Columbia, University of Missouri–Columbia Press.

Prosser, R. (1967) *Adult Education for Developing Countries*. Nairobi, East Africa Publishing House.

Quigley, B.A. (1990) 'Hidden Logic: Reproduction and Resistance in Adult Literacy and Adult Basic Education', *Adult Education Quarterly*, vol. 40, no. 2, pp. 103–15.

Quigley, A. and Holsinger, E. (1993) 'Happy Consciousness: Ideology and Hidden Curriculum in Literacy Education', *Adult Education Quarterly*, vol. 44, no. 1, pp. 17–33.

Rahnema, M. and Bawtree, V. (eds) (1997) *The Post-Development Reader*. London, Zed Books.

Ranger, T. (1983) 'The Invention of Tradition in Colonial Africa', in Hobsbawm, E. and Ranger, T. (eds) *The Invention of Tradition*. Cambridge, Cambridge University Press. pp. 211–62.

Ranger, T. (1989) 'Missionaries, Migrants and the Manyika: The Invention of Ethnicity in Zimbabwe', in Vail, L. (ed.) *The Creation of Tribalism in Southern Africa*. London, Currey. pp. 118–50.

Republic of Botswana (n.d.) *Remote Area Development Programme: Job Description*. Mimeo.

Republic of Botswana (1970) *National Development Plan 1970–75*. Gaborone, Republic of Botswana.

Republic of Botswana (1973a) *National Policy for Rural Development*. Gaborone, Republic of Botswana.

Republic of Botswana (1973b) *National Development Plan 1973–78*. Gaborone, Republic of Botswana.

Republic of Botswana (1975) *National Policy on Tribal Grazing Land*. Gaborone: Republic of Botswana.

Republic of Botswana (1976) *The Rural Incomes Distribution Survey in Botswana, 1974/75*. Gaborone, Republic of Botswana.

Republic of Botswana (1977a) *National Policy on Education*. Gaborone, Republic of Botswana.

Republic of Botswana (1977b) *Lefatshe La Rona – Our Land*. Gaborone, Government Printer.

Republic of Botswana (1980a) *National Development Plan, 1979–1985*. Gaborone, Republic of Botswana.

Republic of Botswana (1980b) *Project Memorandum. Project Title: National Literacy Project. National Development Plan. ED.10*. Gaborone, Ministry of Education.

Republic of Botswana (1982) *National Policy on Economic Opportunities*. Gaborone, Republic of Botswana.

Republic of Botswana (1985) *National Development Plan 6, 1985–1991*. Gaborone, Republic of Botswana.

Republic of Botswana (1991a) *National Development Plan 7, 1991–97*. Gaborone, Republic of Botswana.

Republic of Botswana (1991b) *The Theory and Practise of People's Participation in Rural Development*. Gaborone, Ministry of Finance and Development Planning.

Republic of Botswana (1991c) *Labour Statistics 1990/91*. Gaborone, Republic of Botswana.

Republic of Botswana (1994) *National Report for the Fourth World Conference on Women: Beijing, China, 1995*. Gaborone: Women's Affairs Division.

Republic of Botswana and SIDA (1983) *Agreed Minutes and Report*. Gaborone, Republic of Botswana and SIDA.

Republic of Botswana and SIDA (1984) *Agreed Minutes From the Annual Joint Review of the Swedish Support to Education in Botswana*. Gaborone, Republic of Botswana and SIDA.

Republic of Botswana and SIDA (1985) *Annual Joint Review of the Swedish Support to Education 1985*. Gaborone, Republic of Botswana and SIDA.

Republic of Botswana and UNICEF (1989) *Children, Women and Development in Botswana: A Situation Analysis*. Gaborone: Republic of Botswana and UNICEF.

Riddell, R. (1981) *Ecodevelopment*. Westmead, Gower.

Robertson, C. and Berger, I. (1986) *Women and Class in Africa*. New York, Holmes & Meier.

Rodney, W. (1972) *How Europe Underdeveloped Africa*. Dar Es Salaam, Tanzania Publishing House.

Rogers, A. (1992) *Adults Learning for Development*. London, Cassell.

Rogers, B. (1980) *The Domestication of Women: Discrimination in Developing Societies*. London, Tavistock.

Ronen, D. (1986) 'Ethnicity, Politics and Development: An Introduction', in Thompson, D.F. and Ronen, D. (eds) *Ethnicity, Politics and Development*. Boulder CO, Lynne Rienner. pp. 1–18.

Rostow, W.W. (1960) *The Stages of Economic Growth: A Non-Communist Manifesto*. Cambridge, Cambridge University Press.

Ryan, M. (1982) *Marxism and Deconstruction*. Baltimore MD, Johns Hopkins University Press.

Sachs, W. (ed.) (1992) *The Development Dictionary*. London, Zed.

Samoff, J. (1982) 'Class, Class Conflict and the State in Africa', *Political Science Quarterly*, vol. 97, no. 1, pp. 105–27.

Samoff, J. (1992) 'The Intellectual/Financial Complex of Foreign Aid', *Review of African Political Economy*, no. 53, pp. 60–75.

Sarup, M. (1993) *Post-Structuralism and Postmodernism*. New York, Harvester.

Saul, J. (1979) 'The Dialectic of Class and Tribe', *Race and Class*, vol. XX, no. 4, pp. 347–72.

Schultz, T. (1961) 'Investment in Human Capital', in Karabel, J. and Halsey, A.H. (eds) (1977) *Power and Ideology in Education*. New York, Oxford University. pp. 313–24.

Scott, J.C. (1989) 'Everyday Forms of Resistance', in Colburn, F.D. (ed.) *Everyday Forms of Peasant Resistance*. New York, Sharpe. pp. 3–33.

Seers, D. (1969) 'The Meaning of Development', *International Development Review*, vol. 1, no. 4, pp. 2–6.

Sen, G. and Grown, C. (1988) *Development, Crises and Alternative Visions: Third World Women's Perspectives*. London, Earthscan.

Sharafuddin, A.M. (n.d.) *Women Portrayed in Literacy Materials in Bangladesh*. Unpublished mimeo.

Shaw, T.M. (1986) 'Ethnicity as the Resilient Paradigm for Africa: From the 1960s to the 1980s', *Development and Change*, vol. 17, no. 4, pp. 587–605.

SIAPAC (1990) *Evaluation of Home Economics Programmes in Botswana*. Gaborone, SIAPAC.

SIDA (1972) *Education and Training in Botswana*. Stockholm, SIDA.

Silitshena, R. (1992) 'Availability and Access of Support, Marketing and Extension Services to Small Scale Entrepreneurs and the Informal Sector', in Somolekae, G. (ed.) *The Informal Sector and Small Scale Enterprise Development in Botswana*. Gaborone, University of Botswana. pp. 25–44.

Simkin, C. (1975) 'Labour in Botswana', *Southern African Labour Bulletin*, vol. 2, no. 5, pp. 28–35.

Simon, D. (1992) *Cities, Capital and Development: African Cities in the World Economy*. London, Bellhaven.

Sklair, L. (1988) 'Transcending the Impasse: Metatheory, Theory and Empirical Research in the Sociology of Development and Underdevelopment', *World Development*, vol. 16, no. 6, pp. 697–709.

Smart, B. (1983) *Foucault, Marxism and Critique*. London, Routledge.

Somolekae, G. (1992) 'Women in the Informal Sector and Small-Scale Entrepreneurship: Some Observations From a Recent Study', in Somolekae, G. (ed.) *The Informal Sector and Small Scale Enterprise Development in Botswana*.

Gaborone, University of Botswana. pp. 47–62.

Stalker, J. (1996) 'Women and Adult Education: Rethinking Androcentric Research', *Adult Education Quarterly*, vol. 46, no. 2, pp. 98–113.

Staniland, M. (1985) *What is Political Economy?* New Haven CT, Yale University Press.

Stavenhagen, R. (1986) 'Ethnodevelopment: A Neglected Dimension in Development Thinking', in Apthorpe, R. and Krahl, A. (eds) *Development Studies: Critique and Renewal*. Leiden, E.J. Brill. pp. 71–94.

Stedman, S.J. (ed.) (1993) *Botswana: The Political Economy of Democratic Development*. Boulder CO, Lynne Rienner.

Stichter, S. and Parpart, J.L. (1988) *Patriarchy and Class: African Women at Home and in the Workforce*. Boulder CO, Westview Press.

Stromquist, N. (1986) 'Empowering Women Through Education: Lessons from International Cooperation', *Convergence*, vol. XIX, no. 4, pp. 1–22.

Swartzendruber, J.F. (1988) 'PFP Botswana: A Historical Perspective', *Mmegi*, vol. 5, no. 38, p. 12.

South Commission (1990) *The Challenge to the South*. Oxford, Oxford University Press.

Thomas, A. (1991) 'Relationship with Political Science', in Peters, J.M., Jarvis, P. *et al. Adult Education: Evolution and Achievements in a Developing Field of Study*. San Francisco, Jossey-Bass. pp. 301–21.

Thomas, C.Y. (1974) *Dependence and Transformation*. New York, Monthly Review Press.

Thomas, C.Y. (1984) *The Rise of the Authoritarian State in Peripheral Societies*. London, Heinemann.

Thompson, A.R. (1977) 'How Far Free? International Networks of Constraint Upon National Education Policy in the Third World', *Comparative Education*, vol. 13, no. 3, pp. 155–68.

Thompson, J.L. (ed.) (1980) *Adult Education for a Change*. London, Hutchinson.

Thomson, D. and Larson, R. (1977) *Where Were You Brother? An Account of Trade Union Imperialism*. London, War on Want.

Torres, C.A. (1990) *The Politics of Nonformal Education in Latin America*. New York, Praeger.

Townsend-Coles, E.K. (1969) *Adult Education in Developing Countries*. Oxford, Pergamon.

Townsend-Coles, E.K. (1978) *Evaluation of the Botswana Extension College*. Nairobi, Ford Foundation.

Townsend-Coles, E.K. (1982) *Maverick of the Education Family*. Oxford, Pergamon.

Townsend-Coles, E.K. (1988) *Let the People Learn*. Manchester, Manchester University Press.

Trainer, T. (1989) *Developed to Death*. London, Green Print.

Tsiane, B.D. and Youngman, F. (1986) *The Theory and Practice of People's Participation in Rural Development*. Gaborone, Republic of Botswana.

United Nations Center on Transnational Corporations (1983) *Transnational Corporations in World Development*. New York, United Nations Center on Transnational Corporations.

UNDP (1993) *Development Cooperation: Botswana. 1991 Report.* Gaborone, United Nations Development Programme.

UNDP, Republic of Botswana and UNICEF (1993) *Planning for People.* Gaborone, Ministry of Finance and Development Planning.

UNESCO (1997a) *Adult Education: The Hamburg Declaration. The Agenda for the Future.* Hamburg, UNESCO Institute for Education.

UNESCO (1997b) *Report on the State of Education in Africa.* Dakar, UNESCO Regional Office for Africa.

University of Botswana (1989) *The Young Women's Christian Association: Evaluation Report.* Gaborone, University of Botswana.

Unsicker, J. (1987) 'Adult Education, Socialism and International Aid in Tanzania: The Political Economy of the Folk Development Colleges'. Stanford University. Unpublished Ph.D. thesis.

Uphoff, N.T. and Ilchman, W.F. (eds) (1972) *The Political Economy of Development.* Berkeley, University of California.

USAID (1982) *Why Foreign Aid?* Washington DC, USAID.

USAID (1991) *Botswana Workforce and Skills Training (BWAST) II Project.* Gaborone, USAID.

Van Rensburg, P. (1974) *Report from Swaneng Hill.* Uppsala, Dag Hammarskjold Foundation.

Van Rensburg, P. (1994) Personal communication, 22 November 1994.

Vio Grossi, F. (1986) 'From Project Bureaucracy to the Flourishing of Life', *Convergence*, vol. XIX, no. 4, pp. 1–29.

Visvanathan, N. (1997) 'Introduction to Part 1', in Visvanathan, N. *et al.* (eds) *The Women, Gender and Development Reader.* London, Zed Books.

Walby, S. (1990) *Theorising Patriarchy.* Oxford, Blackwell.

Wangoola, P. (1990) *On 'The African Crisis', People's Popular Participation and the Indigenous NGO in Africa's 'Recovery' and Development.* Nairobi, African Association for Literacy and Adult Education.

Wangoola, P. (1995) 'The Political Economy of Nongovernmental Organisations', in Cassara, B.B. (ed.) (1995) *Adult Education Through World Collaboration.* Malabar, Krieger. pp. 59–69.

Wangoola, P. (1996) 'Alternative Forms of Organisation and Social Action: Implications for Adult and Community Action', in Wangoola, P. and Youngman, F. (eds) *Towards a Transformative Political Economy of Adult Education.* De Kalb, LEPS Press. pp. 321–30.

Wangoola, P. and Youngman, F. (eds) (1996) *Towards a Transformative Political Economy of Adult Education.* De Kalb, LEPS Press.

Welton, M. (1993) 'Social Revolutionary Learning: The New Social Movements as Learning Sites', *Adult Education Quarterly*, vol. 43, no. 3, pp. 152–64.

Wiarda, H.J. (1983) 'Toward a Nonethnocentric Theory of Development: Alternative Conceptions from the Third World', *Journal of Developing Areas*, vol. 17, pp. 433–52.

Wieringa, S. (ed.) (1995) *Subversive Women.* London, Zed Books.

Williams, R. (1976) *Keywords.* London, Fontana.

Wilmsen, E.N. (1989) *Land Filled with Flies: A Political Economy of the Kalahari.* Chicago, University of Chicago Press.

Wily, L. (1979) *Official Policy Toward San (Bushmen) Hunter-Gatherers in Modern Botswana, 1966–1978.* Gaborone, National Institute for Research.

Wolpe, H. (ed.) (1980) *The Articulation of Modes of Production.* London, Routledge & Kegan Paul.

Wood, E.M. and Foster, J.M. (eds) (1997) *In Defense of History: Marxism and the Postmodern Agenda.* New York, Monthly Review Press.

Wood, R.E. (1986) *From Marshall Plan to Debt Crisis.* Berkeley, University of California Press.

Woodhouse, P. (1992) 'Environmental Degradation and Sustainability', in Allen, T. and Thomas, A. (eds) *Poverty and Development in the 1990s.* Oxford, Oxford University Press. pp. 97–115.

World Bank (1981) *Accelerated Development in Sub Saharan Africa: An Agenda for Action.* Washington DC, World Bank.

World Bank (1991a) *Vocational and Technical Education and Training.* Washington DC, World Bank.

World Bank (1991b) *World Development Report 1991.* Washington DC, World Bank.

World Bank (1992) *Annual Report 1992.* Washington DC, World Bank.

World Bank (1993) *World Development Report 1993.* Washington DC, World Bank.

World Commission on Environment and Development (1987) *Our Common Future.* Oxford, Oxford University Press.

Worsley, P. (1984) *The Three Worlds.* London, Weidenfeld & Nicolson.

Wright, E.O., Levine, A. and Sober, E. (1992) *Reconstructing Marxism.* London, Verso.

Young, M. and Whitty, G. (1977) 'Introduction: Perspectives on Education and Society', in Young, M. and Whitty, G. (eds) *Society, State and Schooling.* Lewes, Falmer. pp. 1–15.

Young, M.F.D. (ed.) (1971) *Knowledge and Control.* London, Collier Macmillan.

Youngman, F. (1981) *Adult Education in Botswana 1960 -1980: An Annotated Bibliography.* Gaborone, National Institute for Research.

Youngman, F. (1983) 'The Training of Adult Education Personnel in Botswana', *International Journal of Educational Development,* vol. 3, no. 2, pp. 129–38.

Youngman, F. (1986) *Adult Education and Socialist Pedagogy.* London, Croom Helm.

Youngman, F. (1990) 'The Political Economy of Literacy in the Third World', *Convergence,* vol. XXIII, no. 4, pp. 5–12.

Youngman, F. (1999) 'The State, Adult Literacy and Inequality in Botswana', in Welch, A. (ed.) *Third World Education: Quality and Equality.* New York, Garland. pp. 251–78.

Yudelman, M. (1975) 'Imperialism and the Transfer of Agricultural Techniques', in Duignan, P. and Gann, L.H. (eds) *Colonialism in Africa, 4: The Economics of Colonialism.* London, Cambridge University Press. pp. 329–59.

Index

adult education
  definition of 4–5, 51
  and ethnicity 187–93
  radical tradition of 32–4, 155–6
  role of aid in 110–36, 246
  and social inequality 155–62,
    164–74, 178–85, 194–7, 241–2,
    246
  state and civil society as providers
    of 198–9, 211–17, 219–38, 242–3
  and theories of development 56–9,
    64–6, 70–72, 79–81, 240
Adult Education: A Plan for Development
  (Department of Education and
  Science, 1973), 155
Adult Education and Development
  6
African American Labor Center
  (USA) 117, 236
agricultural extension programmes
  115–16, 124, 166–7, 180–81, 223–5
Ahmed, M., and P.H. Coombs,
  Attacking Rural Poverty 6, 57
aid, role of 96–136, 246
aid agencies 98–100, 107–8, 120–21,
  124–7, 130–35
Alavi, H. 29, 150
Allende, Salvador 64
Althusser, Louis 19
American Federation of Labor–
  Congress of Industrial
  Organisations (AFL–CIO) 117
Amin, Samir 29, 62, 64, 65

Apple, M.W. 35–6, 154, 159
  Teachers and Texts 36
Arias-Godinez, B., and M.B.
  Ginsburg, 'Nonformal Education
  and Social Reproduction/
  Transformation' 157–8

Bakalanga people 186
Bakgalagadi people 186, 187, 189
Baran Paul 59–60, 61, 62
Basarwa people 186–7, 189–93, 196,
  235
basic needs approach 55, 59, 101–2
Bates, R.H., *Toward a Political Economy
  of Development* 82
Bateti people 187
Baudrillard, Jean 28
Bauer, P.T. 68
Bayei people 186
bilateral aid programmes 98, 101
Blundell, S. 160
Bock, J.C., and G.J. Papagiannis, *Non
  Formal Education and National
  Development* 6, 156–7
Boiteko project 236–8
Boshier, R. 159
Botswana, adult education in 6, 8 n2,
  72, 121–36, 165–97, 221–38
bourgeoisie, African 139–40
Bowles, S., and H. Gintis, *Schooling in
  Capitalist America* 34–5, 36, 154
Bown, L. 212
Bratton, M. 208, 218